How Journalists Engage

T0355173

How Journalists Engage

A Theory of Trust Building, Identities, and Care

SUE ROBINSON

OXFORD
UNIVERSITY PRESS

Oxford University Press is a department of the University of Oxford. It furthers
the University's objective of excellence in research, scholarship, and education
by publishing worldwide. Oxford is a registered trade mark of Oxford University
Press in the UK and certain other countries.

Published in the United States of America by Oxford University Press
198 Madison Avenue, New York, NY 10016, United States of America.

Library of Congress Cataloging-in-Publication Data
Names: Robinson, Sue (Professor of journalism), author.
Title: How journalists engage : a theory of trust building, identities, and care / Sue Robinson.
Description: New York, NY : Oxford University Press, [2023] |
Includes bibliographical references.
Identifiers: LCCN 2022060571 (print) | LCCN 2022060572 (ebook) |
ISBN 9780197667118 (hardback) | ISBN 9780197667125 (paperback) |
ISBN 9780197668658 | ISBN 9780197668672 | ISBN 9780197668665 (epub)
Subjects: LCSH: Journalistic ethics. | Press—Public relations. | News audiences—Attitudes.
Classification: LCC PN4756 .R53 2023 (print) | LCC PN4756 (ebook) |
DDC 070.4023—dc23/eng/20230126
LC record available at https://lccn.loc.gov/2022060571
LC ebook record available at https://lccn.loc.gov/2022060572

DOI: 10.1093/oso/9780197667118.001.0001

Paperback printed by Marquis Book Printing, Canada
Hardback printed by Bridgeport National Bindery, Inc., United States of America

*To my husband, Dr. Robert Asen, whose scholarship on
trust and deliberation has been foundational for me
in all the parts of my life as we care for
each other, our kids, our communities, and our world.*

Contents

Acknowledgments

I am indebted to Oxford University Press, the anonymous reviewers of this book, and especially my editor, Angela Chnapko, for all their efforts with the manuscript and publication process. Angela's kindness throughout the process (which happened during the COVID pandemic of 2020–2022) meant the world to me.

Also, did you check out the cover? That was done by the brilliant Shiloah Symone Coley, who went through the University of Wisconsin–Madison's School of Journalism & Mass Communication, coedited *The Black Voice* online magazine on campus, and then went on to a Master's of Fine Arts in Studio Art at American University, graduating in May 2022. She is an artist, writer, cultural worker, and independent scholar with a particular interest in narratives and how we come to believe them. She can be found on Instagram @blckslimshady.

This book would not have been possible without the willingness of the hundreds of consultants, journalists, mediawatchers, engagement specialists, and other change agents to lay out for me what they were doing, why, and how. It is through them that we are witnessing this revolution.

Thanks to the School of Journalism & Mass Communication and the University of Wisconsin–Madison for support, especially financial, without which I would not have been able to write this book. I got research support from the following University of Wisconsin–Madison sources: my Helen Firstbrook Franklin Professor of Journalism endowed research chair, the H. I. Romnes Faculty Fellowship, the Race, Ethnicity, and Indigeneity Fellowship from the Institute in the Research for the Humanities (IRH), the William T. Evjue Faculty Fellowship, and some early money from the Graduate School. The community at the IRH heard the first presentation I did early on in the writing in Spring 2021 and gave me great feedback.

In my department, I am regularly indebted to Jennifer Hart and Rowan Calyx, who helped me deal with all things administrative. I appreciate the support of my school for allowing me to take the IRH Fellowship in Spring 2021 and my sabbatical in Fall 2021 to write it all up. In addition, I received funding from the Knight Foundation to do a study with high-profile political journalists, and I used some of that information in parts of this book. We also combined that data with some of the book materials to publish a couple journal articles and the Knight report we did for industry. These articles included one in *Journalism Practice* in 2020 and one in *Journalism Studies* in 2021. I am indebted to my co-PI on the grant, Dr. Deen Freelon of the University of North Carolina at Chapel Hill, and my research team that summer, including Yiping Xia, Megan Zahay, and Kelly Jensen—all UW-Madison PhD graduate students then.

I received support from the Baldwin Wisconsin Idea Endowment for a project with the UW-Madison Field Day Lab to design and produce an educational video game about journalism for middle school children in public schools. It became a news media literacy project and worked well in Chapter 4 of the book. Thank you to Sarah Gagnon and David Gagnon for asking me to join them on that adventure. We spent 2021 and 2022 together, and I learned an incredible amount from them and their teams.

I was overjoyed to be the research lead on the Citizens Agenda project in 2020 with the Hearken engagement firm, NYU Professor Jay Rosen, and Joy Mayer and her Trusting News team. Democracy Fund, Solutions Journalism Network, and other partners brought that project to fruition with financial and networking support as well as advising throughout. First of all, the whole year—the meetings, the trainings, the thinking, the analyses—was so much fun, especially getting to work so closely with Bridget Thoreson and Jennifer Brandel of Hearken, Jay, and Joy. I adored every member of that team and feel so grateful they all exist in the world. And finally, I was so inspired by the more than 100 journalists who spent hours of their summer getting trained in a new skill set during the most relentlessly newsy year I have ever experienced and then sharing with us, frankly, what they did with that training. My advisee (now Dr.) Steven Wang was an essential member of that team.

Thank you to the following people, who helped me think through concepts in the book; five in particular were so essential in helping me conceptualize parts of the book. Dr. Christine Larson at the University of Colorado read the entire thing, gave me detailed feedback, and as my writing buddy inspired me to write constantly. Dr. Regina Lawrence, associate dean at the University of Oregon and former research director of the Agora Journalism Center, gave me some constructive criticism early on that helped shape my ideas. She herself is a change agent in this ecosystem, working tirelessly to save journalism. Dr. Kiara Childs, an expert in race and media as well as journalism, did a "sensitivity read" for me, looking specifically for places where my whiteness obscured, assumed, or otherwise tainted my analyses. Dr. Andrea Wenzel at Temple University critiqued the full manuscript and spent a bunch of time talking out difficult concepts. And Dr. Anita Varma at the University of Texas at Austin helped me understand solidarity journalism and conceptualize the scope of the built environment as incorporating various movements.

Others who helped me along the way are Drs. Jacob Nelson, Matt Carlson, Nikki Usher, Anthony Nadler, Chris Anderson, and Seth Lewis. Through the course of this thinking, I developed four modules for journalism reporting classes and developed a network of more than 100 instructors interested in blowing up the J-School curriculum, called the Journalism Educator Collaborative. I appreciated all of the resource sharing and mentorship that occurred in that group as well as people's willingness to try something new, even in the middle of a pandemic, and their thoughts on how I could improve my work around trust building through engagement. You all know who you are. Having 14 of them implement the modules in some manner during fall 2020 and spring 2021 helped us refine everything and led to a public-facing website with a 105-page booklet breaking everything down into PowerPoint presentations, discussion prompts, classroom exercises, assignments, and suggested readings. More about this in the appendix, where I detail the methods involved in the data for this book.

The best parts of my gig at UW-Madison are the graduate and undergraduate students I get to work with and learn from. I hired 16 students overall, with different teams for each of the phases of the project (everything from interviewing to coding) and also to help with fact-checking, references, and formatting. The graduate students were Steven Wang, Carlos Dávalos, Kelly Jensen, Megan Zahay, Yiping Xia, Elaine Almeida, Danny Parker, Jessica Schmidt, Jesse Benn, Brandon Storlie, and Michael Aguilar. I also worked with undergraduate students. Some I hired because I was impressed with their coursework, and others I mentored in the Undergraduate Research Scholars program: Enjoyiana Nururdin, Rachel Reingold, Amira Barre, Devon Wanasek, and Seline Wiedemer. I feel particularly sentimental about Dr. Steven Wang, my advisee, whom I hired for several iterations of this project and who helped me—sometimes at the last minute—collect data, analyze, memo, and otherwise shape what this book would end up saying. He is such a gift to scholarship and was truly a full research partner in this venture. Thank you, Steven! And Rachel Reingold was superb in fact-checking the book—fast, reliable, and thorough.

I have a lot of family and friends who listened to me talking about various parts of this, probably ad nauseam. My mom, Gloria Robinson, talked to me nearly every day, asking for status updates and nodding emphatically at all the right times. My besties Linnea Anderson, Dr. Dawn Gilpin, and Dr. Krysten Schuler also endured my sometimes daily chitchat about what consumed those five years. My writing friend and neighbor Sara Alvarado got me over writing slumps, sticking a candle on my stoop in one instance that miraculously ignited the writing flow again. My son, who was 10 and 11 at the time of this writing, asked me every day if I had been "productive," and I found myself looking forward to our evening walks, where I could recount what I wrote about to him. Plus, there was Bini, our perfect Cockapoo, who spent every day snuggled up against me. All of these presences, looking back, seem so pivotal to getting all of this done.

Finally, I dedicate this book to my husband, Dr. Robert Asen, the Stephen E. Lucas Professor of Rhetoric, Politics, and Culture at the University of Wisconsin–Madison's Department of Communication Arts. He has always been the biggest supporter of my work and especially of the research applicable to the profession and our communities. He is cited throughout this book (as well as my other books) for his concepts on trust building in public deliberation and his thinking about citizenship within community. I find him to be a brilliant scholar whose ideas have implications for much of my work. I am honored to recognize him in this small way. He is also a pretty great husband, and I am grateful he is in my life as partner.

Prologue

Early on in my newsroom career, first as a beat reporter and then as an investigative business reporter, I participated in a lot of industry perseverating over how to solve everything that was wrong with the industry. In my master's program at Northeastern University, in the middle of that journalism career, I learned that even back in the 1940s, politicians, educators, academics, and media owners were wringing their hands at the state of journalism. Such a vital segment of our democracy seemed so vulnerable to conglomeration, sensationalism, advertiser influence, stereotyping, pack journalism, and a long list of ailments that needed fixing. Back in the 1920s–1940s, journalists hoped the cure would come in the form of muckraker journalism, and then it was New Journalism's literary style in the 1960s and 1970s, and finally, during my 13-year stint, we were all gung-ho about public journalism in the late 1990s. All of it really, come to think about it, had a single goal: to build more trust in mainstream journalism. At one point, I owned a T-shirt that said "Trust me. I'm a journalist." We wore such things sarcastically, of course.

I left the newsrooms in 2006(ish),[1] finished a PhD in journalism at Temple University in 2007, and landed in Madison, where I became a journalism professor at the University of Wisconsin. During all those previous years, I did not think much about trust or how to build it in any explicit sense. I admit that even by the time I got to Madison, the idea of teaching students how to build trust had not really occurred to me. I was caught up in getting them to understand what the story was, whom and how to interview, how to structure the information, and things like leads and nutgraphs and kicker quotes and the whole when you ASS-U-ME you . . . well, you know the rest. THAT was how we were gonna get the trust. Eventually we started talking more about "audiences" and "social media" as a way to report, as a way to market the stories to new audiences, as a way to build brands. The word "transparency" made the appearance sometime in there in the late 1990s or early 2000s. I never talked about any of this as building trust, though of course it was what I was doing: how to set yourself apart from the other news sites; how to make consumers come back to your brand over and over again; how to build productive relationships that source news and that expand audiences; how to become known as reliable, truthful, relevant, and interesting; how to make a difference in someone's life, in the world.

But as we neared the first quarter of the 2000s, a series of events and forces culminated to undermine the strength and authority of mainstream journalism in Western countries. By then, distrust had plummeted, hitting its lowest scores ever in 2016, rallying a bit in 2018, only to fall again in 2021.[2] Rapid technological changes in the media system were followed by an influential and growing conservative media machine (starting with talk radio in the 1990s) that sowed discontent in mainstream journalism. Then, in the early 2000s, a politicized antijournalism sentiment reflecting a larger-scale, anti-institutional populism swept the globe, proliferating "dark participation."[3] The ways that money and influence changed politics contributed to rampant polarization, disrupting public spheres[4] and creating a new "disinformation order."[5] The surprise election of Donald Trump in the United States in 2016 and the renewed demands for an international public reckoning around sexual harassment (the 2017 #MeToo movement) and racism (especially the 2020 Black Lives Matter protests) intensified the crisis. Western journalists found themselves under attack, culturally, rhetorically, and physically, and feared permanently losing their relevance as well as the authority to tell the day's stories.[6] Publishers and journalists struggled to figure out how to reverse the distrust trends even as they contended with internal critiques, such as the vigorous attack on objectivity as an essentially white supremacist construct.[7]

Meanwhile, civic think tanks, funders, and (some) political leaders became alarmed, worried about the rise of misinformation and the vitality of Western democracy. They began diverting money toward rebuilding trust through a medley of programs, task forces, grants, and other initiatives. At that point, we found ourselves in a unique moment at which the establishment of an entirely new journalistic paradigm was underway, and with it a new toolkit of skills—all with the singular goal of restoring the relevancy of mainstream journalism through engagement and other kinds of trust-building practices. And now it seemed like trust building was all any of us ever considered as journalists, as journalism professors, as journalism students: how to build trust in mainstream information about public affairs so we could save journalism and, in turn, save democracy.

To trust a news article, we knew, involved a combination of factors, although sometimes it was as easy as trusting the friend who shared it on social media.[8] It could also involve a known brand with a trusted reputation, a plethora of evidence and sourcing that lent credibility to the information, or even a transparency sidebar with information about who wrote and edited the story, which sources were used, what ethical decisions were made, etc. However, trusting an individual reporter was another kind of relationship entirely. Trusting a stranger involved more personal characteristics, such as presentation style, intentions (stated as well as assumed), and a consistent presence, as well as expressions of humility, heeding, ignorance, and an awareness of identities. I will go into all of this in the first chapter. Here in this prologue, I sketch out briefly the narrative I will take you on, laying out for you the grand statements I came to as I went through all my data from the past decade, fascinated by what was happening in this industry I have dedicated my life to. Through this narrative, I developed what I had come to think of as the **theory of trust building for journalism**, which was being practiced within a **built environment** that aggregated a series of intentional movements within the industry in response to this crisis of information relevance.

The trust-building theory was not one I made up, per se, but the result after analyzing five years' worth of data collection, considering all kinds of trusting relationships in regard to news and journalists, trying to break down the dimensions of trust as it was being rethought for a world divided, a world globalized, a world in which one's identity constructs were dictating where, why, and how one received and understood news. The theory of trust building as it was playing out asserted three major positions:

1. That trust happened through any number of engagements or other kinds of practices (e.g., radical transparency, minute fact-checking, solutions-based reporting) that created and nurtured personal, organizational, and institutional relationships between journalists, news content, and audiences or communities.
2. That for trust to be built and then nurtured over time, the participants in the information exchange must be considerate of the varying identities influencing and manifesting through the selection of content, sourcing, topics, etc. This *identity awareness* could be done through the practice of an *ethic of care* threading through the engagement practices.
3. This *identity-aware caring* practice via engagement strategies and techniques called for four new journalist roles and eight new or enhanced skill sets for journalists (and also, frankly, for all of us) that center around *learning* and *listening*.

I spend the chapters of this book making the argument for each component, introducing a series of actors in this developing new narrative for mainstream journalism as it was being practiced primarily in the United States between 2010 and when this book was finished in 2022. Many journalists and hundreds of programs, organizations, initiatives, funders, nonprofits, and newsrooms have been frantically trying to retrain the industry at all levels of the work, from the individual reporters to the newsrooms and audiences and the media system itself through policy work. The best part of exploring for this book was meeting all these people who think of themselves intentionally as change agents; these heroes had stepped out of more typical journalistic career paths to take on the saving of the news media in a manner that may not succeed. And there were students, the young, bright-eyed, optimistic ones who yearned to make a difference in this republic, to tell stories and help people make sense of the world. There were villains in the story, and these would be the ones you would expect: those intent on destroying the free flow of accurate information and purposefully tossing chaos into the information mix while undermining what little trust was left for mainstream journalists. But overall, this world comprised thousands of people simply trying to figure out how to *know* through mainstream news media.

It is important to note that these characters and this theory of trust building were already at work, forcing a regime enactment and giving birth to a dominating (though fluctuating) *built environment*. This environment was being ruled by a paradigm centered on trust building for public information exchange—as the primary strategy against all those forces I laid out. The first part of the book makes the case that this environment not only had already emerged but that it was well developed and thriving with a value system somewhat different from traditional journalism's honed routines around objectivity. This particular built environment was constructed, intentionally, to offer a path to journalistic revitalization, even though as yet there is scant evidence that it will work. In this, journalistic engagement and other strategies—some of which were in use before in journalism but many of which were less typical—became part of the toolkit for journalists alongside traditional values and methods such as quotations and attributions and balance and neutrality. This work led to, I am arguing, four emergent roles for journalists (alongside their traditional functions of watchdog and storyteller): *relationship builder, community collaborator, community conversation facilitator,* and *professional network builder.* Furthermore, these roles resulted in the need for eight new or enhanced skill sets to learn: radical transparency, power dynamic accounting, mediation, reciprocity, media literacies, community offline work, needs/assets/solution analyses, and collaborative production. These emerged as a number of submovements within the industry established new protocols and norms, including the fact-checking movement, movement journalism, service journalism, the nonprofit news movement, solutions journalism, community-centered journalism, antiracist journalism, and solidarity journalism.

Unlike other kinds of journalistic movements in the past, such as muckraking in the early 1900s or even the public journalism movement of the 1990s, the work happening with the aim of trust building between journalists and audiences occupied all levels of the media system, from policy and institutions down to the individual reporter at the micro level. As such, this built environment and its accompanying paradigm were more holistic and pervasive than anything that came before. This paradigm I set out to describe here was demanding from journalists an intentionality and authenticity within *trust building* and *engagement* that centered on four components: *identity, an ethic of care, listening,* and *learning.* I think of these as working in tandem; that is, the movers and shakers of this built environment put forward these engagement techniques laced with an identity-aware ethic of care enacted only through deep listening and broad learning.

Engagement with content and between audiences and journalists were the primary tasks, but not as a formula of production (in the way objectivity had become practiced: two sources for, two sources against, and a nice neutral kicker quote at the end). Many of the trainings entreated journalists to confront their own identities before enacting engagement. A big impediment was that journalists were actually taught to compartmentalize or push down these identities as a way to be neutral. This new paradigm could not work without an interrogation of these identities, not only as journalists but as racialized, educated, gendered, aged, classed, politicized beings. By holding explicitly their identities while reporting, journalists could appreciate how any trust-building activity would be influenced by these constructs, the change agents of this built environment surmised.

This kind of identity work practiced an ethic of care, pushing trust building beyond checklist journalism (e.g., "Yeah, I participated in the comments"). Instead, the engagement became a process of self-actualization in relationship to others and also to the content. In practice, this caring paradigm helped journalists to ask metaquestions like, Why did I choose this source? Why did I describe this person using these adjectives? What are my assumptions about this source going into this interview? This trust-building theory posited that such emotional labor on the part of journalists would more likely result in building trust because we knew from the voluminous research about trust that these kinds of relational characteristics tend to be present when trust is present.

I paused here for a moment, thinking about how my former journalist self felt about what I had just declared. Of course, it was not that I never cared as a reporter; the reason I went into the profession was because I cared to make a difference in people's lives. I cared very deeply about democracy. And I cared most of all that truths could be revealed to help us govern, to be productive, and to be happy. But these were abstract forms of caring. What I was talking about here, I told myself, was a more specific, personal kind of caring that evoked identity and promoted relationship building at the core of any journalistic practice.

Indeed, the built environment as it was evolving asserted that this engagement happening via an *identity-aware* or interrogated kind of *caring* could manifest only through *listening* and *learning* on the part of the journalists as well as on the part of audience members and communities. And here again I paused, admitting to myself that I was bristling at the idea that traditional understandings of reporting didn't already involve listening and learning. Throw in writing, and that was the entire job: journalists listened, they learned, and they wrote it all into some compelling story. In truth, I *listened* for soundbites and quotable statements, looking for "turning points." I *learned* in order to write authoritatively, to demonstrate I *knew* enough so as not to mess up context. And this was how I taught, too: listen and learn to produce stories. It was through this kind of evidence-based, contextualized storytelling that built trust in my journalism. Simple, right?

However, the kind of listening and learning in this revised theory of trust building—at least as it was being practiced in the industry at the time of this book—called not on authority but on authenticity, prioritizing not storytelling but connection. The theory fell back not on traditional protocols but on intentionality in a nuanced approach to information and sources. This listening and learning came from a place of *identity-aware care* that valued the process as much as the resulting story product. Engagement through this kind of care-based listening and learning would build trust and restore relevancy and promote connection with publics, according to this theory. By connecting trust building to engagement work with identity-aware care through listening and learning we have been asking journalists to help communities work holistically and *proactively* to be productive.

In this theory, information exchange became less about storytelling and more about solutions-oriented community work. As such, this journalistic work decentered binary "both-sideism" and the tendency to refrain from calling out racism, sexism, etc. because "we trust our readers to make up their own minds."[9] By caring, journalists attended to others; felt an obligation and responsibility to their publics; expended effort and energy to listening and learning; responded and adjusted their reporting based on people's identities, power, and other conditions; and worked in solidarity with communities.[10] When caring was present, listening and learning yielded greater insights, multiple perspectives, and solid links between news and trustworthiness—or so the theory went.

To put it more succinctly as a theory: **trust building happens through the nurturing of personal, organizational, and institutional relationships that people have with information, sources, news brands, journalists, and each other during what is commonly referred to as *engagement*. For trust building to occur, engagement needs to be practiced with *identity-aware caring* and enacted through *listening* and *learning*.** The following six chapters take you through my journey in exploring and understanding how all of this is playing out.

1

How Journalists Trust

Engagement Practices in an Industry Paradigm Shift

I peered into the large ballroom of the convention center in Milwaukee, Wisconsin, where the annual National Newspaper Association (NNA) was taking place in October 2019. "Wow," I thought to myself, "that is a *lot* of white men." Established way back in 1885, the NNA boasted more than 1,800 members as the largest newspaper trade group in the world and nurtured a mission to "protect, promote, and enhance America's community newspapers," according to its media kit.[1] As he passed me in the hall, someone gave me a giant button that read "We ❤ Newspapers." I felt like I had stepped into 1985, watching as NNA prepared for the start of the convention with flags carried by publishers from each state ready to parade in ritual through the center of the ballroom. I hadn't been surrounded by so many white people since I left Vermont and New Hampshire, where I had cut my teeth as a young, white, female reporter. Now a professor at the University of Wisconsin–Madison, I was there in Milwaukee at the NNA's convention to host a couple table talks about digital platforms at the invitation of the NNA administrator. I had agreed as long as I could recruit at the conference for two focus groups about trust building in journalism. I approached several women I saw, hoping to get people other than those who presented as white men in the room, but they told me they were "only wives." I spotted a Black man, only to be told he was a vendor and not a journalist. Resigned, I convinced a dozen white editors and one white female publisher to join me later in the day. Given all of this, I was curious about their engagement practices to build trust with an increasingly multicultural audience—the topic of my focus groups.

At the time, I was in year three of four years of data collection around how journalists build trust through "engagement" and other techniques in news media. Around the country, newsrooms—buoyed by funding from foundations, think tanks, philanthropists, and technology companies—had launched a wide spectrum of initiatives designed to connect them more

How Journalists Engage. Sue Robinson, Oxford University Press. © Oxford University Press 2023.
DOI: 10.1093/oso/9780197667118.003.0001

closely to their audiences. In Washington State, two journalists started a newsletter called *The Evergrey*[2] that hosted road trips to bring liberals and conservatives together to talk. In Florida, a former journalist launched a foundation-funded consulting program called Trusting News to retrain newsrooms in building relationships with audiences. In Pennsylvania, an organization called Resolve Philly[3] started receiving funding from at least five foundations to connect local journalists with different communities in the city, creating collaborations among media and convening forums around local topics of interest, such as economic mobility and COVID racial death disparities. And these are just a few of the kinds of collaborations, programs, and projects that started around 2010 and accelerated after the election of Donald Trump for his one term as president of the United States in 2016. By the time I visited the annual NNA convention in 2019, I was starting to reach research "saturation," the term qualitative scholars use to describe when they start hearing the same information over and over and they know they are done with their data collection. I was ready to start analyzing what I was witnessing.

I had gone into the project back in 2017 interested in exploring how a journalist's identities (racial, gender, age, education, and class)[4] influenced the way they tried to build trust with audiences. But as I dove deeper into everything I could find about the burgeoning movement around engagement strategies among newsrooms, I became fascinated by the vast built environment emerging and evolving, changing the very heart—and professional identity, purpose, and practice—of mainstream journalism today. I designed this research[5] to be iterative, each part building off the one before and culminating in a multiphase, multimethod inquiry at all levels (macro-institutional, meso-organizational, micro-individual) of public content production. I began by collecting as much information as I could about these many initiatives,[6] settling on about 30 of them to look at closely and interview their directors. From these, I paid attention to how power considerations were a top priority and documented the many strategies the news media projects created to build trust with their audiences.

I took these ideals, values, and new skill sets, and through in-depth interviews, surveys, and focus groups, I asked 174 reporters and 160 journalism students what they thought of them. I learned how they thought about their own identities (or not), what kind of engagement they practiced, and their thoughts about how best to build trust with their communities. And here is what I found—yes, many mainstream journalists remained mired in outdated and ineffective protocols, but, after more than a century of troubled adherence to the flawed ideal of objectivity, many in the news industry seemed ready to refocus their efforts on building relationships that prize meaningful (and at times subjective) interactions with community members. And a majority of them were eager (or at least willing) to partake in the massive retraining efforts happening in the industry by the agents of this revolution: the newly established industry consultants, the new engagement specialists being hired in newsrooms, those organizing the various forums and other events to help journalists meet and understand better marginalized folx, and of course professors of journalism like me teaching students how to collaborate, follow through, facilitate, and other techniques alongside how to report and produce content.

The question on your mind, I know, is: Will it work? Will these engagement strategies as implemented rebuild trust between mainstream news media outlets and their audiences in the United States? Will they save an industry that by all accounts is dying, fiscally and morally? Will they result in a renewed sense of trust among the disparate groups who have come to hate journalists? This book does not answer these questions, as important as they are, because we will not know how this turns out for perhaps years. However, how the industry has been trying to answer these questions—and the existential struggles present as we proceed—will determine the outcome. I want to take you into this ongoing inner conflict of journalists, journalism school instructors, and journalism students, as well as those who have dedicated their career to keeping the industry healthy for democracy to understand how this change is happening and what it might mean for the soul of the profession going forward.

In this evolution we all are witnessing—and that many of us, including myself as a newsroom consultant, a journalism scholar, and a reporting teacher, are participating in—we see a new respect and interest in trust building that finally considers the power dynamics, structural racism, and systems of oppression that create inequities, constant microaggressions, and bias against people who have typically been marginalized by news media.[7] Or at least, this is the theory of trust building that is being accepted as truth. This book documents that theory, along with what I am calling a vast "built environment"[8] that operationalizes the theory. This built environment overlays the mainstream news industry and has infiltrated many sectors of it through a number of submovements, from solutions journalism to solidarity journalism, from the fact-checking industry to engagement journalism, and a number of others. The environment, as I will describe in this book, thrives as a constellation of entities, from corporations to governments, traditional newsrooms to innovative community initiatives, extrajournalistic private organizations to high-profile and start-up foundations, as well as scores of committed (and often underpaid or even unpaid) journalists. These actors are networking in pursuit of a major paradigm shift for the profession centered on rebuilding trust in news and newsmaking. Collectively, these people and organizations are pushing mainstream journalism toward relational engagement and other strategies that also aim to create new revenue streams and restore political, commercial, and cultural relevance. This trust-focused network and its growth are facilitated by significant investments from think tanks, funders, foundations, technology companies, media moguls, and big media, but also by thousands of smaller projects undertaken by volunteers and nonprofits at considerable cost and effort in the most comprehensive industry transformation we have seen in a century. It encompasses elements of a vast network, a sophisticated social movement, and a social, professional, and technical infrastructure being built, carefully and very, very intentionally, both within and beyond traditional journalism.

This introductory chapter lays out the four components that make up the dimensions of this journalistic endeavor and the trust-building theory it practices: identity, an ethic of care, listening and learning, and my two anchoring concepts, trust and engagement. I define each briefly here.

- *Trust.* Trust is the outcome when people or things (such as news content) are believed to be reliable, authentic, benevolent, and credible. I will draw from both public, institutional kinds of trust scholarship like deliberation literature as well as the more personal, psychological, and sociological work on trust to understand this well-researched concept in all its dimensions. In journalism, what used to be a formal and distant kind of trust within the institution of the press is now activated on many levels, including between audiences and their news outlets as well as between community members and individual journalists.
- *Engagement.* Engagement is typically defined as participating, sharing, or otherwise partaking in relationship with someone or something. For the news media, engagement practices are interactions between journalists and the news organization with individual community members as well as audiences and work along a continuum from passive (such as click rates on a story) to active (such as hosting focus groups to

listen to community members). I will draw not only from the growing number of engagement studies in journalism scholarly realms but also from the fact-checking, community-organizing, activism, and solidarity work happening adjacent to journalism.

- *Identity.* As with trust, many books and entire scholarly paradigms have explored the concept of identity. For my purposes, identity is the composite of characteristics and fundamental things that make up a person or entity. This research considers identities as race, age, gender/sexuality, class, and education as well as career, ensuring that one's intersectionality is also explored. I will dip into sociology and communication studies as well as race, ethnic media, and gender and women's studies scholarship to explore this concept as it is a variable in trust.[9]

- *Care.* An ethic of care comes from feminist studies, particularly in philosophy and psychology, and refers to a specific morality that emphasizes interpersonal relationships and concern for others. Taking particularly from public enactments of care in democracies and deliberation, I theorize that trusting relationships around news can happen only through caring and being cared for, informationally. To do this, I argue, is to center identities in the caring practice to understand and account for different constructs that affect how, where, and what we come to know—what I am calling an "identity-aware care." Notably the theorized components of an ethic of care include listening and learning before acting.

- *Listening.* To listen is to attend to someone or something. In the literature around listening, including in speech communication and curriculum-instruction scholarship, robust listening demands responsiveness and often results in collaboration. We have always referred to listening in both journalism practice and journalism scholarship: who is being listened to, how to listen so as to ask the right questions, etc. In this book, we embrace holistic listening that transcends singular acts of hearing and encourages a variety of ways to listen, including listening to content, listening to algorithms, listening to teachers, and listening to each other—an actionable value that ensures an ethic of care might be effective.

- *Learning.* Beyond education studies, learning as a research topic can be found in many disciplines and generally means what happens when one somehow acquires knowledge or skills (and then what is done with that knowledge or those skills). In reporting practice, learning has always meant the accumulating of evidence and background research to be able to report with accuracy and context and then to write with authority. In this theory of trust building, however, learning is essential in connecting reporters with communities' histories, understanding the systems of oppression they cover, appreciating identity constructs during reporting, and building lasting relationships of trust.

It is the integration of these concepts that results in this theory of trust building in public information exchange articulated as follows: *Trust building* **happens through the nurturing of personal, organizational, and institutional relationships that people have with information, sources, news brands, journalists, and each other during what is commonly referred to as** *engagement.* **For trust building to occur, journalistic engagement needs to be practiced with** *identity-aware caring* **and enacted through** *listening* **and** *learning.* I know there is a lot to this theory, which is one reason my various reviewers and readers suggested I lay it out in the prologue.[10] Please bear with me as I move from one theoretical strand to the next, showing how each impacts another in the chapters ahead and incorporating them into my overarching framework.

It is important to note that this project is a continuation of my own journey to understand my identities, especially racially as a white[11] person, in relation to journalism, my chosen profession as a practitioner, researcher, and teacher.[12] The data and experiences you will read here reflect my background growing up in a very white New England town of 1,500 people. I went to journalism schools and worked in newsrooms from 1992 to 2005 where I was part of the majority culture, never interrogated my own privileges, and did not consider myself to have a "race." "Engagement" meant letters to the editor or email exchanges or coffee with sources—almost all of whom had the same white skin I did. It was only when I started researching my first book about how we talk about race in public spaces that I realized how ignorant I was about power and privilege in general and how complicit I had been in perpetuating systems of oppression that reified white supremacy through the way that I thought, acted, reported, taught, and studied.[13] I started my personal training in social justice in 2010 and continue that work today, still making plenty of mistakes and still trying to understand what I don't understand.

In addition, the journalism industry and also the academy have recently undergone both a "Me Too" and a Black Lives Matter movement to uncover the sexism, racism, and other biases that have always been a part of these institutions. Both of these global movements—"Me Too" in 2017 and BLM in 2020—forced a massive reckoning for many industries and institutions to uncover oppression occurring regularly and without reparation, unabated. As such, I also consider this book part of those movements,[14] as a way for us to collectively take stock, document, and find new pathways to doing better in this collective journey. Therefore, this book offers a lens of power and privilege to note how these are manifesting in this trust work through engagement practices and to appreciate the omnipresent challenges that entrenched systems throw at any change like this that threatens to topple the status quo.

Finally, one more note of transparency: I believe in this theory and have worked to prove its applicability and relevance. I believe that a vibrant, functional press is an essential part of having a vibrant, functional democracy, so, yes, this book assumes that mainstream journalism is worth saving. As I mentioned, I have operated as a part of mainstream journalism for going on 30 years now. Along with so many, I have felt desperate to find a way to restore trust between journalists and their communities, and for communities to have a working news media that amplify their various voices and help them find solutions to our various problems. And so I have been excited to participate in creating this built environment and in establishing this theory of trust building very intentionally. In addition to studying these concepts, I have collaborated with a number of different change agents and entities to retrain the profession—from establishing newsroom partnerships to overhauling reporting curriculum. I have led a consortium of some 100 reporting instructors and journalism researchers interested in disrupting contemporary journalism skills courses. I have participated in conferences and meetings and forums—sometimes organizing them myself—to establish this particular theory of trust building. I worked with three different projects to administer models of engagement via real-world interventions. In one, the Citizens Agenda,[15] I participated in training and then evaluating how more than 100 journalists rethought election coverage during 2020's spate of primaries and congressional, presidential, and municipal and state elections. In another program, I developed a set of four trust-building modules for journalism curriculum,[16] asked 14 reporting instructors to use them, and then evaluated what worked and did not work through interviews with the professors and surveys of their 160 journalism students. In the third program, I worked with the Wisconsin Field Day Lab on an education video game for a seventh-grade curriculum to teach young people how journalists work. I detail all of these participant ethnographic efforts in this book along with the recommendations for building trust in journalistic spaces.

Trust as a Concept in Journalism

Trust is, at its core, a relational construct. For trust to exist, a *mutual* respect, a willingness to heed on the part of *all* parties, and an active *engagement* must be present, according to public deliberation and other scholars. Trust is the essential ingredient in any democracy in which people must accept that their elected officials are governing effectively and honestly, and in which those officials must trust that the people will see the good jobs they perform and reelect them. When one builds trust, one gains authority in all kinds of realms; this has always been true for mainstream and also alternative reporters. Journalists have believed that the trust between them and their audiences manifests from the norms and routines based on the practices of objectivity, balance, fairness, and freedom from faction as major ethical tenets. This neutrality of the previous century has demanded a critical detachment from communities so audiences can trust that journalists are telling unvarnished truths.[17]

But trust is a fickle thing; it ebbs and flows, depending on the evolution of the relationship as each party enters and exits various experiences, paired with political, economic, and cultural forces. Gallup Inc. takes an annual poll that measures Americans' media distrust; 2021 saw the second-lowest percentage (36%) of Americans saying they have a great deal or a fair amount of trust in the news media.[18] Many organizations have nuanced these numbers: 56% agreed with the statement "Journalists and reporters are purposely trying to mislead people by saying things they know are false or gross exaggerations";[19] "Young adults, Hispanics, and those without a college degree are less likely to have a great deal of trust in their main news source";[20] "Young adults (18–34) today are more distrusting of the media than older adults and report less trust in media than adults their age 20 years ago";[21] "Local news bests national news in earning more trust of Americans for coverage that Americans can use in their daily life (79% to 19%) and in reporting without bias (66% to 31%), among other roles and responsibilities"[22]—to cite just a few. Trust has become highly politicized: "Currently, 68% of Democrats, 11% of Republicans and 31% of independents say they trust the media a great deal or fair amount."[23]

Major reasons for this decline in trust include digital technologies and cable television creating more information sources, less regulation of content on airwaves corresponding with a surge in conservative talk radio and cable news pundits, and newsroom fiscal crises after losing circulation, subscription, and advertising revenue streams, resulting in fewer journalists and less quality content.[24] In the research for my 2018 book, *Networked News, Racial Divides: How Power and Privilege Shape Public Discourse in Progressive Communities*, I heard a lot of the dismay over unmet expectations that people feel toward mainstream reporters as well as why they do not trust their local, regional, or national reporters. I noted especially how people's identities—especially their race and politics—influenced whether and how they engaged with journalists or journalism. This bears out in the polls and reports as well. One very thorough report found that though many Black Americans trusted news media in general, they did not trust mainstream journalists to cover their own communities accurately, believing that coverage of Black people was incomplete and one-sided and that reporters did not know or understand them.[25]

In that research for my first book, I also heard reporters' very cynical views not just of politicians and activists but also of "regular" people and some wariness of the new trust-building/engagement strategies being proposed at every turn. Yet, when I started, very little work had been done around *how and whether* mainstream journalists as discrete individuals trust community members; I want to note, though, that quite a significant subfield of ethnic media scholarship has engaged with identity as a key component of their reporters' paradigm.[26] This is where this book enters. In these pages I explore (1) how different mainstream *reporters* trust people and practice different sets of ethical standards depending on their identities; (2) the different kinds of journalism roles and skills needed for new engagement strategies being practiced, and how feasible these strategies are given the realities of newsrooms and journalism schools today; (3) the metaconversation about what transformative engagement work means for journalism as a moral guide moving forward; and (4) what new practices might build bridges so all people can engage in a vibrant, informed civic, deliberative life within a U.S. democracy in a manner that is morally appropriate. For this last one, we must steep our recommendations in the real-life challenges and obstacles in both newsrooms and J-schools to push forward a new mindset, one that is centrally entangled in issues of power and privilege.

In other words, this book sets out to document how this budding theory of trust building in journalism is being pushed and practiced in the United States today and how we can help it along. In this process of innovation and collaboration, these entities—people and organizations that I dub "trusting agents"—have collectively created a living, growing, thriving "built environment" that networks formerly disparate and competitive democratic players such as newsrooms and foundations. As such, this is also an optimistic book, for in the course of researching it, I have been so gratified and impressed by those giving everything to save this industry, and I find myself a little surprised at the numbers of mainstream journalists now ready to try something different.

But what is really meant by "trust," and how do we know when we have built trust? "Trust" can be defined as a belief that someone or something can be taken at face value in terms of their or its credibility, accuracy, and truthfulness or authenticity. Public deliberation scholars use the concept of trust as a foundation for productive dialogue and break it down into a set of attributes that must be present: that people come with benevolent intentions, that people respect each other, that they heed points, that they deliberate openly and with vulnerability, that people are willing to change their mind, that they offer evidence, that they argue with integrity, and that what they say is accurate or at least not knowingly false. When we apply these ideas to journalism our list changes a bit because traditionally we have not been talking about an *individual* kind of trust but rather an *institutional* kind of trust, where news brands ask audiences to trust their content is true.

Really, though, the journalist/press-audience relationship with trust is complex and involves three levels. The first level is an impersonal, abstract trustworthiness whereby audiences trust that journalism as an institution must exist for democracy to thrive. The second level is an organizational, branded trust for newsrooms.[27] For example, Democrats trust CNN and the *Washington Post* in the same way that Republicans trust Fox News: because of the general reputation and grand narrative of these organizations. Finally, at the third level, the individual reporter must enact a most personal trust in considering how to engage with people, and those people must trust the individual reporter based on no personal knowledge but with significant personal stakes at risk.[28]

The nature of this trust—that is, the dimensions of trust itself, and not just the type of trust—is also at play here. In a blog post, Democracy Fund (a foundation trying to increase trust in democracy via the media, Congress, and elections) declared that any trusting relationship must incorporate both cognitive and affective elements, where "cognitive" refers to logical functioning such as reliability, credibility, responsiveness, etc. and where affective elements include the emotions, vulnerability, and gut feelings.[29] Traditionally, the U.S. press has been mired in the first kind of trust, cognitive, where journalists have offered audiences a kind of contract: we will make sure everything we tell you about the world is as accurate as possible at the time we report it, and we will do so consistently and reliably over time, but you need to accept this proposition by looking at our ads and subscribing so we can make a lot of money. Oh, and please buy our classifieds.

This transactional approach to trust worked for a very long time (with most white people), especially before digital technologies overturned the three-tiered revenue model of subscriptions, advertising, and classifieds and also before people could find news for free on social media. Gradually, news media companies saw profits shrink and responded to demands from shareholders to contract, and massive layoffs began in the late 1990s. The Pew Research Center found that circulations were down 13% and more than 60 news outlets had shuttered between 2019 and 2020 alone.[30] As newspapers closed or published less content, and more specialized, niche content proliferated, the transactional trust model unraveled.

It is important to contextualize here a few things about trust in relation to news media in the United States. One, most polls that have documented how much Americans distrust the news media over time tend to measure only impersonal, abstract, and institutional trust without nuancing whether respondents are thinking about national cable channels or local newspaper outlets, for example.[31] And these evaluations certainly do not get at which dimensions of trust the media are losing or gaining in any given time. Two, as people have turned away from mainstream news, they have turned toward more ideologically driven information sources, starting with cable television's media pundits in the 1980s and conservative talk radio during the 1990s and settling with what friends and family are sharing from obscure blog posts and (sometimes) malevolent bots that are deliberately spreading lies and "fake news" to create information chaos and undermine our democracy.[32] As a result, a polarized information world grew up along with our political polarization, creating such deep divides that people stopped talking about politics with family. This makes sense if we think back to that distinction from the Democracy Fund blog between the cognitive and affective parts of trust. Although for many years journalists were benefiting from cognitive kinds of trust, their audiences now have demanded affective kinds of trust—a kind that reporters did not know how to generate and that they approached with disdain and wariness. Indeed, reporters were taught to avoid getting too close to sources or audiences and to substitute evidence for emotion. Nonetheless, as I thought about my own trusting information habits, this line from the Democracy Fund distinction rang true for me: "The evidence around human cognition and reasoning increasingly points to a counter-intuitive relationship: often, we enter into a new relationship (with a person or a system) with a level of trust that is influenced by the 'bubbles' (i.e. communities and networks populated by like-minded folks) that we in-habit."[33] In other words, journalists need to eliminate their disdain (though it is always good to maintain wariness) and begin appreciating and working within these "bubbles" if they want to reach more people.

The consequence of this information polarization, very bluntly, was seen on January 6, 2021, as Trump supporters believed well-orchestrated lies about a stolen November 2020 election and stormed the U.S. Capitol in an attempt to overturn democracy by attacking congressional leaders who were certifying the presidential win of Joe Biden.[34] A few days later, the Department of Homeland Security[35] issued a rare alert that domestic ter-rorism resulting from "false narratives" was on the rise and threatened the safety of our nation and democracy itself. Trump's removal from office (and subsequent ban from all social media platforms) did nothing to extinguish this countermedia machine or its influence over millions of Americans. Even months after Biden was certified as president and took office, even as all the dozens of cases about election fraud by Trump were dismissed by court after court (including the U.S. Supreme Court), the majority of Republicans believed that Biden had stolen the election.[36] The conservative media outlets that actively put out this false narrative remained vibrant and lucrative as of this writing, and Trump supporters were already working on the next elec-tion. Furthermore, Russia and China continued to undermine mainstream journalism with sleeper information bots that posted lies and misled people to create havoc in our democracy.[37]

All of this is to say that trusting information about public affairs has be-come a fraught and uncertain affair (e.g., not reliable, not consistent), and even journalists sometimes have a hard time distinguishing what is true and what is not. As a result, journalistic authority over information as a democrat-ically essential institution has diminished significantly. It is my assumption that this is a bad thing, not only for democracy but also for knowledge and meaning construction and feelings of community belonging. The industry cannot continue along the path it chose more than a century ago. The refrain I have heard from some traditionally oriented reporters that what is needed is to double down on "accuracy and investigative work and neutrality and show the world what they are really about," as one of my survey respondents wrote, will not work.

This reminds me of a conversation I had recently with ananda mirilli, a queer, immigrant, and Brazilian American working as a community leader, activist, consultant, facilitator, and coalition builder in racial and restorative justice, especially in K-12 education, including a stint on the Madison Board of Education. I invited mirilli into my journalism classes to talk about how reporters could operate with a lens of power dynamics and race, of engagement and care, rather than a false objectivity. I helped mirilli navigate the Madison media scene, and they worked to build relationships with local journalists. During these often-fraught conversations, sometimes journalists expressed exasperation and pointed to diversifying staffs and pervasive coverage of all of Madison's communities. To mirilli, this response seemed odd as many BIPOC communities had stopped viewing mainstream content long ago, even though many of the newsrooms had made huge efforts to make their journalism more inclusive. Indeed, this is a fundamental misconception of mainstream publishers today: any improvements must be intentionally marketed and networked among groups that are not currently paying attention to mainstream media. What this response might look like is the subject of this book, and it has something to do with how mirilli ultimately built relationships with local reporters and editors: One conversation at a time, with journalists who were willing to "show up, with some vulnerability," as mirilli recounted to me. In early 2023, mirilli told me they now felt a profound sense of trust for many of the journalists they had interacted with over the years because of these conversations.

As such, I laser in on the most popular and ubiquitous response—*journalistic engagement*—as a solution to distrust. I describe the thriving built environment pushing engagement work and other techniques in a series of new skill sets for journalists (and also for community members and information purveyors). I point to how journalistic trust and trust building are changing in both conceptualization and in practice, as well as how all of it can be more effective in *listening* and *learning*, how *identities* can entangle good intentions in engagement work, and why we might consider a full embrace of the tender side of these strategies as part of a *caring*, moral exercise that might save both this industry and our souls along with it.

Engagement as a Solution

I want to start with this now omnipresent term "engagement" as it was being used in the United States and other Western countries from roughly 2010 through to the present day in 2023. The trust-building theory for journalism I am articulating in this book demands engagement on some level—with content, with audiences, with other journalists, with technology platforms, with algorithms, etc.[38] Jake Batsell defined engagement in his 2015 book *Engaged Journalism* as journalism that "must actively consider the needs of an audience and wholeheartedly embrace constant interaction with that audience."[39] Others have conceptualized engagement as everything from "collective experiences" with the news brand[40] to "participatory culture and online interaction."[41] For newsrooms, this has always meant tools such as letters to the editor (public) and emails or phone calls (private) in addition to the regular "hanging around" reporters used to do or the community functions that editors and publishers did at the Rotary Club, for example. For years, journalism's engagement metrics included story clicks, Facebook likes and shares, comments under stories, and subscription buying. This kind of engagement is called "reception-oriented engagement," also simply, "audience engagement," because it centers on what the audience does with the content or the news brand and enhances a kind of monitorial journalism.[42]

But in this built environment of trust building, our engagement definition must describe a more robust version of the term, one that calls on journalists and news organizations themselves to be more immersed not only in the content they are peddling but also in communities. Journalists in this industry transformation should be building relationships with the content itself (this means not simply relaying vetted information but also committing to helping audiences fact-check in real time and understand how sources can be evaluated) and with the people in their communities.[43] As Guzmán stated in a 2016 "Strategy Study" online report with the American Press Institute, "At its most powerful, engagement is not a layer to add on top of conventional journalistic practice, but a firmer foundation that links journalism more closely with the people it aims to serve."[44] Some add the dimension of "relational" engagement, meaning engagement that aims to build relationships rather than simply to enhance the brand and boost audience metrics.[45] Newer forms of engagement include memberships, offline forums, listening sessions, online chats, online polls/surveys, and other tactics that take engagement to a more robust level. One study I did with my colleagues[46] (Dr. Yiping Xia as first author) using some of the data for this book found a wide continuum of engagement activities by journalists, ranging from promoting journalism through intense fact-checking sites to actual community building. We theorized that such activities over time "may contribute to the development of greater trust, connectedness, and social capital."[47] Indeed, research has shown that when audiences engage with news content to interact with journalists, they can influence copy[48] and improve their own civic life by participating more.[49] When people engage, trust is generated—either with the people or the content they interact with.[50]

However, if journalists are not willing or able to play their part in engagement because they believe it takes up too much time, for example, or there are not good return-on-investment metrics—as some research has shown[51]—engagement as a trust-building enterprise will fail. Indeed, a 2021 book by Jacob Nelson along with a slew of journal articles[52] he and others wrote sully some of the shine on the idea that this holistic understanding of engagement is going to work in the United States because ultimately, he wrote, we can never know what audiences want.[53] These studies report that newsrooms are feeling overwhelmed and disappointed at how little their constituents seem to want to participate with them. And maybe the biggest problem: engagement has yet to prove it can make money for newsrooms directly.[54]

Despite the lack of proven success models, this theory of trust building through engagement and other kinds of practices was present at every level of information exchange at the time of this writing, whether we are talking about macrosystems and structures where politics, culture, and policy live; meso-level organizations, newsrooms, journalism schools, and consultants; or micro-level individuals intent on pushing engagement work wherever they are at the hyperlocal grade. We can think about trust building along a continuum, with a transactional, commercial-oriented engagement at one end and a more relational (some might call it more authentic) engagement at the other end. Both have to be constantly nurtured and attended to. Along the continuum are different instruments and manifestations for engagement, as practiced at the time of this writing. For example, at least nine journalistic submovements that emerged over the past 15 or more years contributed to pushing the practice of journalism into new realms: engagement journalism, movement journalism, public service journalism, solutions journalism, solidarity journalism, the fact-checking profession, antiracism journalism, community-centered journalism, and the radical transparency movement. Each of these has been responding to the declining trust in mainstream news and the current environment of journalism irrelevancy.

The various submovements based around this trust-building theory created at least four new roles for journalists—relationship builder, community collaborator, conversation facilitator, and professional network builder—and demanded eight new (or newly emphasized) skill sets: radical transparency, power dynamic accounting, mediation, reciprocity, media literacies, community offline work, needs/assets/solution analyses, and collaborative production. These engagement strategies of trust building will be discussed in more depth throughout this book, especially in Chapter 2, which lays out the findings from 30 deep case studies of initiatives, programs, and projects centered on trust building as well as trade press discourse, interviews with the people involved, and hundreds of hours of participant observation in trainings, conferences, summits, and workshops. My evidence details the wide range of engagement work being done by entities founded over the last decade specifically to build trust in journalism throughout the United States, and also by individual journalists alone and in spite of the resistance of their bosses or colleagues.

A number of nonprofits, programs, commercial consulting firms, and think tanks have worked at all of these levels, including one of the stars of this book: an engagement firm called Hearken, founded in 2015 by Jennifer Brandel and Mara Zepeda in Chicago.[55] Using its proprietary software and technology along with community-organizing techniques, Hearken was training hundreds of newsrooms around the globe in new reporting practices that center individual audience members at all phases of content production.[56] As one part of its revenue model, Hearken contracted with these newsrooms on a tiered scale, averaging about $8,000 a year per contract as of 2021. Hearken helped newsrooms move the needle from transactional, reception-oriented kinds of engagement toward more relational ones. I will talk more in the next chapter about how Hearken and dozens of other companies, organizations, and programs were doing this; there I lay out exactly what these engagement practices look like and how these initiatives are trying to connect these strategies to trust building through an intentionally created network of relationships that are technologically enabled and often collaborative in nature.

Journalist Identities

In 2018, I published *Networked News, Racial Divides: How Power and Privilege Shape Public Discourse in Progressive Communities* to explore how and why white journalists stumble in their coverage of racial topics and proposed some ways to rebuild trust with Black and Brown communities specifically. In the course of the research for that book, I heard quite clearly how much journalists' whiteness inhibited them, even though only one or two of the journalists named the term "whiteness" specifically as the obstacle to trust building. For my purposes, "whiteness" represents a social construct, a racialized space[57] that nonetheless constrains the opportunities of real bodies and one that has colored traditional, mainstream journalism—its practices, its content, its functions—since its beginnings in colonial America and in other Western countries.[58] In *Networked News, Racial Divides,* I tracked how whiteness itself became a paradigm for the information flows in midsize progressive-oriented cities in the United States. Despite the best intentions of the progressive information exchangers, from the journalists to the bloggers, radio hosts, and social media posters, the construct of whiteness resulted in challenges to Black and Brown voices and actions such that it was hard for marginalized folx to get a word in edgewise. The white journalists taking part in those information exchanges tried not to engage in race as a lens for reporting, and as such, their own racial complacency propped up a problematic status quo.

In this book, I want to delve deeper into what role identities play in journalism for the journalists themselves and relate that more specifically to trust building. Because one major finding from that work startled me: people do not trust journalists for reasons often caught up in their identities, and *these racialized, aged, gendered, educated journalists reciprocate that distrust in the same ways.* And so, here I introduce identity as a major defining variable in thinking about building trust between mainstream journalists and their audiences. To do this, I have drawn mainly from interviews, focus groups, and surveys with 174 journalists at small, medium, and large news outlets mostly in the United States during 2018–20, asking them how their identities influence their job.

Journalists have long wrestled with identities, both their own and those of their sources and audience members, but open discussions about these identities were discouraged. Editors went to great lengths to keep any possible bias arising from visible or known identities from content and, for example, told Black reporters they could not cover issues explicitly about race, and gay reporters they could not cover LGBTQ+ issues.[59] As our populations became more multicultural, newsrooms more diverse (albeit slowly), and younger, more justice-oriented, socially aware generations participated in news making, journalists themselves began speaking out more forcefully.

For many, this latest iteration of the civil rights movement began in the 2014 protests in Ferguson, Missouri, after the police killing of Michael Brown—two years before Trump became president but well into the far-right Tea Party "populist" neoliberal movement that had been evoking a backslide into incivility, intolerance, and righteous violence (both literal and regulatory) toward those in our communities who were marginalized and disadvantaged. Wesley Lowery (formerly) of the *Washington Post*, who identified as Black, had spent the night in a police holding cell in August 2014 after police shoved him into a vending machine, shot rubber bullets and tear gas at him, and arrested him for being at the uprisings, which he was covering as a member of the press. That next day he called out a white MSNBC reporter, Joe Scarborough, for saying "Next time a police officer tells you that you've got to move along because you've got riots outside, well, you probably should move along." Lowery responded, "I would invite Joe Scarborough to come down to Ferguson and get out of 30 Rock where he's sitting sipping his Starbucks smugly." Thus began the contemporary *public* movement to change journalism from the inside, a movement that Lowery and other journalists of color were leading.[60] It is important to emphasize here that journalists and scholars have for generations pushed for more diverse and less biased newsrooms and journalism.[61] As evidence of this, I point to the spate of high-profile audits of news organizations such as the *Philadelphia Inquirer*[62] and the *New York Times*[63] that was occurring in 2014–22.

Two other journalistic events serve as examples for the pervasiveness of this movement within newsrooms and the metaprofessional discourse about the press. In August 2018, National Public Radio's *Morning Edition* made the decision to air an interview with Jason Kessler, a neo-Nazi and white supremacist who helped organize the UniteTheRight rally in Charlottesville in August 2017. At that rally, a white supremist drove a car into a crowd of counterprotesters and killed a woman. After the interview aired, critics claimed that NPR had normalized this extreme, racist position irresponsibly. Interestingly, NPR's defense demonstrated their deep reflexivity about their own identities as they pondered the decision. The *Morning Edition* cohost Noel King tweeted this: "I'm a biracial woman. Our Executive Producer is a

Black woman. I understand you didn't like this interview; I understand why, but Morning Edition is a notably diverse team who thought long and hard before airing this."[64] In this discourse, we can see that how a journalist engages is the direct result of their identity constructs.[65] All journalists have always made decisions—which stories to write, which sources to quote, which words to use—according to their identities, but to say so in mainstream newsrooms violated the commitment to neutrality.[66] As the United States grappled with a racist president who often said and tweeted racist things, journalists scrambled to respond. To call something racist seemed subjective to many (white) reporters and editors. But by spring 2020, protests all over the country about multiple police killings of innocent Black and Brown people forced an internal reckoning, as Andrea Wenzel documents in a forthcoming book tentatively called *Making News Antiracist*. In June 2020, for example, at least 44 journalists of color signed a petition demanding that the *Philadelphia Inquirer* do better after it published "Buildings Matter Too: Yes, they can be rebuilt, while lives are forever lost. But that doesn't mean they will be" in response to vandalism during some of the riots following the protests.[67] The signed petition read, "Sick and tired of pretending things are OK. . . . The carelessness of our leadership makes it harder to do our jobs, and at worst puts our lives at risk." The executive editor of the *Inquirer* resigned in the fallout. This movement is the topic of Chapter 3, which will delve into how this focus on identity came to be and into the forced evolution that is slowly taking hold in newsrooms today.

"Identity" is one of those terms that academics love to throw around and write books about. At its simplest, identity means how a person thinks of themself in relation to the world. Identity is known to be socially constructed, even as some identities such as race are a physically visible construct, while others like political identity are invisible. Other identities are choices made over the course of a lifetime: to be a parent, to be a leader, to be a sorority member, to be a knitter, to be a dog owner, to be a runner, to be a journalist. Anthony Giddens writes that "self identity is not a distinctive trait possessed by the individual. It is the self as reflexively understood by the person in terms of his/her biography."[68] For Manuel Castells, identity in a postmodernity era reflects participation in the network society and takes place within the context of power—both its absence and its presence.[69] In this book, I am referring primarily to racial, economic, sexual, and gender identity as well as the identity one forms as one begins to "train" in either journalism school or a newsroom to become a journalist.

Much research looks at how different groups of people think about mainstream news, such as how African Americans trust reporters more than their white counterparts do[70] (but not when it comes to covering their own communities)[71] and why conservatives feel mainstream news is too liberal.[72] We know that consumers of mainstream news tend to skew white, middle class, highly educated, and older,[73] and publishers lament their inability to grow their Black and Brown audience as well as younger people. So journalism studies scholarship has already made this connection to identity and trust when it comes to audiences. But what about how the identities of *journalists* influence efforts by newsrooms to build trust with different kinds of communities?

Some research has examined how Black journalists approach their job and have always had to fight for better, more inclusive practices, as recounted in Pamela Newkirk's *Within the Veil: Black Journalists, White Media*. We know that reporters who are not from the dominant culture bring higher sensitivity than white reporters do and a grounding to stories, as Candis Callison and Mary Lynn Young lay out in their excellent book *Reckoning: Journalism's Limits and Possibilities*. We also know from ethnic and alternative media studies how differently BIPOC journalists think about their jobs compared to those working in mainstream newsrooms.[74] In this book, the centering, essential tenet of journalists' identity to be neutral in their striving for an objective ideal is rejected. Instead, I argue that mainstream journalists have used this identity construct to prop up problematic status quos: "Too often under settler colonialism, the 'fourth estate' has served as the rationalizing propaganda wing of the other three," wrote Callison and Young.[75]

In Lowery's provocative June 23, 2020 column in the *New York Times*, "A Reckoning over Objectivity, Led by Black Journalists," he wrote, "What's different, in this moment, is that the editors of our country's most esteemed outlets no longer hold a monopoly on publishing power. Individual reporters now have followings of our own on social media platforms, granting us the ability to speak directly to the public." In the column Lowery wrote that his identity as a Black man bubbled up for him time and time again, despite the mandates in his job to compartmentalize identities such as race and political affiliation. He noted the contradiction that the white reporters who make up 84% of America's newsrooms are never called out for bias because of their race: "The views and inclinations of whiteness are accepted as the objective neutral." Instead he suggested journalists replace this trashed ideal with a "moral clarity" that would encourage them to consider their identities as they choose stories, sources, and headlines: "Ideally, the group of journalists given the power to decide what and whom to give a platform in this moment would both understand this era's gravity and reflect the diversity of the country." I spend a good deal of time in this book, particularly in Chapter 6, positing what this moral clarity might look like in practice. One of my main objectives is to emphatically underscore that white journalists can no longer sit out the conversation about race. They must understand their whiteness in all its dimensions, especially in how it influences their journalism, from how they choose story angles and sources to how they consider context for the news.

An Identity-Aware Ethic of Care

As I was thinking about all of this and trying to develop what I was seeing into a theory about building trust in journalism, I took on a new doctoral advisee named Elaine Almeida at the University of Wisconsin–Madison. Almeida studied visual and social media as places to express "tenderness," a concept deriving from the body of ethical, psychological, and philosophical literature known as "ethic of care." Reading her work about the expression of care and tenderness helped further my understanding of how identity mattered in engagement work that could lead to trust. For Almeida, care was necessarily caught up in identity as she argued that productive responses to expressions of oppression must evoke tenderness. Studying *testimonios* (essentially a form of oral history by marginalized survivors), Almeida asserted that such public discursive work inserts a kind of civic caring, and she cited philosopher Justin Leonard Clardy as defining so-called *civic tenderness* as "an orientation of concern that provides an impulse toward caregiving and protective behavior . . . an emotional disposition that involves the expansion of tenderness among a society's members, institutions, or systems."[76] Thinking about this sort of caring orientation offered a major piece that was missing in my conceptualizing of how the journalism profession needed to change to fully embrace the kinds of engagement and other practices being heralded in the built environment. Through caregiving and care receiving, journalists could set aside the mantle of objectivity and mandated critical distance that I believed inhibited true connection to communities in favor of the offering of a moral voice that is highly aware and appreciative of identities as well as the explicit expression of desire to help communities solve problems and have productive discourse.[77]

Care scholarship has long been steeped in concepts of identity. Its very coining in 1982 came when ethicist Carolyn Gilligan disputed her developmental psychologist advisor's theory about the stages of moral development because she believed it to be too steeped in masculine notions of justice and duty. She developed an ethic of care as a way to differentiate how girls and women view and practice morality as empathy and compassion rather than obligation.[78] Since then many disciplines have taken up care as a way to explain expressions of value and practices of morality— most of them dependent on identity as a major variable.[79] For example, in African American religions,[80] Black feminist studies,[81] and Afrocentric psychology, moral reasoning operates with a deep commitment to empathy, sympathy, and caring that incorporates "syncretistic reasoning" as well as intuitive, holistic, and affective qualities[82] and a "sense of cooperation . . . interdependence . . . collective responsibility."[83] In Jewish studies, care is the operationalizing of the Jewish tradition "We are our other's keeper" and the relationships that Judaism encourages between selves.[84]

Notably, much of the trust-building scholarship in many disciplines surfaces an ethic of care or some version of it as a primary method. Community work, civic engagement, and activism realms such as disabilities studies engage with the idea of caring as a strategic public-relations argument (with some leaders deciding that a "rights" or justice frame is more successful and prompting protest from others, saying it devalues care as unimportant).[85] Nonetheless, in order to become involved and provide assistance, caregivers must build trust, as healthcare workers and community leaders understand well, according to Susan Balloch and Michael Hill's 2007 edited volume *Care, Community and Citizenship*. Community organizers work to build confidence within their groups, help constituents understand complexities, connect stakeholders, and develop alliances and networks—all through "careful attention to building trust and enabling constructive relational dynamics"[86] (basically, the practice of caring). As one of my readers of this manuscript suggested, journalists could learn a lot about a more sophisticated trust building from community organizing, activism and engagement work.

I noted particularly some parallels with journalism in the robust dialogue in feminist studies around how humanity needs the practice of both justice and an ethic of care[87] even as patriarchal society spends more time and resources on justice as the primary objective (with the more female-oriented care work being supplemental).[88] This dichotomy plays out in journalism as well: objectivity as the dominant principle of journalists in Western democracies derives from a rational, logical, analytical, and cognitive Renaissance conceptualization of information exchange around public affairs; objective journalism is that which can be proven according to credentials set up to valorize white, propertied, educated men.[89] This trust-building environment centering engagement, though, developed new guiding norms that encouraged empathy, power sensitivity, relationality, cooperation, nurturing, and self-involvement. As such, a journalism trust theory suggests that this caring, moral work involves a journalist's entire self, including their race, class, and gender orientation as mitigated through personal, professional, and civic networks—a dramatic departure from traditional journalism principles that trained reporters to distance the self and to focus attention on the facts rather than the people involved.

In Chapter 3 I will go deeper into the ways an ethic of care can be practiced with an identity awareness in service of engagement to build trust. I will briefly mention here that I draw from the important work of Joan Tronto about how an ethic of care might be used as a framework for public deliberation and democratic actions through commitment to five values: attentiveness (knowing the needs of others by attending to others), responsibility (feeling responsible for others' care), competence (adopting an ethic of care requires action with appropriate resources and effort), responsiveness (adjusting our caregiving specifically for the person or entity at hand, and not by simply imagining what needs we ourselves might have), and solidarity (collectively understanding and accepting that care is essential to a working democracy and a thriving humanity).[90] It is important to note that this theory as it is working in journalistic spaces calls on both journalists and all of those who would exchange information about public affairs to engage with these commitments—with content and with each other. The two major components of the kinds of engagement that evoke an *identity-aware caring* with the aim of building trust are *listening* and *learning*.

Listening and Learning

Chapters 4 and 5 explore how journalists can listen and learn with an *identity-aware, care-based engagement*, using case studies to illuminate the theory of trust building. In Chapter 4,[91] I offer the example of news media literacies as manifested through what I am calling *listening-to-learn literacies*, which are a group of engagement strategies being employed across a few different initiatives, programs, and projects around the world that center listening as the primary way for journalists and their audiences to better learn. These trust projects expanded the work of media literacy into four spaces: the civic space (which would include K–12 spaces of literacy learning), the journalistic professional space, the social amateur sharing space, and the digital space.

In Chapter 5, I take up two case studies that focus on *listening to learn*. One is the Citizens Agenda,[92] a collaboration between Hearken, Trusting News, and the Membership Project to train more than 100 newsrooms in specific outreach to communities ahead of the November 2020 presidential election. I served as the research lead on the project and helped to survey and interview the journalists who participated after the election. The second is a set of four modules for reporting classes that have PowerPoint presentations, discussion prompts, readings, exercises, and assignments that I created from this data.[93] Fourteen professors and I used some of the modules in reporting classes, and my research team[94] interviewed the instructors and surveyed their students about how it all went in the 2020–2021 academic year. I dive deep into evaluation of these logistics to learn how this trust-focused built environment operates at a granular level, the challenges and strategies to doing the work, and the outcomes for these kinds of applications so that we can revise the models and modules. These applications of the theory of trust building are not perfect by any means, and I will be frank about the challenges, especially because many of these happened during the COVID-19 pandemic that drastically curtailed people's resources and capacities, including journalists, journalism professors, and journalism students. Furthermore, the realities of constraints in newsrooms significantly hamper movement on deeper engagement work.

Those working in the built environment being established are training (and retraining) journalists and augmenting reporting classes for new or enhanced skill sets that focus on listening and learning in a major new paradigm for the industry. These efforts take many forms, and I have aggregated nine specific movements that fall under this trust-building paradigm, although it is not always easy to tell the boundaries and parameters of each one on its own. One[95] movement is the professional and formal fact-checking industry that grew during the early days of the new millennium, dedicated to vetting political claims with "their own rules, routines, and best practices" (discussed by Lucas Graves).[96] This fact-checking movement matured along with an insistent "radical transparency," a second movement that serves as a scaffolding for the trust-building paradigm. Transparency as a trust-building strategy showed up in the 1990s but became formalized and institutionalized as journalists scrambled for ways to convince their publics they peddled accurate and vetted information during the early 2000s.[97] A third, long-time movement pushed newsrooms to be more community based, incorporating local leaders and community members into journalism processes using a variety of approaches, including the rise of nonprofit news outlets focused on the hyperlocal.[98] Arising from this community-based work, a fourth movement, the antiracist movement, has emerged since the 2020 BLM protests that accelerated a reckoning within the industry.[99] In antiracist journalism, the work strives not only to be free of superficialities and bias but to proactively use race as a lens for analysis, call out power dynamics, and educate about systems, structures, and policies of oppression.[100] Part and parcel with antiracism is the fifth movement, public service journalism,[101] when "the reporter's lens moves from the subject to the reader"[102] to provide news that is relevant and useful to readers; the sixth, movement journalism,[103] based on "prioritizing stories that amplify the power of people, producing news that is based on the experiences and identities of oppressed people, and developing shared political analysis between journalists and communities";[104] and the seventh movement, solidarity journalism,[105] which I have described already and refers to a specific type of reporting and writing that works in service to those who are marginalized or suffering with the frame of human dignity and lived experiences.[106] All of these overlap with the eighth movement, the broader engagement journalism that encourages interaction between journalists and audience members and that has been studied extensively in our discipline.[107] Finally, I come to the ninth movement, solutions journalism,[108] led by the nonprofit Solutions Journalism Network founded in 2013. Most of these movements eschewed traditional journalism practices that focused on problems instead of helping communities make progress toward resolutions.[109] For example, in solutions journalism, reporters connect stakeholders, research how others have solved problems, analyze limitations, and suggest possible ways forward through listening and learning that transcend soundbites and pro-and-con lists.[110] Figure 1.1 shows how they are all overlapping and mushed together as part of this pulsating and ever-changing constellation of movements working toward building trust

The Trust-Building Built Environment:
A Constellation of Overlapping, Contemporary Journalism Movements

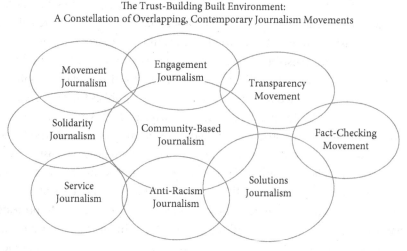

Figure 1.1 Movements contributing to the trust-building built environment

in mainstream information flows. Learning through such approaches is more comprehensive and, most important, demands proactive sharing of data with collaborators. Solidarity journalism centers power dynamics, systems of oppression, and marginalized peoples through grassroots reporting, giving primary attention to people's lived experiences rather than government diplomacy.[111] Both ask journalists to care about the people most affected by wicked problems primarily, and to prioritize listening and learning from them directly rather than through reports, databases, or anecdotes.

Summary: A Theory about Building Trust

Articulated, Modeled, and Tested

As I delved into these trust-building strategies, I began to appreciate some underlying assumptions of the work of engagement. Not surprisingly, the work demands journalists center the public; indeed, many of these strategies have their origins in the public journalism movement back in the 1990s. But the more intense changes would require journalists to be more involved in audiences' lives and their lived experiences than would have been comfortable under more traditional tenets. Because I still identified as a journalist even 15 years after leaving the newsroom, wariness and skepticism reared up for me, and my reflex was to push back on many of the strategies. How can treating sources differently in terms of, say, sending someone (but not everyone) the questions ahead of time be fair and neutral? But as I went through Hearken's engagement trainings, watched people like Joy Mayer of Trusting News work with journalists, and talked to reporters about opportunities for change, my understanding shifted. This is an entirely different industry from the one I entered back in the early 1990s as a teenager.

We need new skill sets, new relationships, and new mindsets. And we have them at the ready. This book documents all of this. The major takeaway will be a complete reworking of trust as a construct in a way that challenges the existing thinking about neutrality, abstract caring, and routines that keep reporters at a critical distance from communities. Instead, we can reimagine trust as something that lives within journalists as individuals who build relationships with communities and themselves and that reconfigures their intentions for content. Furthermore, this book shows how journalists go about engagement practices differently, depending on who they are, what identities they possess, and how they navigate their own biases. Indeed, when they implement engagement strategies, journalists will fail unless those strategies are *proactively* connected to identities not only of the communities they are trying to build trust in but also their own identities, developing an awareness of privilege, bias, and complicity in inequitable systems.

This matters deeply for the kind and shape of response by journalists in their bids to revive this flailing industry. To this end, an entire infrastructure is in place to retrain journalists, a micro-meso-macro *built environment* that operates within a new trust-building, engagement-focused paradigm, combining a handful of submovements, some disparate and some overlapping each other. This infrastructure has now overlaid the mainstream industry, representing a constellation of trust-focused entities such as the Hearken engagement company, programs like Trusting News, academic centers like the Agora Journalism Center and Center for Media Engagement, and a slew of other trusting agents. The actors in this built environment work intentionally to evolve the fundamental identity and practice of journalists through a vast supporting metanetwork of foundations, researchers, trade press, media watchers, think tanks, and technology companies, as well as journalism schools.

The resulting complex theory of trust building that I unveil in this work can be helpful in explaining this moment in journalism. Engaged journalists become immersed in humanity, approaching people, communities, and knowledge with direct and explicit care. Engagement strategies center news work that helps build communities as opposed to watchdog institutions that are problematic for many groups of people. These practices force reporters to ask different questions and privilege outcomes that strive for justice and equity, replacing the view from nowhere to one that is situated perhaps geographically, perhaps topically, but always within community. They move the journalist from witness to proactive collaborator.

Journalists remain the arbitrators of public affairs in the sense that they must still offer accountings with facts independent from politics. It is not their role to "pick sides" in the abortion or the death penalty debates or any other ideological binaries, just as it does not serve truth to provide "balance" and create false equivalencies for topics such as climate change. However, as moral agents charged with seeking justice, journalists do have the responsibility to clearly and directly analyze proposals and events for their real-world impact on all members of communities. Certainly they should not make things worse, as we witnessed during the last decade of the Tea Party followed by four years of Donald Trump as U.S. president—all politicians who played the press like a fiddle such that journalism's conventions normalized a particular political extremism that was neither just nor equitable for all.[112] The concluding chapter of the book lists recommendations that emerged from a working model of trust-building strategies, broken down according to identities, articulated through an ethic of care, and evoked from deep listening and learning.

2

How Journalists Engage

A Theory of Trust Building Applied

"She is clever," I thought as I watched Jennifer Brandel, CEO and cofounder of the engagement consultant company Hearken, open the October 2019 Engagement Innovation Summit (Figure 2.1). On the screen at the gorgeous function hall with its skylights and climbing plants in downtown Brooklyn were the words "Dearly Beloved, we are gathered here to be in a relationship with the public and the community." Brandel, a white-identifying woman dressed in a somber black duster coat with white cuffs, signature glasses, and curly hair, was standing in front of a giant screen evoking the ultimate relationship everyone in the room of 150 people was familiar with on some level: marriage. "The closer you are in a relationship, the deeper you can listen, the more specifically you can respond, the better you can serve, the more valuable your work will be, and the more value you bring to the public." To do this, the summit's panels and presentations emphasized, meant practicing what was being called "engagement journalism."

It was my fifth such conference that year about "engagement journalism"—the latest movement meant to help mainstream journalists build trust with an increasingly multicultural and polarized audience. These meetings all comprised a mix of journalists, engagement specialists, J-school educators, media trust centers, and program directors. I was all in with this kind of journalism, completely committed to the theory of trust building through engagement and other practices being adopted by the profession. The strategies had their origins in other genres of journalism, to be sure, such as public journalism from the 1990s and ethnic media practiced by Black and Brown journalists, as well as trust-building skills used in community activism or public service. However, this was the first time in more than a century we were seeing the mainstream, white-majority newsrooms of the Western world (especially the United States) adopt new skill sets, new roles, and new mindsets at an infrastructural level so ubiquitously.[1]

How Journalists Engage. Sue Robinson, Oxford University Press. © Oxford University Press 2023.
DOI: 10.1093/oso/9780197667118.003.0002

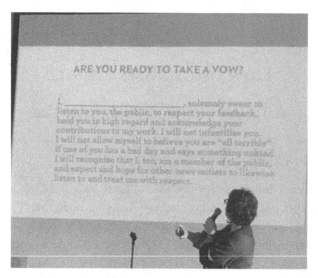

Figure 2.1 October 2019 Engagement Innovation Summit, picturing Jennifer Brandel of Hearken. Photo by Sue Robinson.

As yet, even a decade in, these transformations had yet to be proven successful in turning news profitable. We had to do something to save journalism and, with it, democracy. The industry had come under fire after the 2016 U.S. presidential election campaign's coverage that missed the groundswell of support for Donald Trump.[2] Now, after three years of waging battles between Trump and his far-right supporters, politicians, and media machine, mainstream journalists in the United States felt exhausted and bitter. People were wearing T-shirts in public that read "Rope. Tree. Journalist. Some Assembly Required." Trump and his allies regularly called the press "enemies of the people," and far-right rallies and other events had become dangerous for anyone carrying a press badge. By 2018, Reporters Without Borders for the first time ranked the United States as among the most dangerous nations in which to work as a journalist.[3] So much was at stake already—and COVID-19 had yet to appear during that beautiful fall of 2019. As I sat there, I could sense the desperation of the editors and reporters in the room, with their local newsrooms losing half of their editorial employees and 68% in revenue over the past decade alone and polls showing less than a third of Americans trusting news media.[4]

Brandel and her team at Hearken wanted to slow the steady decline of the profession, and so she had invited these journalists to New York to appeal

Figure 2.2 October 2019 Engagement Innovation Summit, picturing Jay Rosen of New York University. Photo by Sue Robinson.

for a significant change to their coverage of the upcoming 2020 presidential and other elections. Instead of the typical horserace, game-frame election stories, Hearken wanted to help newsrooms implement robust kinds of engagement practices as a way to start reversing distrust. Specifically, Brandel was introducing an elections engagement guide called the Citizens Agenda that provided a blueprint for journalists to ask community members what they wanted the candidates to talk about. The guide was the brainchild of a New York University journalism professor named Jay Rosen, who was most well-known for his piloting of the so-called public journalism movement in the 1990s (Figure 2.2). I noticed most of the journalists in the room were probably too young to remember public journalism, but I had been doing it in my newsrooms myself 20 years ago—inviting community members into focus groups for story-generation sessions, sharing feedback, and acting as the direct conduit for people to their public officials. I had always been a fan, but after a decade or so with some 5,000 news outlets participating in some way or another, the movement petered out as newsrooms contracted and resources dried up and it was all journalists could do to get the daily news out.[5] Here at the conference was public journalism repackaged as a Citizens Agenda exercise.

The journalists around me listened intently, taking notes. Rosen, who identified as a Jewish man and was wearing glasses and a black leather jacket, got up to talk through the guide, joining Brandel on the stage. As the sun streamed down on us, Rosen took us through the Citizens Agenda protocol: set a vision for better coverage of elections, identify stakeholders, ask the voters what they want the campaign to be about, synthesize input, solicit actionable feedback, use the feedback to ask candidates questions, reflect, and adjust.

"Citizens Agenda is a listening plan," he told the crowd. "An engagement map. An editorial product. It is a work of synthesis. It involves art and judgment and not just data. You have to be prepared to take responsibility for what you included and what you left out."

He paused. A hand rose. "How do you avoid being accused of having an agenda?" It was a good question, and people waited for the answer. Rosen tried to be honest: "I don't think we have had enough tries to counter that situation yet." He proceeded to brainstorm a response. Part of the answer, he said, is making sure journalists reach as many groups and platforms as possible, offering surveys and events and Facebook Q/As. "It is every method you can imagine. If you rely on just one, you are going to be disappointed," he warned. If someone along the way complains about missing items, journalists should invite them to revise the Citizens Agenda. Some journalists nodded, while others stared with a blank expression up at the screen, perhaps trying to imagine how such a Citizens Agenda[6] might play out in their cities and towns, if they had the staff to do it, and what other tasks would have to be ditched.

A white woman, Joy Mayer of Trusting News, stood. Where Rosen had a PhD and an academic vantage point for his media criticism, Mayer had the long journalism pedigree born in daily newspapers and had helped create the guide. With her blonde curly hair and jovial personality, Mayer oozed enthusiasm and, like Rosen, lived and breathed engagement. After getting her MA from the Missouri School of Journalism, she directed a program called Trusting News that launched in 2016 and was funded by American Press Institute and the Reynolds Journalism Institute to train newsrooms all over the world in actionable strategies to build trust by demonstrating credibility in the content they produce.

She turned to the crowd and was blunt: "One thing we take for granted"— and I noted the astute use of "we"—"is that we do not get credit for our good service as journalists. The country is actually divided about whether journalists protect democracy or harm democracy. The fact is we believe that communities deserve a shared set of facts. This is a chance to declare publicly what your motivations are: we asked what you thought and here is what we did with that information. That feedback loop is so important. When people think of the media as journalists who help them live their lives, that is when we have succeeded."

She was talking their language. Yes, yes, I could hear my former newsroom colleagues droning in my head: it was just that we have been misunderstood! Lies have been told about us. This Citizens Agenda would reintroduce us to the public, combining this vague, decades-old concept *engagement* with good journalism. There we all were in that spacious Brooklyn ballroom, accepting this fairly radical theory of trust building through relationship-based engagement reporting. (Although, I could not help but think, why is this so radical exactly?) Our collective cynicism and depression lifted at the prospect of this Engagement with a Plan in the form of Citizens Agenda. Surely we shall implement this, and trust will be restored.

I had invited myself to Hearken's summit to, first, ask journalists there to fill out my survey about engagement practices and, second, meet with Dr. Regina Lawrence, a professor and associate dean who was (at the time) the research director for the Agora Journalism Center out of the University of Oregon in Portland; I wanted her to consider collaborating with me on something engagement journalism–related. Lawrence, a white-identifying woman, represented an instrumental agent in not only implementing the trust-building-through-engagement theory but also in filling out its scholarly dynamics as a senior researcher in the field. Agora operated as a research center conducting studies, a newsroom engagement training center, and a networker producing a regular newsletter for all those working in the engagement realm.

Lawrence suggested I meet with the Citizens Agenda team at a table way in the back a few hours after the project debuted with these journalists. There, Brandel introduced us to the petite, white-identifying woman next to her as a "dream wrangler." Her name was Bridget Thoreson, she worked at Hearken, and she would lead the Citizens Agenda project as an organizing force with an incredible eye for detail and a lifelong commitment to relationship building as a journalist. I would come to get to know (and like) Thoreson very well over the course of the next year because, before I knew what I was doing, I had volunteered to be the research lead on the team. This meant I would help in what would become a massive retraining effort for more than 100 journalists ahead of the fall 2020 elections, evaluating these efforts and any outcomes.

Thoreson started that very first team meeting by describing the vision of Citizens Agenda and dubbing us the "dream wrangling" group that could make it happen. "There is a hunger for this kind of work, but how do we turn this hunger into the work?" Thoreson asked. Oh, in that meeting, we created grand visions of in-person workshops, taking the Citizens Agenda guide to newsrooms in a series of free training sessions throughout 2020. We would walk journalists through relational reporting practices to make—we hoped—more public-oriented, engaged, and trustworthy political journalism. (Of course, we had no inkling at that time that the COVID-19 pandemic would make face-to-face trainings—and really, any engagement journalism work—deeply difficult, and in some cases impossible.) We spent the rest of the meeting talking almost entirely about the logistics for how these trainings might come to fruition, thinking about possible funding sources (Brandel's job), training organization (Thoreson's job), training content (Rosen, Mayer, and Thoreson's jobs), and research (Lawrence's and my job).[7] And we left Brooklyn feeling optimistic, like we were doing *something*.

As I flew home to Madison, I spent the hours pondering what I had just witnessed. One of my research questions going into this project had been: **What is the relationship exactly between trust and engagement?** This is a conceptual question, but also a scholarly one, that first demands a deep dive into what we mean when we say "engagement," logistically, and so the first part of this chapter explores how these new trust initiatives like Citizens Agenda have been advising journalists to rebuild trust through specific engagement practices. What are the assumed dimensions of engagement and its intrinsic value as a trust-building mechanism? What new journalistic roles and skill sets must emerge in this work? To answer these questions, I collected data on almost 100 of the programs, projects, centers, commissions, consortiums, and initiatives around the world that aim to build trust through some kind of engagement strategies. My research team and I took on 30 of them as deep case studies. The trust initiatives I looked at—from small to large in scope, from Washington, DC, to Washington State, Turkey, and Paris[8]—consider "engagement" broadly and operationalize "trust building" at all macro-institutional, meso-organizational, and micro-individual levels. We analyzed all the digital content produced by and about these projects and also interviewed the managers of them.

In the process of this analysis, I landed on the certainty that what I was seeing was a trust-focused new paradigm for the profession with what I am referring to as a "built environment" that encompasses elements of a vast network, a sophisticated social movement, and a collaborative professional and technical infrastructure being built both within and beyond traditional journalism.[9] This built environment, already developed, already entrenched, overlays the news industry and has infiltrated many sectors of it. Communication studies lacks adequate terminology to describe and explain this transformation, but I employ this "built environment" term to represent this constellation of entities from corporations to governments, traditional newsrooms to innovative community initiatives, extrajournalistic private organizations to committed (and often underpaid or even unpaid) journalists, all of which are networking together with great intent. Collectively, these people and organizations are pushing mainstream journalism toward relational engagement and other strategies that aim to build trust around their information production, create new revenue streams, and restore political, commercial, and cultural relevance. This trust-focused network and its growth are facilitated by significant investments from think tanks, funders, foundations, technology companies, media moguls, and big media, but also by thousands of smaller projects undertaken by volunteers and nonprofits at considerable cost and effort in an attempt to save journalism. Operating at all levels of the media system (macro, meso, and micro), it is a dramatic response to a series of events and circumstances colliding in the short space of a few years, roughly 2010–20, including a number of polls showing steep declines in trust toward mainstream news sources especially in the United States but also in other Western democracies.

This chapter is dedicated to showing how and when this trust-building movement started and how these groups are forming their own collaborative networks to breathe oxygen and energy into it, intentionally and at scale. I document this built environment by describing each layer and level of trust building by analyzing the case studies' list of strategies and techniques. What is the scope of trust building for the industry? I report what journalists, journalism instructors, and journalism students thought about trust building and this engagement movement. Has this relational engagement skill set been widely embraced by the profession? What has been the connection to trust building, according to these practitioners? What have been the challenges? These trust strategies have become a new calling card for many journalists as they scramble to find the particular transformation that will save the industry, economically and culturally.

The answers to these questions helped fill out my working theory of trust building around mainstream information exchange for news: *Trust building* happens through the nurturing of personal, organizational, and institutional relationships that people have with information, sources, news brands, journalists, and each other during what is commonly referred to as *engagement*. For trust building to occur, journalistic engagement needs to be practiced with *identity-aware caring* and enacted through *listening and learning*. This chapter provides the evidence for this emergent world centered on relational trust building through a continuum of engagement practices. First, I provide the documentation for the built environment as it is playing out at the macro, meso, and micro levels of the Western media system. Second, I detail the new skill sets and roles journalists have begun to adopt to make the built environment thrive, including relationship builder, community collaborator, conversation facilitator, and professional network builder, taking on eight new (or newly emphasized) skills: radical transparency, power dynamic accounting, mediation, reciprocity, media literacies, community offline work, needs/assets/solution analyses, and collaborative production. Finally, I bring in "an ethic of care" and the theoretical framework that helps explain the intentionality behind the engagement (re)trainings by using Joan Tronto's five values associated with public caregiving: attentiveness, commitment, responsibility, responsiveness, and solidarity.[10] To build trust, journalists can be guided by these five values through the production process of listening, the caring and caregiving process of information exchange, and the outcomes toward learning.

The Built Environment: A Paradigm of Trust Building

Between 2010 and 2017, as I was researching and writing (and rewriting) my first book about how white reporters can build trust in Black and Brown communities, I began getting invitations to media trust summits and noticed an increasing number of well-funded projects centered on rebuilding trust— a trend that accelerated after the 2016 journalistic debacle that was the coverage of the U.S. presidential election. Of course, all of us paying any kind of attention to media knew (and studied, taught, lamented) about the increasing information polarization happening in Western worlds, but suddenly the ramifications slapped us in the face with the surprise election of Donald Trump to the highest U.S. office in 2016. Journalists struggled to holistically and compassionately cover the blatant lies, explicit racism, and sexism of politicians; their norms of objectivity had evolved into practice that forced binaries and false equivalencies. The industry faced an existential crisis about their increasing irrelevancy to many groups. Revelations about widespread sexual harassment and assault pinged our social media feeds in what came to be known as the #MeToo movement, started by a Black woman named Tarana Burke in 2006 and going viral globally in 2017. This was followed by increasing mainstream anger at the continued police killings of Black and Brown people, culminating in intense and global Black Lives Matter protests in 2020. Newsrooms along with civic think tanks, academics in political science, sociology, and communication, and democratic foundations scrambled for a response that would pick at the rampant distrust problem, especially among conservatives and people of color. We saw a slew of initiatives dedicated to new kinds of *listening* and also new kinds of *learning.* And we all started exploring new ways to engage and connect with these audiences through relationship building, community collaboration, conversation facilitation, and industry networking—both internal within the industry and external with communities.

Take, for example, First Draft.[11] I had a chance to catch up with Aimee Rinehart, the deputy director of First Draft, in January 2021 to learn about this expansive consortium of technology companies and newsrooms as well as academics all bent on stopping the spread of fake news and misinformation. Google News Lab worked with nine groups to launch the for-profit organization in the summer of 2015.[12] Its mission page stated, "Everything we do starts with collaboration. We bring together a global network of journalists to investigate and verify emerging stories. We work with our partners to conduct innovative research projects and develop pioneering training programs. And we share cutting-edge digital tools to help both content creators and the public make better-informed judgments about the information they encounter online. By standing up for truth in a polarized world, we can build more trust in society and help every community to thrive."[13] In this iteration of the trust-focused built environment, First Draft sought funding for individual projects all over the world in which they organize specific and timely collaborations to, for example, combat disinformation during the October 2019 presidential election in Uruguay[14] and the global problem of intentionally misleading content about the coronavirus and its vaccines.[15] Another core element is helping their newsroom partners rethink traditional sources: "What 2020 has taught us is that the authorities are not necessarily the authorities anymore. You have to not be the stenographers; you have to check into everything they say. When the president is no longer an authority, then who else is no longer an authority? When a police department has something at stake, an officer who has been charged with a crime, it is the journalists' job to interrogate that information. Who is the expert now?" To do this, First Draft built out and nurtured a series of mini-networks that pop up for a specific need and then disperse by establishing collaborations between a set of news partners in a particular area for a particular event all based around some kind of fact checking that demands intense engagement with the circulating content. "First Draft offers a neutral hub for these partners," which would otherwise be competitors, Rinehart told me in our interview. Part of their work includes in-person training sessions for reporters not only on how to spot fake news and debunk it quickly but also on how to work together. "What I love to see at our events are when business cards start flying and we see those relationships being made," Rinehart added.

While First Draft represents a largely professional-focused, internal effort, other projects turn toward building relationships, collaborating, facilitating conversations, and networking with communities externally. For example, on August 26, 2017, Fiona Morgan and Alicia Bell helped organize and facilitate an exchange between 80 community members and journalists in Charlotte, North Carolina, for a conversation about reckoning with the city's racial and other kinds of disparities.[16] There, city residents pointedly asked reporters to make the effort to deeply understand their past and also to help the city find resolutions. The event was a reckoning for journalists, who participated, listened, and talked through possible partnerships with community members as they worked to develop a less hierarchical and more collaborative manner of news production. The journalists left with an armful of stories to co-create, new voices to amplify, and new alliances with other media around the intractable problems of disparities.

It was exactly the kind of trust-building work Morgan and Bell, who had organized the event, believed was necessary to reconnect community members with their local journalists. As the Journalism Program director and organizer, respectively, at the national advocacy organization Free Press, Morgan and Bell had been trying to reinvent local journalism—its news roles, its democratic responsibilities, its community relationships—through a project called News Voices. In the terminology of News Voices, the project centered racial equity, "honored and uplifted" people of color's voices, and created journalism focused on "community-driven solutions" to wicked problems such as addiction and homelessness. Morgan brought the perspective of a former journalist and policy researcher, while Bell brought the perspective of a seasoned community organizer committed to racial justice. By 2020, the News Voices team had expanded their efforts from New Jersey and North Carolina to Colorado and Pennsylvania, helping other communities and their journalists network and collaborate to produce more complex, solutions-oriented journalism and to combat misinformation. In 2018, Morgan transitioned from journalist to engagement consultant, founding Branchhead Consulting as a way to help the profession strengthen this intricate "ecosystem of information," while Bell shifted to addressing racial justice and media reparations work, leading Free Press's Media 2070 project.[17] For my purpose in this book, Morgan and Bell represented the new journalistic paradigm.

Four years after First Draft launched and two years after Morgan and Bell were nurturing engagement journalism in Charlotte, I was feeling overwhelmed as my search uncovered more and more trust-building projects. It was 2019, and I was not the only one feeling this way. How could we avoid duplication in our work? How might we learn from each other's initiatives? In late August 2019, I arrived at the University of Texas–Austin's Center for Media Engagement for another Engagement Trust Summit, this one amid sweltering heat (Figure 2.3). I was curious about the small but powerhouse group Dr. Natalie "Talia" Jomini Stroud had gathered. All the "regulars" from trust-building news work I had gotten used to seeing

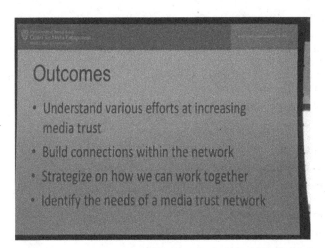

Figure 2.3 August 2019 Media Trust Summit at the University of Texas at Austin, picturing a slide about the summit's anticipated "outcomes." Photo by Sue Robinson.

were present, and Stroud, the founder and director of the Center for Media Engagement as well as a professor in the Department of Communication Studies and the School of Journalism at the University of Texas, told me she intentionally set out to build a vibrant network during this 2019 event.

"This is a chance for people to come together who are working on the same project," she said to the group of about 20. "We need to think about and understand the various efforts at increasing media trust, build connections within the network, strategize on how we can work together, through identifying the needs of a media trust network. Are there ways to move our work forward, together?"

She had taken a survey of us before the conference, asking what would be most helpful (see Table 2.1). The group was made up of academics and researchers like myself, center directors; a few reporters involved in engagement work; nonprofit groups like Reporters Without Borders; a few media entrepreneurs like Jim Spencer, who had his hands in everything from Ask Jeeves and AOL's news platform to helping media companies launch new digital projects; funders like Democracy Fund and Knight Foundation; and media analyzers like the Pew Research Center.

These influencers started ruminating on the possibilities of formalizing this trust-building network, including creating databases and a common glossary as well as some kind of structure to improve communication among

Table 2.1 PowerPoint Slide by Center for Media Engagement

Networked Logistics for Trust Entities in Engagement Built Environment	
In your opinion, what would be useful for those working on media trust?	
Database of the key people doing work on media trust	73%
Database of survey questions that have been used to measure media trust	68%
Data set tracking media trust over time	59%
Regular newsletter including news, research, and meetings	50%
Calendar of meetings, releases, events	50%
Regular, virtual meetings to coordinate efforts	45%
Regular, in-person meetings to coordinate efforts	23%

Source: Center for Media Engagement, informal poll of those working in the media trust space, August 2019.

all the entities working in the engagement space. All in the room agreed that the unifying themes had to do with a desire for a (widely) shared set of facts and to cure the information disorder occurring in the public sphere, and that the best way to do this was to build trust in mainstream news. But some of us also felt a keen sense of dismay at how few of us were connecting regularly about what we were learning. Stroud expressed her concerns: "It's such a mess: There are so many groups doing so many things. And no one is actually talking to each other. It's kind of tragic when you think about it. What if everything we are doing is actually missing the mark? This could be the case if we are not doing the research about what works and what doesn't. In this room we might have a solution, but it does not get out there and it is not shared enough. How do we get it enacted in the world? That is a scary fear."

She paused, then asked the room, "What can we do to collaborate completely?"

Then she revealed an informal "adjacency matrix" networking map she had done of the 19 of us in the room, showing all of our mutual linkages and possible connections: 2,922 possible connections comprising this built environment. The informal map sparked something for me, and I knew finally what I wanted to demonstrate and document in this book: this burgeoning built environment around trust building in the journalism profession.

Defining "Built Environment"

I want to step back here to define what I mean by built environment, which is a term that comes from urban design and has been taken up by disciplines such as computer intelligence and public health. A book chapter by Kaklauskas and Gudauskas about "intelligent decision-support systems and the internet of things" defined the built environment as "a material, spatial, and cultural product of human labor that combines physical elements and energy in forms for living, working, and playing."[18] In public health, scholars and practitioners consider health through modalities and access to healthy living, such as hospitals, clinics, running/biking paths, grocery stores, vitamins, and health education.[19] Typically in this literature, the built environment is fundamentally about physical structures that enable a particular kind of aesthetic or worldview. However, many scholars have also documented how built environments constitute life cycles that depend on everything from climate to energy sources, policy decisions, and system design. For example, the built environment of energy incorporates policy decisions, educational structures, social/cultural/ethical decision-making, economic concerns, quality of life, comfort and aesthetics, behavioral and life styles, air pollution and other health impacts, carbon emissions, technical infrastructures, legal and regulatory situations, microclimates, and psychological factors.[20] This chapter documents the various elements of the built environment being created around trust building for credible information about contemporary public affairs.

This thing I am trying to capture could probably go by a lot of names. I was going to go with "ecosystem,"[21] a term many other journalism studies scholars were evoking,[22] but I rejected it for two reasons. One, the term had become so ubiquitous and was applied to so many different situations that it had lost its conceptual power. And two, although actors in an ecosystem can be intentional and even subversive, the concept alludes to a landscape that has organic properties and generally exists outside of intentionality, as Anthony Nadler pointed out. In addition, the metaphor implied media entities were not hierarchical or politicized and assumed that "news will flourish through the grace of an invisible hand" and that "benefits will emerge."[23] In some ways, though, I still lament the decision to discard the term "ecosystem" because I like that an ecosystem always embodies a complex, interconnected network of associations, linkages, and relationships pulsating together as a working world—which captures what is happening here. Had I gone that route, I would have considered this thing as an *environmental ecosystem* with different levels of actors and forces, movement and evolution. Whatever this is, it is marked by old and new organisms working proactively for the health of the news media system. Nonetheless, ultimately those two problems continued to nag, and I moved on from "ecosystem."

I considered and then rejected a number of other terms. After his critique of "ecosystem," Nadler suggested that the term "infrastructure" be used to describe media systems. But "infrastructure," as useful as it is in pointing toward human agency in creating media systems, ironically doesn't point toward the human networks essential to creating new practices, philosophies, and technological tools for trust building. (The same could be said of the terms "movement," "paradigm," "landscape," and "sphere"—although all of these are incorporated into a built environment, of course.) Moreover, "infrastructure" connotes "hard" systems—systems that may age and atrophy—rather than an evolving, highly interactive system. Also, all of these terms represent something more fixed and rigid than what is happening; it is important to capture how interconnected all of the actors are within the system, how experimental the work is, and how fickle the sustainability of any one agent or initiative can be, even as new norms and protocols around trust building are being codified by newsrooms big and small as well as by journalism schools.

The only term that seemed to survive all of these interrogations was one that Nadler also suggested in that 2019 *Journalism Studies* article: "built environment." By 2022, Dr. Andrea Wenzel at Temple University was adopting the term "built environment" in her developing book manuscript she was calling *Making News Antiracist*.[24] Her book proposal, which she sent me after I had heard about it and reached out, laid out how journalists needed to change to be antiracist in their fundamental practice. Interestingly, her proposed book offered a documentation of a part of the very movement I was also investigating. I called her, and she generously offered to include me in a Zoom with Nadler[25] to explore the different terms. Wenzel and I agreed we wanted to use the same concept so as not to confuse an already concepts-crowded field. This conversation gave me a lot to ponder, and eventually I came around to the fact that what I was describing here was indeed a *built environment*.

One aspect about "built environment" that resonated with me as I plunged into books and articles from urban design, computer intelligence, and public health was its malleability combined with intentionality. People could establish built environments ethically, with benevolent goals and a sense of community.[26] Of course, importantly, we all know of built environments that have been created for nefarious purposes. Here I am thinking of the U.S. criminal justice system, with its foundational policy work dating from colonial times establishing the legal superiority of white, propertied men with bulti-in discrimination toward everyone else.[27] Or how redlining and other discriminatory practices created a racist built environment in housing and real estate.[28] But by 2022, change agents all over the world were working to disrupt such environments through policy, alternative spheres, and other mechanisms of equity.

Journalism itself has always been a built environment in the sense that its norms and routines developed as a result of innovative publishers responding to available technologies, commercial interests, and the demands and needs of audiences. Objectivity did not organically become a thing for journalists. Much research has shown how news organizations settled on neutrality to sell more product;[29] one scholar even called it a "strategic ritual" employed to garner authority.[30] Over the years, various entities have added—or tried to add—new parts to the infrastructure.[31] And sometimes entirely new foundations have been built, such as the conservative media sphere that enraptured half the United States with its misinformation campaigns, constant jockeying for information authority, and explicit antagonism toward mainstream news through the first part of the 2000s.[32] Indeed, the trust-building one at hand grew, at least in part, to counter this far-right built environment.

Wenzel's *Making News Antiracist*, due out in 2023 or 2024, investigates Philadelphia's community-centered media activism and, specifically, attempts by legacy news organizations to be antiracist. She explicitly lists the challenges, obstacles, and failures but documents also the centering of care and equity, coupled with the decentering of whiteness and white-orienting journalistic habits and practices in newsrooms. Essential to creating a successful built environment, her book proposal claims, is calculated transformation not only at the level of the individual reporter choosing sources and framing stories but also at the news organization level, such as hiring practices and also the institutional plane of leadership, funding, and what she calls "collaboration and power-sharing."[33] The built environment around trust building that is the focus of my book includes the one that Wenzel describes, but also all the other kinds of work that is meant to appeal to more groups, from rural conservatives to immigrants and African Americans. Like Wenzel, I conclude that without keen introspection about its own complicity in the broken systems around us, the journalistic infrastructure being so carefully crafted and its distributed, omnipresent paradigm of (what I am calling) an "identity-aware care" will fall into shambles.

As of 2022, though, this trust-building environment had been established within mainstream journalism, its roots extending more than a decade before. At the time of this writing, it comprised vast networks of connections, associations, and relationships backed by way more money and energy than any of the built-structural attempts of the past. And, like many built environments, the one I describe changed patterns, losing and gaining (and losing again) vitality through a multitude of new, old, and emergent circumstances. These circumstances include the existence of new funding through powerful players such as Facebook and Google and the adoption of engagement practices like newsroom-sponsored community forums about polarizing topics like gun control and abortion. In comparison, urban design scholars have noted how most built environments are "diverse regarding different living standards (influencing the space per capita), climate conditions (influencing the cooling and heating demand, and envelope design), and construction technology (influencing the material choice, construction system, and fabrication). The choice of construction systems, construction technique, building components and materials is usually based on a multi-criteria approach and should cover different aspects, including: Functionality, Technical Performance, Architectural Aesthetics, Economic Cost, Sustainability, Durability and Maintenance."[34] The trust-focused built environment encompasses all of this: the choice of source selection, how an interview is conducted, the cost of defending itself against a lawsuit, the sustainability of trust efforts, and where the community forum would be hosted. Architects of this infrastructure include Brandel from the engagement consultant and technology firm Hearken and her colleagues who introduced this chapter—all working to disrupt the status quo of traditional reporter values and norms, such as de-emphasizing objective measures and retraining for skills in community conversation facilitation. What I describe here became a significant and dominant set of forces that transformed the overarching media infrastructure in the United States in the first major paradigm shift for the profession in more than a century. In the next section, I detail the components—and the people who crafted them—of this environment.

Working toward Multilevel Change

In Figure 2.4, I show the macro-meso-micro levels at work in this movement. At the macro level of political climate and institutions, this built environment has been fueled by various intentional efforts to change the very culture of news within the industry and beyond it. For example, the Knight Commission on Trust, Media, and Democracy (2019) gathered top media publishers (e.g., Google News, PBS *Frontline*, CNN), academics (MIT Media Lab, University of Pennsylvania, Yale University, etc.), CEOs (e.g., from Kickstarter, the cleaning company SC Johnson), and other leading figures—including former secretary of state Madeline Albright at one meeting—to study what could be done to shore up democracy by instituting policy changes, boosting media literacy, and making other macro-level structural changes.[35] In another example, the Europe-based Ethical Journalism Network worked with

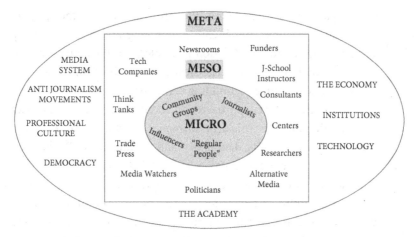

Figure 2.4 Trust-focused built environment at meta-meso-micro levels

policymakers, media owners, and media support groups throughout the globe to establish collaborative ethics policies to guide journalist-politician interactions. These groups worked at the policy level to intervene in institutional ways through powerful partnerships. Such projects changed the cultural and political backdrop that enable trust building. At the meso level of trust building, the creation of new organizations and the evolution of long-standing ones emphasized cross-professional collaborations as part of a growing infrastructure to support trust-building work. These included consultancy and training firms as well as academic centers and nonprofit entities. As an example of how these intervene at the cross-organizational level, the Oregon-based Agora Journalism Center developed a platform for engagement journalists called Gather that offered trainings, networks, and news about community engagement and trust-building strategies for newsrooms. Industry-adjacent centers executed studies with participating newsrooms to test trust-building strategies, while journalism schools incorporated trust-building skills into new curricula.

At the micro level, individual journalists, from high-profile political reporters to the one-person newsrooms in tiny towns across the United States, spearheaded projects on their own and partnered with community organizations or journalism schools on trust-focused initiatives such as revamping commenting sections to be more interactive, creating public conversation forums, and gathering direct input from communities to drive their coverage of challenging issues. Individual academics have

Table 2.2 Trust-Focused Built Environment at Meta-Meso-Micro Levels

Level of Media System	Trust-Building Goals
Meta level	• Cultural change • Industry change • Widespread media literacy • Political harmony • Trust in the media system • Democratic relevance • Addressing systemic oppression
Meso level	• Organizational (e.g., newsroom) change • Transparency work • Community relationship with news brands • Journalism school curriculum revision
Micro level	• Mindset change • Community member relationships with journalists • Audience relevance • Reporting class overhaul

taken it upon themselves to create singular classroom experiences that help students gain a foundation of relational engagement journalism before entering news production spaces. Table 2.2 lists the levels, the goals of the trust-building at each level, and some examples of projects that fit into each level.

Facilitating all this work at each of the three levels was an unprecedented financial investment aimed at shifting the culture and practice of journalism. Foundations and think tanks have been working in the media trust space for decades, but their efforts exponentially grew during this time period. Facebook, Google, and other corporations with deep pockets also entered this space and started pouring money into the trust problem. An exact figure is hard to come by (despite my attempt to quantify these efforts), but to give some sense of the scale, Craig Newmark, founder of Craigslist, between 2015 and 2019 donated more than $40 million to journalism initiatives to shore up the industry's relevancy, according to the *Chronicle of Philanthropy*.[36] His contributions included a $20 million endowment to the CUNY Graduate School of Journalism in June 2018 that thrived at the cutting edge of engagement journalism education.[37] Such swelling resources were revealed in other high-profile projects, such as the 2021 call for proposals by the National

Science Foundation's Convergence Accelerator, titled Trust & Authenticity in Communications Systems, offering $750,000 in the first phase, and ultimately $5 million to a handful of projects in 2022–23.

A Case for Multilevel Change: The Trust Project

Let's take a look at how these people get networked through two different trust-building entities, one establishing a vertical infrastructure involving everyone from researchers to community members as well as newsrooms, the other a more horizontal platform for newsrooms to collaborate across brands. I will start with the work of former journalist (and Peabody Award–winner) Sally Lehrman at the California-based nonprofit Trust Project, which she started in 2014 with an infusion of cash from Newmark. The idea drew from Lehrman's experiences more than a decade earlier when she organized a group called the Northern California Society of Professional Journalists' New Media Executive Roundtable and Online Credibility Watch to confer about the problem of clickbait and the ethics of online news. When she realized that the same problems discussed then were persisting into 2013, she convened a similar but larger group to consider how to reinvigorate journalism ethics online. That meeting inspired Lehrman to start working on a technological solution to support ethical news distribution and consumption, and so, through her professional networks, she reached out to friends at Google News and Twitter who could advise her on online systems algorithms. Lehrman spent the next two years building a consortium of senior news executives to develop what became eight Trust Indicators, which news sites use on their pages to show the people and policies behind their organization and its journalism. Over the next five years, she expanded the network, collaborating with funders, technology companies, researchers, and members of community groups. The Trust Indicators were designed to be used by the public to assess news sources and to prompt news search algorithms to privilege accurate and credible information. The goal was to reach three types of community members—avid news users, engaged news users, and opportunistic news users—and to help those engaged with misinformation to reconnect with accurate, reliable news.

"The Trust Project built the Trust Indicators by asking people what they value in the news—and what wins and loses their trust," wrote Lehrman on the website. "Then we married their insights with bedrock journalism values to come up with eight core disclosures that every reader, listener and viewer deserves to know." Figure 2.5 outlines the eight Trust Indicators: best practices for journalism, journalist expertise, type of work, references, methods, locally sourced, diverse voices, and actionable feedback. Once a news outlet had committed to abide by these indicators, they could use the "Trust Mark" logo as a kind of ethical shorthand on each news article.

By November 2017, Lehrman had launched the initiatives to work with news outlets all over the world to implement the indicators on their platforms. As of the time of this writing, the indicators were being used by more than 245 news sites around the world and were used as guides for Google, Facebook, Bing, and other big-tech companies as well as news aggregators like Nuzzel, and as a news literacy tool by the Economist Educational Foundation, Arizona State University's News Co/Lab, and others. The project has had five major funders for continued implementation: besides Newmark, they are Google, Democracy Fund, the Knight Foundation, and Facebook. The Markkula Center for Applied Ethics supported the project as a fiscal sponsor and institutional host in its earliest years. Consider all of the entities involved in just this one project (remembering that there were dozens and dozens of these kinds of initiatives by 2021) and all the major agents within the trust-building built environment that are connected in this work, from technology companies and funders to academics and researchers.

Through the years Lehrman nurtured this network, always making sure trust building in newsrooms was ethics-based and involved deep engagement with content and audiences. Key to the project, said Lehrman in an interview with me, was building "a community of journalists sharing what we do and how we do it." And because of this network and the mandated commitment to *all* the Trust Indicators until they are given permission to use the Trust Mark, the newsrooms find themselves revisiting ethics policies they had not touched in 25 years or forced them to create policies around diversity and inclusion, as one organization in Brazil found they needed to do. "In principle, they did have a commitment to diverse voices," Lehrman told me, "but they didn't have a policy stated to the public or even internally, and so the first step was they created a new policy. And honestly, at first, they weren't sure, 'Do we need to do this at all?' And then they kind of thought about, well, okay, the Brazil context. And, well, yeah, there are very diverse populations in Brazil. And then they went a step further and created a person responsible

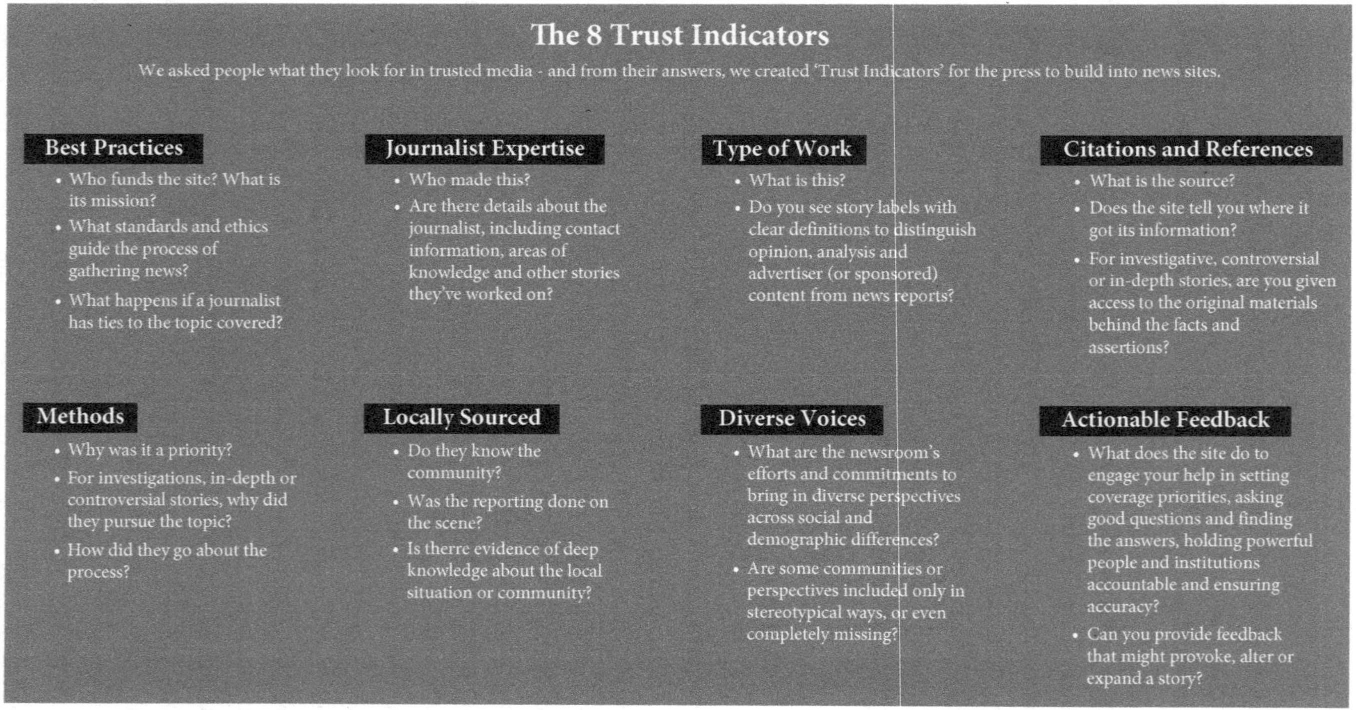

The 8 Trust Indicators

We asked people what they look for in trusted media – and from their answers, we created 'Trust Indicators' for the press to build into news sites.

Best Practices
- Who funds the site? What is its mission?
- What standards and ethics guide the process of gathering news?
- What happens if a journalist has ties to the topic covered?

Journalist Expertise
- Who made this?
- Are there details about the journalist, including contact information, areas of knowledge and other stories they've worked on?

Citations and References
- What is the source?
- Does the site tell you where it got its information?
- For investigative, controversial or in-depth stories, are you given access to the original materials behind the facts and assertions?

Methods
- Why was it a priority?
- For investigations, in-depth or controversial stories, why did they pursue the topic?
- How did they go about the process?

Locally Sourced
- Do they know the community?
- Was the reporting done on the scene?
- Is there evidence of deep knowledge about the local situation or community?

Type of Work
- What is this?
- Do you see story labels with clear definitions to distinguish opinion, analysis and advertiser (or sponsored) content from news reports?

Diverse Voices
- What are the newsroom's efforts and commitments to bring in diverse perspectives across social and demographic differences?
- Are some communities or perspectives included only in stereotypical ways, or even completely missing?

Actionable Feedback
- What does the site do to engage your help in setting coverage priorities, asking good questions and finding the answers, holding powerful people and institutions accountable and ensuring accuracy?
- Can you provide feedback that might provoke, alter or expand a story?

Figure 2.5 The Trust Project's Trust Indicators

for diverse voices in editorial. So, to me, that was a fantastic example of how working together as news organizations around the world, responding to the public, we can really make amazing advances in our own work and build the structures."

I saw The Trust Project as an integral part in creating a scaffolding for the built environment—a scaffolding that imbued the work across the profession with a keen, intensive transparency around news information with the explicit goal to build trust in that news content. Furthermore, Lehrman worked with teachers, librarians, civic leaders, and others in local communities in what she called "public influencer workshops" to brainstorm ways the Trust Indicators might be useful in those spaces. So this built environment is overlaying not only the journalism industry but also civic realms.

In January 2021, shortly after the election that pushed out Trump, Lehrman and her team produced a report on user research they had conducted the previous summer to assess, among other things, their progress in trust-building strategies. In the first set of interviews they conducted in 2014–15, the team noted typical expressions of engagement with the brand and the news content. "In our second round, we found engagement had deepened and yet still needed to grow. For instance, perceptions about comment sections have radically changed. Instead of toxic cesspools, they are now seen as useful public spaces for discussion and learning about other perspectives." In a project like this, the emphasis is on one or two singular tools—in this case, the Trust Indicators and the Trust Mark (see Figure 2.6)—that gets distributed widely through the built environment by marketing done by the program as well as

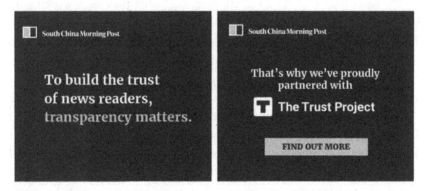

The South China Morning Post partnered with The Trust Project just as it was updating its internal newsroom policies.

Figure 2.6 The Trust Mark. Courtesy of The Trust Project

written up in the trade press, through education with journalism instructors (such as at the Arizona State University's News Co/Lab or used as a case study for students to engage with the Trust Indicators, as I did in my advanced reporting classes), and through implementation by the newsroom partners. This is a more vertical utilization of the built environment because it involves engagement at every level of the infrastructure: the public, journalists, funders, and researchers. Engagement happens in the form of exchange between reporters and audience members but also between journalists, technology platforms, community members, and the content itself.

Connecting Trust with Engagement through New Skill Sets and Roles

The shape of successful trusting relationships often served as a source of disagreement in the industry. This was the topic at the very start of the conversation during Talia Stroud's Center for Media Engagement trust summit in August 2019, just two months before Hearken launched Citizens Agenda in Brooklyn (the opening scene of this chapter). Opening the meeting on that hot day in Texas, Stroud said, "You can diminish fake news, but at the same time you need to have something else to turn to. Some things are moving the needle and some things are not. It is important to take a step back and look at all of this."

She paused and took a breath before asking, "What do we even mean by the word 'media trust'?"

The participants, about 20 in all, described what they were working on and with whom. And then Joy Mayer spoke up. As I mentioned earlier, Mayer founded and headed Trusting News, which offered free trainings to journalists and educators. She was a pivotal player in the emerging built environment, and every time I heard her speak, I found myself nodding emphatically. She did not disappoint on this occasion.

"I have started to hate the word 'trust,'" she confessed. "I am interested in keeping our conversations really specific. It is so different across different fields. I want to drill down. Are we talking about national politics or local news or what?"

All the participants agreed on what they wanted the outcome to be: whatever engagement strategies we implemented, we needed credible information that was relevant for people to use in all their social, professional, and civic lives *and that was accepted by all publics as trustworthy.*

I sensed a mood shift in the room. That last part represented the key ingredient in trust-building work. Jeff Jarvis, a professor at CUNY and longtime media writer, spoke up: "I see a string building here. The end goal is to change the metrics under which journalists work. Right now, we are doing clickbait. But to get there you have to have some sense of what is valued in a community, and out of that you are going to build a feedback loop."

This brings us to what we mean by "trust building through engagement." What did this look like in practice? What exactly were the components of a "feedback loop"? How did one determine what was "valued" in a community? And perhaps most important, what were the new skill sets and roles that journalists must learn to make all of this happen?

The adoption of entirely new skill sets as well as the roles journalists were playing marked significant departures from traditional journalism routines by centering work around caregiving of information, audiences, and each other. Reviewing the data from the trust initiatives and then within the interviews, focus groups, and surveys, I came up with a list of engagement strategies that were being implemented in the name of trust building. In Box 2.1, I've separated them into low- and high-commitment efforts. The techniques in this list, which range from responding in commenting sections to mediating conversations, form eight categories of skills and four new roles. First, I will describe these skill sets, which much scholarship has already explored and which my case studies have also revealed as being taught and practiced:

1. Radical transparency[38] (e.g., highlighting who was involved in story production, the contributors' identities, ethical decisions etc.).
2. Power dynamic appreciation[39] (e.g., acknowledging in reporting and in content production the power dynamics at work in the community/institution/issues). This also refers to the power in the newsroom and within the reporter's own self, such as understanding one's identities and places of bias and the newsroom's problematic practices.
3. Mediation[40] (e.g., helping people find common ground/values and moving beyond polarization).
4. Reciprocity and feedback loops[41] (e.g., following through with sources and community members, checking in with people constantly.

Box 2.1 Engagement Strategies

Basic (Low-Commitment) Engagement Strategies

- Respond to comments proactively, ask discussion questions, redirect conversations when they get off topic or vitriolic, help connect people in comments, institute ratings systems for comments and encourage community surveillance.
- Provide readers with information about how the story was conceived, where the story came from, what funding/advertising helped pay for it, what sources were used, and who contributed to its development.
- Detail any ethical deliberations and decisions that took place in the newsroom related to the story, along with the formal ethical principles of the company with each story/project.
- Provide readers with reporters' identities/biases such as private-life activities that might have informed or shaped the way the story came out.
- Loop back around to any people who contributed information to the story to let them know what happened to the story, linking to the publication and explaining how their time/effort helped its production.
- Allow someone such as from a marginalized community who is not an official to be anonymous because they are worried about retribution if they speak out critically. Explain that decision in a sidebar. Consider power dynamics between different kinds of sources and what harm could come to anyone involved who is vulnerable.
- Give people not used to speaking to the press (especially those in communities that do not trust the mainstream press) interview questions ahead of time. Allow them some control over how the interview goes.
- Practice solutions-oriented journalism that pushes community toward resolution and does not keep them mired in binaries or blame games (e.g., Whose side are you on? stories).
- Directly connect community members and elected officials.

More Intense (Higher-Level Commitment) Engagement Strategies

- Collaborate with community members. For example, let them help write pieces of the story or create a companion piece for it, being transparent with audiences. Let profiled people see the story before publication. Crowdsource stories.

- Break up entrenched routines. Experiment with different sourcing techniques, such as using Google forms, providing a suggestion box in a well-trafficked place for community input, or holding newsroom meetings around the topic in community centers or public libraries.
- Connect with topical influencers for entry into marginalized communities. Ask them to co-host virtual and real-world meetings with you. Ask them to introduce you to more people in different parts of communities. Spend time in that community both virtually and physically.
- Market engagement initiatives beyond the branded website, email listservs, Facebook, etc. Make sure to tag key influencers and get the content in front of people not already in your audience.
- Personally train in social justice, innate bias, and privilege on a regular basis. Mandate staff/colleagues to train as well. Acknowledge ignorance and apologize when mistakes are made.
- Approach every story and project with a lens of power (who has it, who doesn't) and not a lens of objectivity.
- Learn histories from community members, especially the relationship between the news outlet and them. Understand and acknowledge those histories when approaching people from marginalized communities.
- Collaborate with nonprofit organizations, university departments, ethnic media on wicked problems facing communities for introduction to communities, cosponsoring community forums and events, etc.
- Think creatively about story formats and consider less traditional types, such as photo collages or poems from community members.
- Report and write mindfully, understanding where biases might be coloring content or framings. Consider focus groups made up of diverse audience members to give consistent feedback on coverage.
- Incorporate into stories that most disparities are a result of problematic structures and systems.
- Involve communities at every production step. Tell people they are needed and make them feel their significance as more than a check of a box. Allow community members to feel they have some ownership over content.

- Actively help the community come up with solutions to its problems by not only writing stories about them but also facilitating forums on the topic, connecting stakeholders, researching solutions, etc.
- Help people bridge their differences by moderating the conversation, calling out trolls, redirecting conversations, and setting up expectations and structures.
- Spend more time in communities, professionally: holding "office hours" in informal spaces, hosting potlucks, cosponsoring community events and functions, etc.
- Spend more time in communities, personally: volunteering, attending functions, getting to know different kinds of people, frequenting stores and businesses in many parts of the communities.
- Steep yourself in culturally relevant modes, languages, customs, expectations, etc. Understand that people do not think alike or necessarily share the same set of values and priorities.
- Create private spaces for topically interested folx to gather and deliberate more in depth. Spread out the responsibilities for moderation and facilitation among staff, but reporters should understand that this work is now part of journalism.

** Remember that some of these will fail the first time they are implemented. Learn from the mistakes and continue to evolve.

Sources: Agora Journalism Center, Hearken, Citizen's Agenda, Trusting News, Membership Puzzle Project, Center for Media Engagement, Reynolds Institute, Ethical Journalism Network, Solutions Journalism Network, Gather, Ground Truth, Maynard Institute, The Conversation, The Journalism Trust Institute, Building Trust in Media in Southeast Asia and Turkey, Your Voice . . . , Ask A . . . , What's Next, Coral by Vox Media, Evergrey, Listening Post, Journalism That Matters, Spaceship Media, Voting Block, The Banyan Project, A Year of Listening, the Knight Commission on Media, Trust & Democracy, Google News Lab, The Trust Project for News on Facebook, Democracy Fund and Associated Projects, News Integrity Initiative and Associated Projects, Resolve Philadelphia, London School of Economics Truth, Trust & Technology Commission, Knight Foundation and Associated Projects, The Trust Project.

5. Media literacies[42] (e.g., everyone, from K–12 teachers and parents to tech companies and journalists, has to help people recognize good information.
6. Community offline work[43] (e.g., visiting schools, hosting forums).
7. Needs/assets/solutions analyses[44] (e.g., proactively helping community stakeholders to listen for a community's various needs, recognize

the existing assets and potential partnerships, connect groups and policymakers, and work toward solutions to problems.

8. Collaborative production[45] (e.g., partnering with other news media or community groups to develop shared ethical guidelines around information exchange or asking people to crowdsource and even produce content.

I designed Table 2.3 to incorporate the definitions and examples of how these skills are being promoted through this built environment. These must be conducted through the identity-aware care in service to trust building, as laid out in this book. These skills overlap, of course, and are not all-inclusive. Furthermore, just as with the demand for learning multimedia skills, not every journalist will be adept at all of these. Indeed, it will be impossible for someone to completely embody them. Just as with multimedia, it will be important for journalists to master a subset of these skills and for editors to remember that not everyone is good at everything and that there are only so many hours in the workday. Furthermore, the data show that though these skills are being touted and taught frequently and pervasively through trainings, schools, conferences, and other kinds of workshops throughout the mainstream industry, they are adopted and practiced unevenly, with some journalists taking them on with eagerness and others half-heartedly (and haphazardly), while still others reject them outright. That said, these are the myriad skill sets that the theory of trust building through identity-aware care demands. The idea here is that for trust to be built again in mainstream journalism, reporters need to learn to listen through the wielding of these different techniques.

These skills group into four new kinds of roles that journalists take on in this trust-focused built environment: *relationship builder, community collaborator, community conversation facilitator,* and *professional network builder.* These four roles crystallized for me after multiple conversations and writing an International Communication Association 2022 conference paper about all of this with Dr. Regina Lawrence at the University of Oregon and Agora Journalism Center.[46] In Table 2.4, I show the relationships between these roles spread among the layers of the built environment.

Relationship Builder. The trust-building movement encouraged *relational* engagement—focused on building sustained and deep interaction with audience communities. Transactional strategies "treat engagement primarily as a

Table 2.3 Trust-Building Skill Sets

Skill Set	Definition	Example
Radical transparency	The act of revealing all the sources, editing process, evidence, and identities involved with the production of the content as well as the ethical and other policies or guidelines influencing outcomes. (Transparency as a value has been around for decades, of course, but what we are talking about here is much more robust and demands a public accounting.)	Many projects represent this skill set, including the entire fact-checking industry. The Trust Project with its eight Trust Indicators: expertise, labels, references, local, diversity, actionable feedback, methods, best practices. Another example is the PBS *Frontline* Transparency Project that aggregates the original source material for stories, etc.
Power dynamic accounting	When journalists account for the various power dynamics at work among those in the story, stakeholders, and communities affected. This might include understanding systems of oppression, contextualizing histories of discriminatory policies/practices, and changing protocols for sources to allow for vulnerable populations to have their voices amplified. This skill set also includes journalists being introspective about their own biases and identities and how those influence the story process.	The various audit projects happening at news outlets documenting coverage that stereotypes, excludes, and is unidimensional. See the audit reports at the *Philadelphia Inquirer* or the *New York Times* for examples.
Mediation	The skill of being able to facilitate conversation and deliberation among people who hold divergent and polarizing viewpoints. This skill must include how to deal with microaggressions, how to make sure all voices are heard, and how to move from ranting to needs/asset assessments, strategies, and possible solutions.	Your Voice Ohio is a journalism collaborative that hosts community conversations to explore solutions to challenges such as opioid addiction. Another is Spaceship Media, which trains journalists how to listen and create "journalism-supported dialogue."
Reciprocity	The mandate to follow through with sources and communities before, during, and after story production, to demonstrate how expended efforts mattered. This might include sending notes to all sources (regardless of whether they made it into the story) to let them know what happened with their words. It incorporates outreach tactics to make sure groups not within the existing audience are contacted. This skill incorporates regular feedback, perhaps through focus groups of community members who are not subscribers. The notion of reciprocity develops a more relational—rather than extractive or transactional—skill set.	The Citizens Agenda project in 2020, followed by Democracy SOS and other Hearken-led initiatives show journalists how to involve community members in creating a news agenda, how to use the agenda to hold politicians accountable, and how to circle back to communities to keep the agenda fresh and inclusive.

Table 2.3 Continued

Skill Set	Definition	Example
Media literacies	The civic/educational, technological, professional, and social learning about how information is produced, disseminated, circulated, and manipulated that must happen for journalists, news consumers, voters, politicians, platforms, and others to have accurate information. For journalists, this has typically meant being the educator. These efforts have intensified, such as with the fact-checking movement (e.g., First Draft). Now journalists themselves also have to gain new literacies, such as critical-thinking training about algorithms, polarization, histories of oppression, problematic systems, and community complexities.	The Ethical Journalism Network, based in Europe, joins journalists with policymakers and others to train in ethical principles of information exchange, human rights, and good governance.
Community offline work	The skill of learning how to navigate spaces as a community member as well as a journalist, and working within communities through the hosting of forums, conversations, and other work that may not be directly related to content production but that remains central to building trust between journalists and their audiences. In essence, this involves adopting a skill set similar to community organizing, such as listening, connecting, and outreach tactics for hard-to-reach populations. It involves navigating between a lot of different personalities and agendas and to help people stay focused on common goals to improve their lives. This may entail volunteering in community centers or schools, hosting forums and conversations, connecting stakeholders, and researching solutions to wicked problems.	Trusting News trains journalists and newsrooms in how to incorporate offline conversations into reporting routines. See their Road to Pluralism project to explore how journalists can help communities overcome polarization.

(continued)

Table 2.3 Continued

Skill Set	Definition	Example
Needs/assets/ solutions analyses	Learning to assess community needs and assets in the search of possible solutions, as well as framing content so that it advances the conversation about community problems, connects stakeholders, investigates proposals, and otherwise helps improve the situation in a way that resonates with community members (as opposed to what those in power think the community needs). This skill rejects the common he-said-she-said or pro-con binaries found in reporting, replacing them with the outcomes of authentic outreach to marginalized groups and analysis of potential solutions to problems by working within these communities. Journalists must be taught to go beyond the typical three sources; this means learning to find and analyze models for change and articulating areas of value consensus (e.g., we all want to feel safe) to establish a nonpolarizing space for deliberation and dialogue. This skill entails learning how to assess the needs of any given "source" as well, such as posing less interrogative and more productive questions, using trauma-informed techniques to avoid doing more harm, and rejecting assumptions based on status-quo thinking.	Solutions Journalism Network hosts training, creates curriculum, and maintains a database of stories—all focused on helping communities move forward to overcome shared problems. The San Francisco Homeless Project, a 70-plus newsroom collaborative, highlights ongoing social injustice, amplifies the perspectives of those in need of support, and identifies possible resources and action steps to fulfill needs.
Collaborative production	This skill involves rejecting traditional autonomy protocols in favor of collaborating and co-creating/producing with community members on solving problems. This may entail crowdsourcing or the sharing of writing/multimedia, etc. so that community members feel a sense of ownership of the journalism. This skill must prioritize the giving up of power over content to some extent and prioritize lived experiences (as opposed to officials). It may mean collaborating with competing news outlets by sharing resources, promoting each other's content, etc.	Resolve Philadelphia works with newsroom partners to host workshops and listening sessions, co-creates newsletters, builds collaborative relationships to better tell the stories of marginalized neighborhoods and issues of Philadelphia.

means to other ends (i.e. engagement as 'selling' the news)," while a "relation-ship" approach treats engagement "as a more substantive relational endeavor to bring the public in to deciding what the story is and how it should be told."[47] The emphasis on retraining acknowledged the fairly radical shift in mindset required to do relational engagement—work that required journalists to step away from the bedrock "independence" value embedded in American jour-nalism and toward a notion of themselves *as* community members.[48] While the notion of being actual *members* of the communities they served had yet to be widely accepted, this relationship building role emanated from many of these projects and initiatives.[49] For example, this line of thinking showed up in the opening anecdote of this chapter with the kinds of questions Jay Rosen was getting about Citizens Agenda from journalists concerned they would be seen as having an agenda for the community. In my newsrooms—all my newsrooms, whether it was the tiny family-owned weekly in Derry, New Hampshire, the midsize state paper in Vermont, or the midsize re-gional, Gannett-owned daily in Cherry Hill, New Jersey—community *participating* was banned. No political signs. No volunteer work. No covering of family or friends. This had never been realistic, and today many consider it to be unethical. The role of relationship builder included being accessible and responsive, reaching out and following through to community groups and community members, describing the sourcing, ethics, and funding of news work, and showing journalists' personalities. Such tactics highlighted improving trust by providing the transparency, reliability, and relatability that have been the basis of trusting relationships.[50]

The growing sense that journalism is about relationship building and earning trust was evident in an ever-widening circle of journalists. In my survey of 106 journalists conducted in 2019, nearly half (48) agreed with a dynamic definition of journalism as engagement and relationship-building. As one wrote in an open-ended question, engagement "means getting out of the newsroom and into the communities we cover to find what people want to know without assuming we already know the answers. It also means having real conversations with people about the issues that matter to them and being willing to hear their answers." Another said, "Engagement is about me and my writers engaging with the community—connecting people with news, events, information, and engaging them in dialogue with us—but it is also about engaging them with one another in a productive way and con-necting people." Overall, about 70% of the respondents in the survey agreed with the statement "It is part of my job to interact with audience members and develop relationships with them over local news." As a reporter, I used to go to the local diners and coffee shops (er, and bars) and "interact with audience members" as well, of course. And I listened for stories all the time. But building actual relationships with the people I encountered? Well, all of us turned down invitations from community members on our beats lest we be accused of conflicts of interest.[51] But by 2022? We had moved to "reciprocal" journalism with "direct, indirect and sustained" kinds of mutual exchange[52] to create, as its goal, vibrant community. Whoa. That felt quite a bit different from what I had done.

Community Collaborator. Journalists were also being encouraged to produce news collaboratively with communities, such as crowdsourced projects.[53] Research indicated that journalists could find it challenging to engage collaboratively with the public because of their own professional resistance, the public's lackluster response, or insufficient resources.[54] Thus, foundations and others have been spending boatloads of money to train newsrooms on how to leverage public input more effectively. And, startlingly, journalists were all in on this idea. My survey asked journalists from around the United States about "partnering and collaborating with community groups on stories"; some 71.4% said they would be willing to partner, and 53.9% thought they could realistically implement such a partnership—a huge shift in routines for mainstream journalists (although only 32.5% had ever done so).

As one respondent wrote, "It's creating the news with people rather than for them. I believe involving my audience in the story, the more invested they can be in the project, and the richer and more popular the coverage can be." The survey also asked how willing respondents would be to "act as an intermediary between your community and local resources (meaning connect stakeholders who are all working on the same problem together, linking people who are working through a problem with resources to fix it, etc. in a very proactive manner and NOT just through a story)." About 60.3% of the sample said they would be either extremely willing or willing to operate in this capacity (though only 33% said they would be able to incorporate this role into their daily work and only about 20% had ever practiced in this way). That two-thirds of this sample of journalists embraced the role of community connection-builder signaled to me a noteworthy shift from the traditional journalistic stance of "independence" toward community.

Community Conversation Facilitator. Related to both relationship building and community collaborating, the role of community conversation facilitator asked journalists to serve as an intermediary among audience members, especially around polarizing topics. Importantly, a primary goal of this role was often not to generate news content as much as to facilitate understanding among community members across difference and give "voice" to those typically marginalized in such discourse. "Engaged journalism projects often have engaging a community in civic conversation as the primary goal and informing the audience as a close second," according to one overview of a trust project.[55] Such facilitation work could resolve polarization as people come to understand each other's partisan ideas, suggested journalist Mónica Guzmán in her 2022 book, *I Never Thought of It That Way*.

One example of this type of effort was the work that Fiona Morgan and Alicia Bell launched with the Free Press in Charlotte in 2017, mentioned earlier. Another, Your Voice Ohio, a project of the Akron-based Center for New Democratic Processes, brought together newsrooms from across the state to host dialogues about challenging issues in local communities. According to its website, the project used "engaging, authentic, and accessible solutions-driven community conversation to rebuild trust between Ohioans and Ohio media." The initiative was founded in 2015 by a dozen legacy media outlets that agreed they needed to experiment collaboratively with new ways to represent diverse voices in democratic practices. Since then, the network has grown to about 60 traditional, start-up, and minority news organizations and has held nearly 90 conversations meant to advance solutions to local problems, including addiction, community visioning ahead of local elections, race and representation in reporting, and building vibrant communities. For example, in 2017 journalists from four news outlets sat down with dozens of community members over the course of three nights to tackle the issue of opioid addiction, resulting in a 30-page report with a series of possible solutions toward resolving the crisis. In my interview with Doug Oplinger, the director, he asserted, "The trust comes only by being useful to helping them make their daily lives better. . . . At the end, after they've had this conversation in which they almost always feel good about what just happened in these two hours, there is this thankfulness and this realization that the news media did this for us. . . . The editor in [one] community came up to me afterwards and said, 'I've never felt this kind of goodwill in my community.'" Simple acts of facilitation help the community feel cared for.

Table 2.4 New Journalist Roles and Their Associated Skill Sets

Journalist Roles	New or Enhanced Journalism Skill Sets within an Ecosystem	
Relationship builder	• Listening reciprocally • Partnering with other media (negotiating, compromising)	• Collaborating with community members • Boosting other journalism
Community collaborator	• Moderating difficult conversations	• Connecting community stakeholders
Community conversation facilitator	• Helping people come to understand their differences • Creating inclusive spaces	• Responding to community members and following through • Practicing extensive transparency
Professional industry networker	• Nurturing multiway channels of communication	• Being introspective and reflexive

In our focus groups and interviews, reporters and editors told us about the many community events they had facilitated around big problem issues as well as the listening sessions they engaged in. For one reporter in a focus group at the Online News Association in 2019, holding live events done around community issues was "all about this idea of us being a part of the community." More than 80% of journalists I surveyed said it was part of their job "[t]o host and facilitate community forums around important topics facing the town," as my survey phrased it. Another 79% said they were willing "to proactively find ways to bridge differences, especially polarization, and facilitate a more moderate conversation through . . . journalism." As with the relationship builder and community collaborator roles, the number of journalists who reported actually doing this kind of work, though growing, was less than the number who agreed in principle with playing these roles. In regard to facilitating conversation, 61% of those we surveyed were not regularly hosting community forums, and 56% said they had never or rarely helped their community overcome polarization through conversation.

Professional Network Builder. A final major role change brought forth by this movement has been a focus on establishing a more connected and cohesive professional network that spanned all the levels of the built environment, from the metajournalistic culture to the individual reporter working collaboratively with other reporters. Journalists have always networked, of course; much scholarship documents the "interpretive community" that the industry created.[56] However, within this built environment focused on trust building, entities have acted much more in concert, intentionally reaching out to different organizations to build partnerships where none had existed before. Hearken's cofounder and CEO Jennifer Brandel told me in our interview that she had intentionally set out to develop a unique professional network, which she compared to an "interstitium" of connectivity across fields and professions around trust building through engagement at all levels. As she was talking in our interview, I was frantically looking up "interstitium," which is a thin layer of "fluid-filled super highway" that carries biological information throughout the body as kind of connective tissue. Brandel used this organ to think metaphorically about the trust-focused built environment: "The solutions for this work won't be found in any one vertical or any one organization. It has to be a networked approach. There are common patterns and problems across so many industries that support democracy. So I try to see Hearken as one bridge—to connect the insights from an organization like the Center for Tech & Civic Life—which helps train election officials—to journalists. Or bringing in voting rights scholars from Common Cause to help journalists understand the history of voter suppression and be able to bring more context to their reporting. So often journalists just look to each other for ideas and innovation, but if we go one altitude layer up, and look across industries to what others have learned or are trying, we can evolve far more quickly to meet this very critical moment."

Brandel paused and asked permission to go on a tangent. She remembered when she was at WBEZ's Curious City in Chicago, before Hearken was a reality, when she wanted to do work that was connected to audiences for a more robust impact on journalism. She approached a news organization to expand the work of engagement to other news organizations or to spread the gospel beyond Chicago, where she was based. She was turned down. She thought to herself at the time, "Okay, this isn't a fertile ground to plant the seed in. We're helping out this organization [but] we can't help the ecosystem." So, eventually, she founded Hearken.

"How can we play this role as an interstitium on the democracy level? Because we see the health of the organ of journalism cannot survive without better connection to the other organs of philanthropy, organs of governance, all of the organs that support civic infrastructure," she added.

I felt like clapping after Brandel finished talking this out with me. And if you follow the dots as I have done in this chapter of looking at how these organizations are starting to interconnect and collaborate around some common goals (e.g., help journalism and, thus, democracy survive), you can see the bubbling up of this interstitium. In 2022, this built environment and its tangents were still pretty messy, but it was all also so remarkably more organized than it had any right to be considering an inauspicious beginning and that everyone's personal goals were not aligned. I was also surprised because mainstream journalists have traditionally been difficult to herd, having a strongly developed competitiveness. I remember when I first got to Madison, checking out a multi-newsroom consortium determined to start a collaborative project called All Together Now to cover healthcare issues in 2007. Fascinated, I watched as everyone's good intentions and desire to produce something huge resulted in a few stories individually published here and there. A lack of resources and territorialism stymied true partnership. But now financial pressures made such activity not only appealing for its resource distribution but also essential for survival.

The survey findings indicated widespread acceptance of this collaborative posture. More than 80% of our respondents said they were willing or very willing to collaborate with other journalists on bigger community issues, and almost half the sample (46%) reported having done some kind of partnering work already. In our interviews and focus groups, journalists talked about how constrained they felt in newsrooms to accomplish the kind of big-think pieces they wanted to do without partnering with other news organizations. And there were numerous examples in the entire data set of journalists working together on bigger community events to tackle a single issue such as economic hardship. In fact, in a Knight Foundation project that included interviews with nearly 50 high-profile political reporters, done in collaboration with Dr. Deen Freelon at the University of North Carolina in 2017, I was startled to hear a majority of our participants talk about boosting other journalists' content as their primary use of Twitter.[57]

It brought to mind how Brandel's vision played out back at the October 2019 Engagement Innovation Summit. Even then, she was already plotting how they could turn this Citizens Agenda and Election SOS project into a grand networking interstitium program that helped elevate newsrooms from the myopic vantage point they were currently mired in—playing constant defense against political and other attacks (sometimes actual, physical attacks), appeasing cranky shareholders and publishers, and trying to do more with so much less. She wanted newsrooms to see themselves as an integral part of a vibrant network that included Hearken, other engagement specialists, and civic and voting organizations and also throughout their communities. As they distributed physical copies of the 40-page Citizens Agenda guidebook in that Brooklyn reception hall, Brandel and her team made networking in the built environment an essential component to engagement, working it into every part of the conference and, as such, modeling the infrastructure that she believed necessary to save journalism.

For example, at one of the breakout tables during the summit, Mia Sato, engagement editor at the Better Government Association, was helping the participants think through how to network the engagement within the newsroom. "So, it sounds like you have a decent amount of people to throw their work behind it," Sato was saying to one of the guests trying to figure out logistics for election engagement, "but you need a web developer and at least you need three partners minimum. You need engagement tools. Front-end development. You would probably want nonprofit groups or community service groups that have the contacts with people. What else? You need someone to spread the word. You need partners who have committed to prioritizing that coverage." Indeed, the ethos of the entire day was how to avoid isolating the work of trust building in newsrooms with one or two individuals and make it a more holistic undertaking that connects all journalists in the newsroom in a common purpose. In a promotional video that summarized the event on Hearken's webpage, Brandel says in the voiceover, "We are really trying to take away the artifice that engagement only happens within an industry vertical, because it is something that is universal, that so many different people are solving for in fantastic and innovative ways. And, we wanted to cross-pollinate and share that learning."

This framing differed drastically from conferences I had attended as a reporter all those years ago. During those days and even as a journalism professor later on, I of course thought and nurtured and taught a lot about the importance of sourcing networks. All journalists "work the beat," as we used to call it, so that when something happened, we would know about it first from that very carefully primed network. However, this intensely collaborative paradigm that Brandel and others in the built environment heralded seemed much more holistic about journalists' obligations not only for these sources but beyond the source network and inclusive of audiences as community members and also of each other, within and outside of individual newsrooms. For this built environment to succeed in the creation of trust between journalists and their many constituents, we needed to distribute efforts and eschew competitiveness. In other words, for it to succeed, we needed to start *caring* differently—about the very norms and routines we had come to see as entrenched and immutable, about how we considered sources, about the roles in this evolved information environment.

Interestingly, these four new roles mirror the kinds of roles community leaders and activists have typically taken on in cities and towns, and journalists could learn from the copious research in that field. A quick scan of the literature found that much knowledge already exists about the kinds of environment that relationship building, collaboration, facilitation, and networking need. Key, according to some of this scholarship, is that the news organization's goals and intentions be transparent and that the means to those goals be well resourced and logistically competent.[58] Furthermore, these roles must be thought of as intertwined, each action in them done with the larger community needs and capacities in mind, whether the circulation area or the profession.[59] When organizations such as newsrooms engage as proactive agents with notions of collectivity in mind, they can help communities build capacity and develop more relevant and sustainable solutions to community problems,[60] even overcoming intense disagreement among community members.[61] For community leaders, such organizing work demands multiple agents operating in solidarity at the grassroots level.[62] This solidarity typically derives either from a shared community (often, neighborhood) identity and steeped in a collaborative ethos, or it grows as a result of some external threat, and in community organizing, it can often be harnessed to mobilize constituents and/or policymakers in some way.[63]

Indeed, "solidarity journalism," mentioned in the introduction, asks reporters to work from this grassroots level, within community, and not as an entity that stands apart: "What would it mean for journalism to think of itself as an institution committed to aiding in the construction of a community defined by the solidarity of its citizens with one another," asked Garry Pech and Rhona Leibel in a 2006 journal article. By 2020, a journalism studies professor, Dr. Anita Varma, had founded the Solidarity Journalism Initiative at the Markkula Center for Applied Efforts, before it moved with her to the University of Texas at Austin Center for Media Engagement, where she became an assistant professor. Varma drew from this community practice work[64] this concept of solidarity as an explicit commitment of social justice action applied to journalists "as a foundational moral principle from which journalistic duties take root."[65] In this kind of journalism, Varma argued, journalists move away from the typical stories that may evoke empathy from audiences but that do not develop concrete paths for addressing persistent problems. Instead, solidarity journalism would center the perspective of marginalized voices, value their lived experiences, and help people find shared beliefs and interests (e.g., the desire to feel safe) even within polarizing issues—work she terms "radical inclusion."[66] For Pech and Leibel, writing in solidarity with a newsroom's community necessitates an ethical processing that is based in caring about humanity. Does the content dehumanize anyone? Does it promote "a sense of our human connectedness with other human beings?"[67] These roles as I have described them in this chapter combined with the eight new skill sets reflect this call for solidarity journalism that Varma, Pech, and Leibel advocate because they focus on people in addition to factual information and in violation of the critical distance mandate. As such, central to any solidarity movement or community work, including the kind of trust-building actions we are asking of journalists in this built environment, must be an ethic of care.

Applying Care Theory to Engagement Practices

As I put together these new skill sets with these new roles centered in the intentionality behind the work, it seemed fundamentally transformative to me that journalists were being taught to not only care about communities but to act as a caregiver and to take on that role of caregiving enacted through relationship building, collaborating, mediating conversations, and networking. Trust building for and with communities, this work demanded, could happen only through relationships engaged in the practice of care. I defined an ethic of care in the first chapter, but here I mention that it offered for me a huge body of interdisciplinary scholarship from its origins in developmental psychology. This literature on care explored everything from the different moral stages between men and women to the more public understanding of an ethic to guide democratic and civic life. I borrowed from the political scientist Joan Tronto to reassert a definition of "caring" as "a species activity that includes everything that we do to maintain, continue and repair our world so that we can live in it as well as possible."[68]

Traditionally, reporters were taught to care only in the abstract—about democracy, audiences, government institutions, etc. They were taught a "Grand Virtue" kind of caring, with dominant values like objectivity and the American Dream, which reinforce whiteness and its harmful practices. They were taught not to care about individuals or groups, to be neutral. Any evidence of this kind of "caring" resulted in discord within the profession, such as when Black reporters at mainstream news outlets were told they cared too much about Black people to cover Black Lives Matter movements.[69] The profession, operating under this paradigm, failed. And, actually, all of our public institutions, with the exception of the military, had long been losing trust. The press's failure had many reasons, including its slow response to digital technologies and social media, but at its core was a breakdown in staying relevant with communities for whom the American Dream did not work out so great. This rhetoric operated in a care deficit, defined as an incapacity to meet needs.[70] As news outlets lost relevancy, they died off quickly.[71]

The engagement strategies revealed in Box 2.1 with the goal of building trust between journalists, audiences, sources, and information will not work without significant commitment to the nurturing of all the trusting relationships. The new roles that journalists are being asked to play invoke building, collaborating, facilitating, and networking—all actions demanding that journalists partner in solidarity with nonjournalists; in other words, the people formerly known as sources were now considered partners.[72] A common element for this built environment and its acting entities lay in their networked interdependency at the meso-organizational and the micro-individual levels of information exchange. This built environment, as documented in this chapter, represented a complex professional ensemble of a diverse set of actors focused on moving the mainstream journalism profession toward a more relations-based (and less transactional) industry—and trying to figure out new revenue streams in the process. And the actors in this built environment do this through relationships, collaborations, facilitation work, and networking—all core characteristics of caring.

When engagement toward trust building is embraced in full, journalists move away from an approach based in neutrality, where they operate from a distance with abstract, indirect caring for stories, democracy, and information. These engaged journalists instead become immersed in humanity, approaching people, communities, and knowledge with direct and explicit care. As such, this evidence leads me to argue that trust-building work is about relationship building guided by an ethic of care that results in a fact-based moral voice for journalists. This chapter delved into what this has looked like in the practice of these engagement strategies enacted through eight skills—radical transparency, power dynamic accounting, mediation, reciprocity, media literacies, community offline work, needs/assets/solution analyses, and collaborative production—as practiced through four new roles: relationship builder, community collaborator, community conversation facilitator, and professional network builder. The idea of *listening* in order to *learn* threads through all of this work as the theory posits that it only through this kind of practice can journalists help communities and their members move forward and the process of this solidarity work build trust.

In practice this would look like the attentiveness, responsibility, competence, responsiveness, and solidarity that Tronto proposed in *Caring Democracy*:

- Attentiveness (we must know the needs of others by attending to others)
- Responsibility (we must feel responsible for others' care)
- Competence (adopting an ethic of care requires action with appropriate resources and effort)
- Responsiveness (we must adjust our caregiving according to the needs at hand, for the person or entity specifically, and not by simply imagining what needs we ourselves might have)
- Solidarity (we must understand and accept collectively that care is essential to a working democracy and a thriving humanity)

Here we can think about *attentiveness* as listening and learning, and *responsibility* as taking on the mission of community builder in addition to storyteller. In this built environment, reporters and newsrooms must have the *competence* to commit to engagement as a fundamental part of the job, of the calling, and not merely as a box to check off. Being *responsive* to different constituents means appreciating that each story affects different populations according to power dynamics. All of this work, this relationship building, collaboration, facilitation, and networking, has meant reporting and producing in *solidarity* with communities to help cities understand the problems, connect stakeholders, and research solutions—all while immersed within a sense of a shared humanity.

Table 2.5 Care Qualities with Engagement Work

Care Quality	Engagement Work
Attentiveness	Listening, being present
Responsibility	Relationship building
Competence	Commit resources, network productively
Responsiveness	Reliability, follow-through
Solidarity	Community problem-solving, collaboration

Now when I think back to that warm October 2019 day in Brooklyn at Hearken's Engagement Innovation Summit, it seemed all of these dimensions were clicking into place for me as I listened to Jennifer Brandel compare engagement journalism to marriage. Citizens Agenda for those fall 2020 elections represented a first step in getting newsrooms moving toward more involvement with audiences. Would it work, though? Would newsrooms even be interested in taking six weeks out of their schedules to (re)train in these unproven practices? Based on the surveys I was collecting at that time, my answer was a tentative yes. But to replace the familiar norms and routines that had felt "objective" through the employ of binaries and official sources with a journalism so . . . engaged? Though clearly commitment to this work had materialized, we still seemed quite far from a full application of these roles and skills. In the next chapter I dive deeper into exactly how the trusting agents in these projects and initiatives were trying to convince journalists of a different set of values, a different kind of routine through an identity-aware care so essential to this theory of trust building as it was playing out. Key would be reteaching journalists—and all of us—how to listen to learn and how to learn to listen.

3

How Journalists Identify

The Practice of an Identity-Aware Caring

One day toward the end of 2018—about a year before that October 2019 Hearken Engagement Innovation Summit—I finished Phase 1 of my project and had compiled the list of engagement techniques. I clicked "Print" and watched the list slide out of the printer, then took it with me to the living room, where I camped out every day to sort through data and plan the next iteration of this multiphase study. What I had in front of me did not seem like much, just 24 bullet points with a line or two for each. (See Box 2.1.) But each bullet point had been culled from the 30 trust-building case studies— websites, background materials, evidence from studies, trade press reports, and interview transcripts with those involved. Each bullet point offered either a brand-new or enhanced technique that had been researched as an effective way to improve journalism—and specifically, to restore journalistic trust. Separated into low-effort and high-effort, the list ranged from the simple to the complex and could be classified into eight skill groupings: radical transparency, power dynamic accounting, mediation, reciprocity, media literacies, community offline work, needs/assets/solution analyses, and collaborative production. All of these trusting tasks represented some kind of engagement, broadly defined, in the following ways: They asked the reporter to build a relationship with audiences, and they asked audiences to build relationships with the journalism. They asked the reporter to engage with histories and systems of oppression, and they asked audiences to demand journalists educate themselves and to be discerning, introspective, and critical. They asked reporters to work with communities on forward-moving solutions, and they asked community members to contribute effort by showing up at forums, connecting with stakeholders, and caring about truthful information. They asked everyone involved in the republic to show up, to listen, to learn, and then to act out of a shared sense of humanity.

Whether or not these strategies would succeed in saving the industry could not yet be known on that day in late 2018, but those acting in and

How Journalists Engage. Sue Robinson, Oxford University Press. © Oxford University Press 2023.
DOI: 10.1093/oso/9780197667118.003.0003

contributing to this trust-focused built environment were banking on it. The mainstream journalism profession and the journalism education system had embarked on a widespread training effort to make these new skill sets around engagement journalism ubiquitous and entrenched, paving the way for a new kind of information exchange in Western countries—one centered on community deliberation, feelings of connection, and relationship building around mutual care in addition to facts. Gazing at the list that represented a year's worth of data collection, I endorsed all of them, and I would spend the next three years implementing them as best as possible through trainings, consultations, reporting classes, journal articles, and other kinds of profes- sional sharing. I would build reporting course modules around them. I would develop research projects inspired by them. I would write a book about them.

But in that moment in 2018, reading over the list, something tugged at me. In truth, it had been tugging at me since I was a reporter in the news- room, when we would occasionally get calls from a researcher at some fancy university wanting us to take a survey or answer a few questions. They inev- itably wanted to know why exactly Big Bad Gannett[1] paid more attention to advertisers than to communities. We stopped talking to researchers, feeling the general animosity many reporters felt for academics. This derision was one reason my editors tacked "Dr." onto my name in the newsroom even though at that time I had only an MA degree; it was not done out of respect, let's just say. At any rate, what bothered me about those researchers was this intractable problem: these academics assumed we journalists were all the same—that we worked with one mind, with one set of biases, with one kind of training and background. And that bugged me even then, even when I had yet to fully accept that I had a race as a white woman and privileges and power that I did not earn. Some reading I had been assigned in my PhD program would make sweeping statements about why the news was like this or like that, and I would think, "I bet instead it was that the reporter couldn't reach the person they wanted to reach, and the editor was breathing down their neck, and their partner on the desk had left early to go skiing," and so on.

That was way back in the early 2000s, but here I was in 2018 feeling that familiar tugging again as I thought about these strategies, which I and many both inside and outside the profession were spending a lot of time and money on. Weren't we forgetting something? The assumption had been in this trust- focused built environment that better listening and more attention would re- solve disconnection from all communities. However, not everyone listened in the same way. Not everyone built trust in the same way. Not everyone engaged in the same way. Indeed, what it came down to was that not everyone *cared* in the same way—not about facts, not about each other, and certainly not about mainstream journalism. Individual reporters entered newsrooms bringing with them histories of trusting, engaging, and caring—personally and professionally. And these differences resulted in nonuniform manners of trust building and a hodgepodge mixture of engagement practices. I came to realize that reforming journalism would require a specific type of care, one which I call "identity-aware" care.

In this chapter I explore the last two additions to my theory of trust building: **Trust building happens through the nurturing of personal, organizational, and institutional relationships that people have with information, sources, news brands, journalists, and each other during what is commonly referred to as engagement.** *For trust building to occur, engagement needs to be practiced with identity-aware care and enacted through listening and learning.* This paradigm shift has been led by people of color and women in newsrooms, spurred on by social movements such as the 2017 #MeToo sexual harassment reckoning and the 2020 Black Lives Matter protests, both of which became global. The shift for the white-majority mainstream newsrooms reflected a way of doing journalism that had already been the norm for the alternative press and ethnic media. It was beginning to be encapsulated in submovements like "solidarity journalism" mentioned in the previous chapter. The shift was long overdue, one that many, many journalists, scholars, activists, and others have called for over the years, asking the press to reckon with itself in the way it propped up structures that hurt entire groups of people, in the way it had become a system of oppression itself. This chapter attempts to situate this emerging trust-focused built environment and its "engagement journalism" into that history while documenting the changing mindset.

Central to such a reckoning must be the anchoring concept of identity. It is only through identity that one finds the perspective necessary to effect change, be it a Black columnist calling out objectivity as racist in the *New York Times* or a white queer woman helping to train journalists in engagement strategies or a young, white, cis, liberal reporter eager to help the industry evolve. In this focus on identities, we necessarily must bring our full selves into the process of journalism and also journalism education—to not only care about audiences and their facts but, importantly, to *care for* and also to *care with* communities. This chapter considers journalists as individual trusting agents who are navigating this new paradigm and their evolving role in the profession. I ask here: **How do different reporters trust people and practice ethical standards according to their identities? How do reporters of different identities engage in order to practice trust building? How are journalists themselves thinking about and practicing the connection between their own identities with their engagement and trust-building work?** I draw from hundreds of hours of ethnographic participant observation at engagement trainings, workshops, summits, and panels as well as in-depth interviews, focus groups, and surveys with 174 journalists and a review of the explosion of journalistic metadiscourses around identities. I strove to collect a diverse sample, and so more than a third identified as BIPOC. I will delve first into how identity has traditionally played out with journalists and then into the data from the surveys, focus groups, interviews, and participant observations about how different kinds of journalists consider engagement work with an ethic of care toward trust building.

I argue that how journalists trust is guided by whatever dominant identities they hold most dear, especially their racial identity, their gender/sexual identity, and their professional identity. Those journalists who identified as white, cis-gendered, and heterosexual and who who went through J-school thought about audiences, practiced reporting, and believed in the role of journalism in different ways than those who identified as being from a typically minoritized group or who came to journalism through another career path (not journalism school). Just as developmental psychologists who came up with care theory found differences between how men and women developed their moral selves, this work highlights how different engagers manifest different kinds of caring through different kinds of newsmaking relationships.

What It Means to Be Identity Aware

A core part of this trust-building paradigm incorporated identity work on the part of journalists. I saw this clearly in my first book as white reporters opened up to me about feeling their skin color keenly while reporting on race, so much so that they often held back in reporting so as to "not make anything worse" in relation to race in their communities, as one print reporter told me. They felt reporting on race as a white person got "tricky" and "sticky" quickly. Another white reporter told me during that data collection, "I am not Black, so I do not have a sense for what it is truly like to be a minority in the metro school district." A white editor from that same sample added, "At its most basic level can white reporters really report well on race?" As mentioned in the introductory chapter, journalists have been trained to bracket their identities as they report and write. Identity led to bias, which led to journalistic failure—or so the training mindset was. In the pursuit of objectivity, identity must be shelved or compartmentalized because subjectivity—that is, reporting that stemmed from one's identity—turned content into something other than straight news reporting; it turned content into opinion, or so the thinking has been. The opposite of objectivity had always been subjectivity. And subjectivity was bad. Very bad. It was here that I diverged from my more traditional colleagues both in the newsrooms and in the journalism schools: I did not believe that the opposite of objectivity was necessarily subjective opinion. Instead, this book posits a more complex understanding of what a nonobjective journalism might look like through engagement techniques that are apolitical yet intensely individualized and involved with explicitly stated agendas for co-creating better communities.

The dominant identity that many mainstream journalists have held has been their professional identity, often formed during time at journalism schools[2] or from training in the newsroom itself. Scholars have spent much time documenting how this identity became entrenched and codified across Western democracies in many newsrooms.[3] This identity has comprised the following kinds of statements: reporters have a shared set of practices centering on evidence and truth-telling via interviews, eyewitness accounts, databases, and other collection and analyses tools; they strive to be neutral and responsible with their truth-telling; they think of their job as a calling and an essential function of democracy; and they abide by ethical tenets and principles that have been uniform across the industry from newsroom to newsroom. These norms and values of mainstream journalism have also required reporters to refrain from conflicts of interest, to not do harm, and to provide people with enough information to self-govern.[4] There's more to it, but you get the gist. Furthermore, all of this has been taught in J-schools since the 1900s. As journalists moved between different information channels, that identity-shifted with them, always coming back to certain stalwarts of objectivity and evidence-based exchange.

This standard, as it has endured in mainstream journalism, reflected what some would consider to be a "colonized" position in which the reporter operates from a "detached and neutral point of observation," while the journalism "maps the world and its problems and classifies people and projects"[5] according to a white-privileged hierarchy. This entrenched, so-called rational and empirical way of knowing has been called "the hubris of the point zero"[6] for its declaration that truth derives from objective observation—a false connection that Ilia Rodríguez named as a central problem in journalism. The answer, according to many of the essays in Daniels and Blom's 2021 *Teaching Race* volume, is a pluralistic, intersectional lens for the communication industries, especially as taught in universities and trained in newsrooms: "We should plan on checking our opinions at the newsroom door but not our life experience. Instead, we should try to leverage diverse experiences to build a better news product,"[7] wrote Elliot Lewis, a professor of practice at Syracuse University. But for the most part, the professional communication industries' mainstream members have not done this, in part because the status quo as experienced by these mostly white journalists did not disappoint. The status quo worked well for them and, as such, seemed reasonable and fair.

Much research has lambasted the press for its lack of diversity and perspective, which many have argued led to rampant stereotyping, marginalization, and failures to investigate problematic institutional systems ever since U.S. journalism began in the colonies more than 400 years ago.[8] In 1988, the *Kerner Report*'s fifteenth chapter noted how homogeneous its newsrooms were back then: "Along with the country as a whole, the press has too long basked in a white world, looking out of it, if at all, with white men's eyes and a white perspective. That is no longer good enough. The painful process of readjustment that is required of the American news media must begin now. They must make a reality of integration—in both their product and personnel."[9]

It did not get much better, staying at around 13% journalists of color until around 2018, when the American Society of News Editors reported 22.6% in their Newsroom Diversity Survey identified as people of color.[10] American newsrooms lack other kinds of diversity as well, including age, sexuality, class, and political affiliation.[11] The industry's newsrooms also had become full of reporters from upper-middle-class backgrounds—who else could afford the long hours with low pay and often unpaid internships and the need to have a car without outside financial help?[12]

And, per much criticism and accusations, especially from conservatives, these mainstream newsrooms seemed very liberal.[13] Brisbane journalism studies scholar John Henningham found that Australian political journalists skewed left, and he determined that "a shared liberal consensus among political journalists, especially those in the national capital, may result in general acceptance by them of a liberal agenda."[14] Similar findings have been revealed in other countries as well, including Ireland[15] and Hong Kong,[16] as well as the United States, Great Britain, Germany, Italy, and Sweden.[17] I do not engage very much with political identity as an influence on reporters; indeed, I did not find any significant differences in how journalists with different political identities answered the questions about engagement and trust-building strategies. And there was an obvious reason for that: only 5 of the 106 survey participants identified as Republicans, the rest identifying as Democrat, Democrat-leaning, or independent. This is a significant limitation for this research, and one I hope to rectify with my next set of research studies. Of course we know that people definitely judge individual reporters and their news brands based on their assumptions and perceptions that they are overwhelmingly liberal, which has been a core reason for increasing distrust.[18]

But it is the ubiquitous whiteness of reporters in U.S. newsrooms that has operated as a dominant, sometimes invisible, but always present and universal trope that influences how a person operates according to a paradigm of white superiority and oppression for everyone else.[19] As such, whiteness as a category has necessitated the existence of "others" who are somehow lesser, has allowed the normalization of discrimination, and has created and perpetuated systems and structures that primarily benefit the dominant group.[20] Journalists growing up in this society of whiteness played along, if subconsciously. In his 2011 dissertation, "Whiteness and News: The Interlocking Social Construction of 'Realities,'" Kevin Dolan asked white journalists, "[W]hat does it mean to be white?" They had no answer. Dolan found that when journalists of color try to raise concerns about racist structures in their journalism, they are accused of "having an agenda," but when white reporters do so, "they can be seen as looking at the big picture."[21] Dolan also connected the practice of objectivity to the whiteness of newsrooms, writing, "'Objective' journalism, through all its practices, discourses, and defenses, is consistently disingenuous, truth evading, and duplicitous. It is disingenuous in how it avoids questions of values, it is often truth evading with its constant reliance on empty platitudes such as 'the right to know' (avoiding the values in deciding which issues or subjects where the right to know is absolute), and duplicitous in how it avoids accountability in its constant reliance on procedures as defenses for news judgments (we treated it like any Census report or story on a conflict of interest)."[22] Dolan called this problem one of "white incumbency," meaning that journalism's racism problem is about the inability of newsrooms—no matter how diverse they are getting—to move away from a white mindset and a white-cultural approach to journalism.[23] In these white, mainstream newsrooms, wrote Pamela Newkirk in *Within the Veil: Black Journalists, White Media*, "Black journalists, then, are forced to compromise their own sense of fairness to satisfy the journalistic standards of news editors whose own objectivity is clouded by their own subconscious assumptions about race."[24]

Many journalists of color have long rejected this whitewashed way of doing journalism and embraced an identity-aware reporting. Consider that the first Black-led newspaper, *Freedom's Journal*, began in 1827 as a way to challenge racism, launching a long history of media criticism centered on identities.[25] Sarah Jackson documented how Black celebrities could use both mainstream and Black press to expose disparities in societal conditions.[26] Indeed, they often left mainstream newsrooms that refused to change as the United States became more and more multicultural. For example, even as recently as 2022, journalists of color left National Public Radio—once considered one of the more progressive news organizations in terms of diversity—in droves, some saying they were not able to be innovative and creative in their identity-aware journalism.[27] These journalists exited not only for ethnic media outlets like the *Chicago Defender* that had been producing identity-aware news accounts for more than a century, but also for the thriving alternative public sphere of Black and Brown digital media like The Root, Black Twitter and other spaces. In addition, journalists holding identities within the LGBTQ+, Hispanic, Native American, different kinds of Asian, disabled, and other realms created other kinds of counterpublic spheres wherein their own identities and sensibilities—from framing to sourcing and topics—could flourish: "because perceptions of race and justice influence the way we see the world, it obviously matters who presents 'facts' to the public."[28]

Identity guides people in everything they do, from their job to their social life, from their politics to their personal ethics, and it is the intermingling of different identities combined with professional norms that can form a paradigmatic belief system that influences actions and behaviors. A belief system, according to Philip Converse, writing about public opinion research back in 1964, is the "configuration of ideas and attitudes in which the elements are bound together by some form of constraint or functional interdependence."[29] If identities are indeed influencing actions, then we can understand that they also inform and "constrain" choices; in other words, we can predict behavior based on these influences.[30] "For example, a journalist who has a more liberal and progressive political outlook, for example, is likely to place more emphasis on the watchdog role of the press, and a journalist who sees social inequalities as a huge problem in a society is likely to place more emphasis on the advocacy role of the media," according to Tang and Lee.[31]

This has created tension for reporters who hold different kinds of identities, whose belief systems create friction with the mainstream journalism norms such as objectivity within a media system rife with oppression, from its histories to its policies that produce false equivalencies and assign legitimacy from within a white-liberal-elitist paradigm. Consider, for example, how Black journalists' presence in newsrooms influenced coverage, even as they chafed at the normative constraints and cultural resistance from editors— such as when Bryant Gumbel at NBC thought up and produced a series on Africa, spending more than $2 million in 1992.[32] We can extend this line of thought into other important public realms, such as that of citizenship, as rhetoric scholar Catherine Squires studied, arguing that "there are different modalities of *racial citizenship,* and that with their power to influence and set boundaries for public discourse, news media are major players in drawing lines between identity groups, and between acceptable ways of doing race, doing citizenship."[33] It is only by centering race and their racial identities (and also their gendered identities) through creative engagement practices that BIPOC people have defined their participation in civic life, according to Squires. And this has included reporters who have also been members of populations typically marginalized by mainstream journalism.[34]

To be identity-aware, then, is to call out bias and oppressive conditions with evidence-based facts revealed within an identity framework that encompasses a racial/power lens. By saying this, I am not evoking terms like "neutral" or "balance" or "fair" per se, because these terms too can lead to false equivalencies and/or confusing standards.[35] If, as a white, straight-A student, I approach a story about racial achievement disparities, can I ever be neutral about the school system's inadequacies? I can get closer to the truth if I call out my identities that will influence how I approach the story and constantly interrogate them as I report. Fairness, too, may be a lovely idea, but in reality we should commit instead to *equity.* In equity, every person is allotted the conditions of reporting that they need (as opposed to equality, when all sources are treated the same, as if no power dynamics were present).[36] One way this may play out, according to the engagement techniques the built environment encourages, is to take more care in reporting with BIPOC sources who are not in a position of authority, allowing them to interview the reporter, allowing them to see their quotes ahead of time, allowing them, even, to be anonymous yet vetted.

Let me give an example that happened as I was writing this in spring 2022 and teaching a beginning reporting class. Several of the students were working on K–12 racial achievement disparities in Madison, and I messaged the class a local story, "A Perfect Storm: The Pandemic Has Exacerbated Long-Simmering Troubles for Madison's Public Schools. Critics Say the School Board Is Part of the Problem."[37] Up high in the story was a quote by a former school board member and high-profile progressive named TJ Mertz: " 'I think we've allowed the school board to become purely about symbolism.' Symbolism is important, he adds, 'but it can't stop there. The board should guide decision-making and ensure policies are being implemented successfully.' " I wrote to the students that the context left out by the reporter was that Mertz, a white, highly educated male, had lost his seat years before to the first BIPOC woman to get elected, a Brazilian American, and soon after, the board for the first time in history became much more representative of the school district, with a minority of white officials. "Pay attention to the TJ Mertz quote up high. Problematic?," I messaged to the students after pointing them to the story. "Knowing that context is important because now his use of the term 'symbolism' becomes code for 'BIPOC people.' And NOW doesn't that change the tone and meaning? THIS is what it means to approach a story with a racial lens." Would pointing out this background be "fair" or "balanced"? I think Mertz would say no. But it would be more contextually accurate. It would be identity aware, so to speak.

A Mainstream Movement towards Identity Awareness

The identity-aware journalists have spurred the current mainstream revolution in the news industry. By 2020, the industry, still reeling from the #MeToo movement around gender inequalities and sexual harassment in 2017–18,[38] headed into a racial reckoning emboldened by the Black Lives Matter protests that spanned the globe.[39] The impetus was yet another killing of a Black man, George Floyd, in May 2020 at the hands of a white policeman in Minnesota. However, the movement had begun earlier, with the killing of 17-year-old Trayvon Martin in July 2013 and the acquittal of the white man who murdered him; at the time American writer and civil rights leader Alicia Garza posted, "I continue to be surprised at how little black lives matter. . . . Black people. I love you. Our lives matter." This was tweeted out by a community organizer named Patrisse Khan Cullors with #BlackLivesMatter as a tag line.[40] With this building movement erupting, Floyd's killing was captured in its entirety on social media: people videotaped the man's pleas as the police officer kneeled on his back for almost nine minutes until Floyd died, on camera.[41] Something that had been entrenched broke. For months people around the globe took to the streets, social media, and journalism to call for change. And the mainstream news industry as a whole began its own reckoning in earnest.

The metadiscourse for the news media profession centered the industry's complicity in discrimination and racism, with a series of high-profile journalists calling out the press, projects aimed at self-investigation, and renewed commitments to doing and being better. Black and Brown journalists threaded the public conversation with stories of blatant intolerance. Consider this Twitter thread by Brent Staples, a member of the editorial board at the *New York Times* and a 2019 Pulitzer Prize winner, on June 4, 2020:

> White newsrooms only hired Black reporters at all because of the civil unrest of the 1960s. African American reporters at the time could actually tell you which riot got them hired. (1/3) We came in under suspicion of "split loyalties." Early in my career, I criticized coverage in the paper where I worked at the time. A manager called me in and said—without even a hint of irony: "We worry that you are here pushing a Black agenda." (2/3) In other words, I was welcome to stay—only if I subscribed to what critical race theorists would later describe as the "white normative view" of world events. (3/3)

This discourse laid bare many stories that starkly demonstrated the industry's collusion in society's constant oppression of people of color.[42] What we were seeing here is the continuation of generations of journalistic "black witnessing" that Allissa Richardson described in her 2020 *Bearing Witness While Black: African Americans, Smartphones, and the New Protest #Journalism*. Long have African Americans in particular[43] found ways to illuminate the atrocities done to Black people in the United States and elsewhere through media, from Ida B. Wells with the *Free Speech* newspaper and her *Southern Horrors* of the late 1800s to the smartphone at the beginning of the 21st century. Indeed, Richardson noted how Western African drummers relayed their people's histories and current events as the "first black witnesses."[44]

And so we come to June 23, 2020, when Wesley Lowery penned a column titled "A Reckoning over Objectivity, Led by Black Journalists" that served as a catalyst for that metaconversation already happening and that went viral through various digital platforms. He wrote:

> [A]s protesters are taking to the streets of American cities to denounce racism and the unabated police killings of Black people across the country, the journalism industry has seemingly reached a breaking point of its own: Black journalists are publicly airing years of accumulated grievances, demanding an overdue reckoning for a profession whose mainstream repeatedly brushes off their concerns; in many newsrooms, writers and editors are now also openly pushing for a paradigm shift in how our outlets define their operations and ideals. While these two battles may seem superficially separate, in reality, the failure of the mainstream press to accurately cover Black communities is intrinsically linked with its failure to employ, retain and listen to Black people. . . . The views and inclinations of Whiteness are accepted as the objective neutral.

Lowery linked such problematic practices of journalism as stereotypes and missed coverage to a lack of perspective within the newsrooms themselves. But he did not stop there. Next up was his takedown of objectivity as it had come to be practiced by mainstream journalists:

> Neutral objectivity trips over itself to find ways to avoid telling the truth. Neutral objectivity insists we use clunky euphemisms like "officer-involved shooting." Moral clarity, and a faithful adherence to grammar and syntax, would demand we use words that most precisely mean the thing we're trying to communicate: "the police shot someone."

Immediately longtime media watchers criticized Lowery for trying to move the profession from "objectivity" to "subjectivity."[45] How would mainstream journalism differentiate from other subjective content? Objectivity had been in place for both cultural and commercial reasons and had been key to helping the press attain authority over the day's news—simply because, in part, the reporters were supposed to be free of faction. Tom Rosenstiel[46] in a series of 22 tweets on June 24, 2020, laid out what a moral voice might sound like for the news media, saying that he was striving for more "clarity": "If journalists replace a flawed understanding of objectivity by taking refuge in subjectivity and think their opinions have more moral integrity than genuine inquiry, journalism will be lost." For many journalists, this stream of thought was a tricky one to follow all the way through. Journalists knew that the minute they revealed their identities, especially their racial and political identities, anything they wrote would become suspect and their work dismissed out of hand.

One striking bit I noticed in the Lowery piece was in this subhead: "What's different, in this moment, is that the editors of our country's most esteemed outlets no longer hold a monopoly on publishing power." This underscored one of my arguments: we were at a pivotal moment of this reckoning, one that is forcing transformation. We have seen such reckoning before, but these moments tended to be dominated by inadequate handwringing that resulted in a lot of reports and panels but not much actual change. In the March 2021 report of its own practices around race, the *New York Times*—the U.S. flagship, legacy news outlet—revealed that, although it had made progress in diversifying its staff, its culture remained mired in whiteness.[47] The report provided evidence that its BIPOC peopel on staff, especially its Black and Brown employees, found the *Times* a difficult and sometimes impossible workplace. The three authors of the report—editors Amber Guild, Carolyn Ryan, and Anand Venkatesan, identifying as two people of color and a white woman—wrote, "For many, this report is long overdue. For others, it will be a new and uncomfortable portrait of The Times. For all of us, it is a call to action." BIPOC people within the industry were increasingly in positions of power to effect change at fundamental levels, but the change would come only with acknowledgment of the role identities play in newsmaking. It is my argument that we need to move toward a more nuanced understanding of how the meaning construction of news changes depending on who we are—whether we are authoring the material or simply reading and sharing it. It is only through revolutions in fundamental institutional practices to focus on power and privilege and *decenter* whiteness that any of these calls to action can be successful.

Becoming More Identity Aware

When I worked at a Gannett newspaper, we reporters were given a racial quota: the combination of sources in our stories needed to match the percentage of minorities in our states. As a (very) young, (very) white business reporter in Vermont, I rolled my eyes at this quota: good luck to me, I thought, trying to find people of color in my beat in *Vermont*.[48] Also, we covered the entire state, and I did much of my reporting on deadline, talking to sources over the phone. I agonized over how to discern the race of someone on the other end. Asking someone bluntly at that time in my life seemed impossible, mortifying, and racist, having been raised to believe that pointing out race was inappropriate and that I needed to be completely colorblind. My face heated, and I would blurt out the question I had settled on: "Can you tell me what your heritage is?".

This memory came back to me as I read through our 174 transcripts with journalists across the United States. White people often had a difficult time when the topic turned to race. Many insisted that they had no biases. One respondent said his identities influenced his reporting "very little. My job is to present facts and accurate quotes from all sides present. My identity should not play a factor in that job." Most of the responses about identity referenced nonracial and nonpolitical categories such as their being an atheist or a Catholic, a parent, lower income, a sexual assault survivor, LGBTQ, an immigrant, or female. One even described their identity as a cat owner. Several talked about times they had been accused of being racist or inappropriate in their coverage but spoke of the incident in defensive tones or said it made them back off and try to "play it safe." About half of the white journalists we talked to said their identities either did not influence them or that their identity—as a parent, a Catholic, a survivor—worked positively, making them more sensitive to topics that involved their identity. These people believed everyone must be "treated the same": "I always make every effort not to let my own personal views get in the way of my writing. I try and ask difficult questions, even of groups I personally agree with, on contentious issues, to represent both (or all) sides fairly." Others said they "tend to stay away from race, sexuality, class, religion and politics." Another white reporter said, "I'm more affected by the way people behave (or misbehave) than by their identities, or mine." These participants' goal in doing their journalism centered on finding, verifying, and publishing accurate information that could help communities improve.

Three-quarters (74%) of our white participants espoused a more traditional role for journalism and went about trust building by enacting the normative reportorial practices and values, such as "presenting clear, accurate information and to be responsive to feedback." When it came to trust building with people who did not share their identities, it seemed sometimes to be more about checking boxes: "Quote people from these communities to show that you have considered their viewpoint," wrote one person in a survey. These reporters operated outside of community, helping to build *for* the community rather than *with* them. Often their responses were steeped in the traditional, ingrained lexicon of storytelling, democracy, and information exchange, with a tone of pride and the sense that this was a calling: "I want to help keep our readers informed. I want to hold powerful officials accountable. I was to explain complex issues to readers. I want to shine a light on wrongdoing, corruption and malfeasance." Transparency was a key attribute in these passive actions toward trust building without relationship building.

But then there was the 26% of our white sample who talked more frankly about the privilege their whiteness and other identities such as being able-bodied and heterosexual gave them and how they tried to be more aware of these "fault lines."[49] They spoke of trying to be a voice for the voiceless, of participating within their communities, and—most frequently—listening. I was impressed to see fully half of all of our participants rethinking journalism's function in a society and proactively changing how they reported. These responses considered their role to be helping communities solve their problems and even suggested that journalists themselves should roll up their sleeves and work alongside communities to do so. These respondents purported a more proactive approach to build communities *with communities* and wrote longer answers about power structures. And while transparency was also listed as important to trust building, these respondents recognized that the existing antijournalism culture meant they needed to "show them that I'm a normal person and not an enemy of the people"—a very active statement. Whereas those in the more traditional group mentioned that they tried to make sure community members knew how to reach them, these reporters were more focused on going into neighborhoods and being more present in different kinds of spaces. As one respondent wrote, "I try and show up in person to places in the community on days where I am not reporting out a story. . . . This works when you hone [sic] in on one or two neighborhoods at a time. I also try and meet and talk with community stakeholders at grass-roots organizations to try and better understand the work they're doing, to see if there's a place for me to fit in my work as a journalist." This type of expressed engagement offered an intentional and deliberate nurturing of community relationships. These more identity-aware white journalists talked of the importance of being introspective and of interrogating their mistakes. One journalist described creating focus groups of community members who regularly analyzed their coverage, specifically around issues of disparities, bias, and stereotyping.

A sample of our participants (36%) identified as Latinx, African American, Native American, Asian, or mixed race, and most of these participants were very used to talking about their identities. For these reporters, their identities—especially racial[50]—loomed over every aspect of their job, as one Filipino-American-identified woman said: "Frankly, I work in a geographic area that is very white and conservative so my mere presence may set off alarms for some people." They described their encounters with racism both internally in newsrooms as well as externally and said they were often the arbitrators and facilitators of their news outlet's racial interactions.

PARTICIPANT: There's this one story in particular where it was an older, white man who is a really great storyteller [who] . . . covered a Filipino-American event, but used comparisons that just were not . . . It was just very insensitive.

RESEARCHER: He probably didn't even realize.

PARTICIPANT: He didn't realize it, and then when he got called out on it, he still was like 'I don't see the problem.' And I'm like, as a Filipino-American in the newsroom, one of the only ones, we had to really explain it. . . We invited members of that particular organization and community to come in to also speak about it to kind of, to better explain just to even the higher-ups because even his editor didn't see it at first.

RESEARCHER: So what could have gone differently?

PARTICIPANT: We could have actually tried to find a reporter in the newsroom that was a person of color, even if it wasn't an Asian person, just maybe a person of color who could be a little more sensitive to that.

RESEARCHER: To read the story before he produced it? Or to actually do the story?

PARTICIPANT: To actually do the story.

RESEARCHER: Oh, okay.

PARTICIPANT: But then also, yeah, an editor. I mean I'm an editor, and he could have easily pinged me.

Many of our BIPOC journalists as well as our LGBTQ+ reporters described to the research team situations like this, where they had to take on responsibility for the newsroom's soul and expressed dismay at how much work was still needed in these places of whiteness. In analysis of these, I noted how much extra labor this work entailed for journalists of color in these newsrooms—having to educate their colleagues and audiences, having to constantly be on the lookout for copy that was insensitive to their communities, having to navigate the ignorance of white reporters and editors (especially bosses), and having to serve as a checkpoint for many stories about race or other groups that were not well represented in the newsroom. Scholars have studied this phenomenon in diverse disciplines from community organizing to higher education and have dubbed it "racial battle fatigue," as coined by educator William Smith.[51] The concept well encapsulates the unrelenting negative energy involved in fighting oppression in all its forms: microaggressions, outright racism, and all the physical, psychological, emotional, political, social, and other forms of trauma associated with that constant battling. This idea bubbled up in these focus groups and interviews with journalists of color.

These participants also reported valuing transparency, accuracy, integrity, and respect as means to trust building. However, their professional goals inevitably reflected identities in some manner, often centered on empowering communities through solutions-oriented journalism that integrated emotion and humanity, as one Hispanic-identifying reporter recounted in an open-ended survey question:

> In my current role, I cover criminal justice systems across the state. . . . I aim to write stories that connect individual narratives and experiences with systemic underpinnings to better inform the civic lives of [residents] (as voters, as taxpayers, etc.). More broadly, as a journalist, I hope for my work to heighten public awareness of certain systemic issues: to be a product of bearing witness to folks who entrust their stories to me; and to be a document of the times. More and more, I strive for my work to be "useful"—to be for, rather than about, the communities I cover—in this instance justice-impacted people and their families/larger communities.

This stated aim revealed a deep, intentional function to amplify people and issues that have typically been marginalized in mainstream information outlets. These journalists integrated their professional goals with the identities of their sources or how the institutions and other entities they were covering oppressed people holding certain identities. In addition, they pulled in their own identities. "Representation matters, and I think it's important that viewers not only see me, but know that I'm bringing my own stories and humanity to the editorial meetings and chiming in when necessary," wrote one Black journalist. These responses revealed a keen sense of obligation on the part of these journalists to ensure sensitivity and effect change. One person who identified as Asian felt she had a "moral obligation to bring forward stories that are overlooked by other members of the media who don't have my perspective." These reporters talked and wrote very openly about their expressed intent to "add the dimensions that were omitted" when stories about their communities, such as immigrant groups, were written in the mainstream press.

Journalists as Identity-Aware Caregivers

At a Citizens Agenda training, a Hearken engagement consultant and trainer named Bridget Thoreson[52] talked to reporters about how their own identities needed to be considered as they went about building trust with audiences. She told a story about being in a newsroom as a white, young, gay journalist, and the Supreme Court had just made gay marriage legal. Thoreson had a lot of story ideas but was told by her editors she was too biased to cover LGBTQ issues, making her feel marginalized and offended. "But heterosexuals covering heterosexuals is fine?" she remembered thinking to herself. On this particular day in May 2020, I watched as she started telling her story to the 26 reporters and editors on the call in a virtual training as part of the Citizens Agenda[53] project:

> The day that the U.S. Supreme Court ruled that gay marriage was legal was one of the most isolating I had ever experienced in the newsroom. Colleagues were coming up, they were congratulating me and I felt like crying instead of cheering because they didn't understand the struggles that my wife and I had been through to patch together the legal protections for our relationship while this whole conversation was happening. Our coverage as a newsroom had not reflected the nuances of the struggle that I knew existed for the LGBTQ+ community. My colleagues—whom I respected tremendously—did not even know what they didn't know, and what's worse, they had never asked. I share this experience today because

it's incumbent on all of us to do better when it comes to reaching out to underrepresented or marginalized communities. That starts from coming from a place of vulnerability and curiosity, and of being willing to admit that you don't know what you don't know, that you need to understand that members of these communities will have barriers to trust that you must consider in your outreach.

Thoreson's co-trainer, Malii Watts Witten, nodded in support as Thoreson finished her story. Witten called herself an "impact entrepreneur" for culturally diverse environments at her consultancy, Engage Between, identifying as U.S. American Black and heterosexual and not as a journalist at all. The Zoom was part of the first of five cohorts of newsrooms cycling through free training that Hearken was doing in conjunction with (white, cis, female, heterosexual) Joy Mayer of Trusting News and (white, cis, male, heterosexual) Jay Rosen of New York University and the Membership Puzzle Project in an effort to get newsrooms to "people power" their election coverage. Each training month had a session specifically on identity—the identity of the journalists. That May 2020 cohort comprised a majority of white reporters; about 20% identified as races that were traditionally minoritized. I was the researcher on the project, but I had my video on as Witten had requested of all participants to lend a sense of intimacy to conversation about personal identity among virtual strangers. I considered myself a participant observer in these trainings, where I found my whole self, my past journalist self, and my present academic/researcher/teacher/trainer self engaged. Yet another part of myself—my white self—felt uncomfortable already, knowing what was coming, despite my own racial journey. Certainly, before embarking on my quest for self-interrogation about race, I had no idea what I did not know. But I would learn that day and in subsequent interactions with Thoreson and Witten the connection between identity and an ethic of care when building trust as journalists.

My first book[54] centered on identity, investigating the relationship between how people in Black and Brown communities trusted white reporters, especially when news coverage had to do with race. In that book I made a series of recommendations for white reporters on how to build trust better in traditionally marginalized communities. I encouraged reporters to interrogate their own identities, privileges, and biases, for although many newsrooms offered diversity trainings, they tended to focus on the logistics of building trust and did not treat reporters as having racial identities themselves. But that book was more about relationships between white reporters and Black people specifically. A feeling that I could go deeper sparked this book.

I forced my thoughts back to the training at hand.

Witten began the facilitation, asking for reactions to Thoreson's story. Right away, a Black reporter shared:

> I had a neighbor outside of Baltimore who is a lifelong public radio consumer, and we were having a conversation about violence that he was witnessing as an emergency room surgeon. And he made a statement that I, because I was Black, probably had been exposed to that kind of violence but that that was something he had never seen before. It struck me that he was a lifelong listener to public media who would hold a belief like that and feel comfortable articulating it. . . . We've done a poor job of informing our core listeners about the world around them.

Witten thanked her for sharing and then launched into a homily that was completely unexpected, even though by this point I had attended, hosted, or organized dozens of trainings around identity in all my professional and civic capacities. She introduced to the cohort the Hindu faith Brahma to suggest that in channeling one's spirituality, one remembered the basic human function of community nurturing and connecting. Here the task of the reporter was not about truth-telling in the strictest sense of the word, as a fact-finder or stenographer, but rather as a facilitator and problem-solver, and even closer: an interpreter of needs. She continued, trying to tie the idea back to reporting protocols and introducing the idea of reporting transformation (or maybe evolution): "How else can we reach beyond our own understanding to explore intersectionality, to explore nuance, to create depth to our stories? Bridget mentioned one idea that was about vulnerability. I know . . . you are told that you're supposed to be objective. You're trained to be a neutral party, but what if you weren't? What if you created—at the head of your story or your coverage or your interviewing—a bit of a commentary about who you are coming into this story?"

But when she asked for reactions, only two engagement consultants and I spoke up. Others on the call were silent. In a conversation later with Witten, she told me white people asked to interrogate their own identities were often silent: "I felt like people were grappling with their own assumptions about what journalism should be when it comes to engagement. . . . It was a challenge conceptually and certainly in practice. There's a thought out there that the only way to do big journalism is to take yourself out of it. [In the Citizens Agenda cohorts] we were talking about very much putting yourself *into it*, right?"

To talk to Witten was to talk to someone whose engagement paradigm occupied her entire being, and she strove to model that in her training facilitations. Bringing up spirituality represented a strategic choice completely new to journalism. She called objectivity "a very white Anglo-Saxon-Protestant construct." By evoking a more spiritual, less rational approach to journalism, one can reconnect oneself to humanity in a more holistic undertaking. Much research backed up this idea that objectivity resulted in propping up a dominant culture privileging whiteness.[55] To move away from this distancing is to move toward a more global, multicultural engagement edict but also must mean an identity centering for reporters. This will not be easy, given journalistic training to compartmentalize self-identities.

In identity centering, the ethic of care represents a fundamental value in the journalistic trust-building work, requiring deep listening—to the self, to the content, and to others—around bias, privilege, and power. In the decades after the "ethic of care" scholarly debut in the 1980s, care theorists like Joan Tronto have used the philosophy to move morality studies away from universal applications and toward "moral particularism." Moral participation recognized that individual situations and experiences demanded contextualized ethical approaches.[56] Undergirding this theorizing was the idea that the more one knew a person and their life experiences, the more connected one felt to them, and the more one cared for them.[57] In giving voice to underrepresented people and in amplifying their needs, journalists can place facts into the development of a moral fabric shared by all communities. The developmental psychologist who coined the term "ethic of care," Carol Gilligan, and her co-author Janie Ward wrote in a foreword to an edited volume titled *Race-ing Moral Formation: African American Perspectives on Care and Justice* that such work could illuminate "how a person's inner world can come into the outer world and how the outer world (the voices of others) can enter the chamber of the self, like breathing out and breathing in."[58]

Caring centers on connectedness *and* justice, which through the 1970s and 1980s were considered to be incompatible as values because justice demanded equality through impartial determination (the very tenet upon which journalism's objectivity rested) while caring as an ethic needed involvement.[59] But through the late 1990s and into the 2000s, scholars in Afro-American studies and other fields theorized away the false boundaries of the two concepts care and justice, and it is at this intersection where journalism can benefit. The scholarly work to incorporate these once conflicting value frameworks[60] broadened the information-exchange conversation and served to reconcile the seeming contradictions between good journalism and good trust work and engagement.

As some journalism studies scholars took up an ethic of care, they suggested that journalists' adoption of an ethic of care in their professional work could represent an essential virtue toward improving the human condition in general. "Modern journalism, including all the technology it entails, can be an important vehicle for ethical caring in a complex and disparate world,"[61] wrote philosopher Maurice Hamington in 2011. Communication scholars Mohammad Delwar Hossain and James Aucoin in 2017 took up the thread that Linda Steiner and Chad M. Okrusch began in their 2006 journal article "Care as a Virtue for Journalists."[62] Both of these pieces, along with a book chapter that Steiner wrote in 2009, suggested that journalists would do well to incorporate caring behaviors such as listening into their hitherto justice-oriented norms and routines. In doing this, Steiner and Okrusch suggested, they could revise the "journalism mythology in ways that give them permission and validation to do what they, as human beings, already may want to do and even try to do—to care about problems and to acknowledge that they care that their work has impact, produces caring responses and actions. A caring ethic enables journalists to be ethical decision makers as well as moral agents."[63] Hossain and Aucoin advanced this argument by suggesting that this might be a "universal ethic" as a "moral philosophical foundation" for all journalists across the globe to adopt and adapt as their contexts deem appropriate: "A journalist who is in a caring relationship with their city also would be in caring relationships with their state, country, region, and world, each on different, but important, levels."[64] In this principle, journalists were to envision a more just future in the face of present crisis and to report and produce content within a *caring* framework.

In my sampling of journalists talking about engagement practices, this ethic of care was rarely made explicit. Yet, a strong ethic of care existed implicitly within the stories they shared about their process of reporting. Not only did engaged reporters talk about attentiveness and responsiveness with communities—that is, caring for constituents—but they also spoke of moments when they themselves felt uncared for, either by others in the newsroom or by audiences. One survey participant wrote, "My experiences as a survivor impacted me while covering a child porn arrest. It was extremely triggering and I'm thankful that I had a flexible deadline that allowed me to process what I was writing. My experiences allowed me to be more careful about my word choice and how I selected which sensitive information to include in my story." Her own caring needs—based upon her identity as a survivor—made her reciprocate caring. In my sample, these engaged, identity-aware reporters often used the words "kind" or "kindness," saying that building trust was about "having human conversations, like asking about their families, before launching into interviews. It involved face-to-face meetings and checking in regularly." One Latino man had this to say:

> Mainly I just try to make every interaction lean on the side of relational instead of transactional. When I interview someone, I want to listen well, show that I care, follow up, explain things about journalism they may not know. I think getting the public to trust you starts with being trustworthy. It's about making your intentions explicitly known, and following through with fair, balanced, and accurate reporting. With people who aren't direct sources, I just try to be a nice man. And I see an opportunity to correct a misunderstanding they have about how news orgs function. I do so inquisitively and kindly.

A caring kind of journalism for these people rejected the "fast, 'extractive' approach," explained one reporter. Instead, trust building was about "taking a slow, relationship-building approach." These identity-aware, caring reporters focused their perspective on their communities, as opposed to the stories themselves. "[I] constantly think about the people who will read my stories and how they will feel about the way they're being described," one Black woman reported. Primarily, journalists practicing an ethic of care wanted to help communities feel and be nurtured themselves. "I would like people to care about the world around them," said one engagement reporter.

In 2002 journalism ethicist Kelly McBride wrote a piece for Poynter, a nonprofit journalism training center, that placed these ethics side by side as they played out in journalism and connected them to identities, even citing Gilligan's classic work *In a Different Voice*.[65] As I have already argued, I do not see objectivity and subjectivity or emotion and evidence as being incompatible, and I suggest that the adoption of an ethic of care on the part of reporters would incorporate a justice-oriented frame essential to help move communities forward in equity. What matters most would be for journalists' intentional proaction and engagement toward justice through caring, not only by trying to evoke empathy for others—as journalists have always done—but also to help disrupt problematic institutions and the status quo through an identity-aware kind of caring that ultimately resulted in action—such as solutions-oriented journalism.[66] For Hamington, this would entail a significant social obligation for reporters: "Journalism can provide the imaginative link to caring. However, with that reporting comes tremendous moral responsibility."[67] This would demand both a caring and a just integration that celebrated identities while also fighting disparities and exclusions. Hamington, who had been studying the ethic of care for decades as a philosopher, offered up three components that must be incorporated into caring: inquiry, connection, and action,[68] and he suggested that journalists operate at a critical and convenient nexus between community, policymakers, and the public sphere to orchestrate an ethic of care in all they produce.

Engagement techniques in journalism must be used along with justice-oriented, fact-based paradigms that maintain mainstream journalism's essential identity and its claim of information authority. Table 3.1 shows the alignment between an ethic of care, identity awareness, and journalists' well-established justice-oriented norms and routines. Let me return to those five ethic-of-care values from Joan Tronto broached in the previous chapter: attentiveness, responsibility, competence, responsiveness, and solidarity. Now I pair them with the ways in which engagement work has unfolded in the trust-focused built environment I reveal in this book. We know from Chapter 2's analysis of trust-building work that these techniques call for eight new kinds of skill sets: radical transparency, power dynamic accounting, mediation, reciprocity, media literacies, community offline work, needs/assets/ solution analyses, and collaborative production. These created the need for new journalistic roles: relationship builder, community collaborator, community conversation facilitator, and professional industry networker. Many of these caring qualities already align with justice practices of journalists such as quotations, attribution, contextualization, relevancy, source vetting, and accuracy. In these ways we can see how journalists can learn caring practices that also combat fake news in the process of building trust in their information.

Care theory asserts that it is on the journey toward knowledge and other outcomes where caring can be particularly meaningful.[69] Journalists have a unique positionality as knowledge purveyors to instill an ethic of care as a

Table 3.1 Care plus Identity plus Justice Demand New Journalism Skills

Care Quality	Engagement Work	Identity International	Justice Qualities (Mainstream Journalism Conventions)	Skills Needed
Attentiveness	Listening, being present	Empathy, explicit compassion	Attribution or background vetting, quotations, networking among stakeholders, asking community members to evaluate coverage	Power dynamic accounting
Responsibility	Learning, relationship building	Know histories, research systems of oppression	Diverse sourcing, contextualization, background work through lived experiences and not only past journalism	Media literacies, community offline work
Competence	Commit resources, network productively	Be present, amplify voices, expand sources/ audiences	Triangulate evidence and sourcing, fact-check within communities, make transparency declarations	Mediation
Responsiveness	Reliability, follow-through	(Self-)identity, introspection, checking in	Mediating poststory dialogue, offer neutral platform for dialogue, forums	Radical transparency, reciprocity
Solidarity	Community problem-solving, collaboration	Collaborate/ partner with different groups	Embracing the "neutral" facilitator role through factual information, source connections, partnerships	Needs/assets/ solutions analyses, collaborative production

major tenet of their work. However, essential on this journey toward knowledge must be an awareness and appreciation of power dynamics and other forces that stem from individual and group identities. For example, Thayer-Bacon emphasized the need for inclusive exchanges as well as respect for "the other" in caring relationships.[70] Otherwise the learning can never fully be achieved. In this evidence, we can see a blossoming movement happening among those for whom trust building is fundamentally about relationships, engagement, and listening because of a commitment to caring. Integral to this trust-building work is the awareness and interrogation of the identities at play as acts of caring. We see in the ways these journalists talk about what they do and who they do it for reflections of their worldviews shaped by their social identity constructions, such as race and sexuality, as well as by their identity role of reporter or engagement journalist. We know from the communication theory of identity that communication is an enactment of identity,[71] in much the same way that culture and communication[72] are entangled. Identity-aware journalists talk about their jobs in more relational ways that evoke an intense caring for the people and communities they cover, in addition to more traditional journalistic caring about facts. We see in these manifestations a more holistic ethos conveying a sense of connection to fellow humans and a desire for all of us to think about and nurture one another, as opposed to more distant expressions that center content, information, and journalistic standards.[73]

Summary

The journalism profession, operating under the traditional paradigm as critical distance from communities, has been failing. Its failure has stemmed from the industry's slow response to digital technologies and other dire economic and political conditions, but has had at its core a breakdown in trust between news brands and their audiences. As fewer and fewer people have felt less cared for in many parts of their lives, they have lost trust in the institutions that were supposed to provide safety nets for them. This played out in the news media as well; as politicians and others have perpetuated the narrative that mainstream news publishers cared only about profits and "liberal agendas," half the population turned toward Fox News and other conservative sites that peddled fear and stoked resentment, playing up self-care for the individual rather than care for the whole. Engagement might help to move us back to the encouragement of fulfillment of care for all, so that all information needs can be met.

The kinds of engagement being proposed in the trust-focused built environment documented in this book would require journalists to be more involved in audiences' lives and would evoke their own lived experiences in ways that might be uncomfortable under more traditional tenets. As I read through the list of techniques for trust building, I still felt a familiar wariness and cynicism. Because I still identify as a white journalist even 15 years after leaving the newsroom, my reflex was to push back on many of these strategies emerging from this built environment. How can treating sources differently by, say, sending them the questions ahead of time, be fair and neutral? Tell everyone our biases in a sidebar? What the heck?

But as I observed these journalists in their engagement trainings and as I talked to reporters about possibilities toward change, my understanding shifted. I began to appreciate some underlying assumptions of the work of trust building. Not surprisingly, the work demands journalists center the public; indeed, many of the strategies promoted have their origins in the public journalism movement back in the 1990s. In that movement, about 5,000 news outlets in the United States privileged listening and constant interaction with the public in story development and production. The movement—always unevenly practiced and not universally accepted as being helpful in the industry—fizzled as newsrooms began contracting in the early 2000s. In that Poynter article I mentioned earlier, ethicist Kelly McBride also turned back to that public journalism movement as a possible teaching moment toward an ethic of care. This would represent a paradigm shift away from newsrooms as autonomous entities and toward a professional world in which journalists operated from within communities, caring for and with people.

In the follow-up interviews and surveys that my research team did with Hearken[74] of the journalists who participated in the Citizens Agenda trainings during spring and summer 2020, we were pleased to note that the month of intense retooling toward engagement strategies moved the needle on identity work as well.[75] The guide prompted more newsroom introspection about how those in marginalized communities were being disproportionally affected by the pandemic and the Trump presidency, which was extraordinary for its hate-fueled policies and explicit racism. One participant said, "We could always do better, but I think it also made me more mindful to like, 'Who am I talking to, what sources?' 'Am I always talking to white people?' . . . And so, just trying to be mindful about what other organizations that are being led by people of color are out there doing this work? And how can we highlight them? So, I tried to do that."

Another organization partnered with a community group of Spanish speakers to solicit Citizens Agenda questions for the candidates. I will go deeper into these case studies in the next two chapters but will end this chapter with this frank insight from one of the Citizens Agenda training cohorts in a posttraining evaluation with a (white, bisexual, female) public radio producer and her (white, heterosexual, male) co-worker:

RESEARCHER: How do you deal with race, when you say you want to better represent Black and Latinx communities?

PARTICIPANT 1: We're still thinking through . . . I don't know if I have a good answer, because it is sort of a large and existential question.

PARTICIPANT 2: Yeah, it's like, we're not going to fix it all with this election, right? This is a beginning of a longer-term effort on our part.

PARTICIPANT 1: . . . I feel like it affects every level of our journalism organization. It's about what stories you cover; it's about which people you hire. I think we have one Black reporter, a single Black reporter in a city whose population is about one-third Black. How are we supposed to tell stories from those communities if none of us are from there? How are we supposed to have the background and the history and the sourcing? . . . I feel like journalism like this can be more responsive to communities. And traditionally, when you have top-down journalism run mostly by white dudes, what do you get? You get where we are right now. That's what you get. And we shouldn't be particularly shocked by that, because we've been at the top, so we're the ones doing the top-down business. It's people like me. And that is such a fundamental change that absolutely has to happen, that will take time and will take growth and will take a lot of big, scary changes. But I actually feel like this is the thing that keeps getting us excited, if I can speak for our little cadre about this [Citizens Agenda] project, is like right now, this feels like a meaningful piece of journalism we can do. I don't know how to get my head around this moment and what we can do to help the world, but just listening to people and trying to get them information they want feels like a thing we can do. It feels like a really good place to start.

Listening to learn to help the world seems like a really good place to start, indeed. In the next chapter, I surface a strategy that has long been used to build trust in information: news media literacies. However, I reimagine how we can use literacies in the practice of identity-aware caring for this new trust-building theory.

4

How Journalists Might Care

Trust Building through Listening-to-Learn Literacies

Aiden White described the meeting in Turkey as being . . . awkward.[1] In the room were journalists, editors, and people from various official organizations who were there to work out a collaborative ethics policy of information exchange. The meeting was part of the work White was doing with the Ethical Journalism Network, a global ethics media support group based in the United Kingdom. The Network's mission was to strengthen journalism via projects aimed at enhancing ethics, good governance, and self-regulation, globally, especially between news organizations and governments. As of 2023, it represented a coalition of more than 70 groups of media actors, including press owners and media support groups all over the world. White (of International Federation of Journalists fame) founded the EJN in 2012, really at the cutting edge of this kind of work, and had worked most of his life in journalism, especially as an advocate for standardized journalism ethics.

I bring up White's work with EJN here at the start of Chapter 4 to exemplify how journalists might care through *listening* and *learning* exercises with their sources, audiences, and other constituents. I want to show how difficult listening to learn can be for all journalists, who are often used to much more neutral (and sometimes even acrimonious) relationships with anyone not a journalist. At this Turkey meeting that White described, tensions had cut through the EJN negotiations because Turkey had begun arresting and imprisoning journalists; many of the journalists in the room had known people persecuted by the government, some by the very officials with whom they were supposed to deliberate ethics. A journalist approached White, clearly upset. "We cannot allow this meeting to go ahead because someone in the room representing the Turkish Practice Council has given evidence against the journalist in a trial," the journalist said. "And that journalist was sent to jail."

How Journalists Engage. Sue Robinson, Oxford University Press. © Oxford University Press 2023.
DOI: 10.1093/oso/9780197667118.003.0004

White remembered responding, "Well, I don't know why that person gave evidence against the journalist. And I don't know why they were called. But that's not really our issue. Our issue is we're trying to bring people together."

White continued with the meeting, brokering a set of ethical guidelines on a Turkish-language website and creating a series of workshops and seminars on investigative journalism, the ethics of data journalism, and computational journalism. He told me, "For the very first time groups around the table who had never previously worked together to support journalism—employers, unions, human rights groups, press freedom groups, fact-checking organizations, media rights campaigners—were sitting together, committed to a common approach in getting Turkish journalists to report ethically and professionally. And that is excellent. It never happened before. And it's now being driven by Turkish journalists themselves. . . . We're trying to be an agent of change, encouraging at a national level coalition-building and practical actions to strengthen journalism." White and EJN's hope was that by strengthening universal ethics around truth and accuracy such as independence, humanity, and accountability, journalists could reeducate people on the press' essentialness to democracy through open dialogue and transparency. Explicit in this work was the grounding in shared understandings of human rights and promoting dialogues between the profession and civil society—but it was complex work, filled with mine fields and thorny histories where past "listening" had failed.

"My own view is that the future of journalism will depend upon building trust in the way that journalism works, the content of journalism, and its transparency," White explained in his interview with us. EJN taught journalists how to work through difference while being more introspective about their own shortcomings. In Cypress, he added, EJN helped local media produce a glossary of hate speech in collaboration with officials. The process became fraught, with journalists bristling that politicians seemed to be telling them what to write. White saw the friction as huge progress in a place mute on its own divisions:

In fact, this had a positive effect. It got journalists and editors talking about the issue. By starting the debate in newsrooms, it immediately contributed to new thinking inside journalism. Before we published this glossary, there was no discussion in Cyprus about the divisions on the island. There was lots of hate speech. There was a lot of pejorative terminology used, which was really unhelpful. Now, suddenly, there was a debate. And that debate was heated. But it was very useful, and it has begun to lead to change because now there is a recognition of the problems. We come from the outside to say, "You guys have got lots and lots of things in common, although you don't talk about them and you don't work together. Let's find a way in which you can talk about them and in a practical way draw up programs where we can begin to try to address some of these issues." So that's exactly what's happening.

For White, the major takeaway of this anecdote from the work of the EJN was the creation of shared journalistic goals and debate over public information practices with competing information actors in spaces that had never existed before. Key was to build ownership for a set of common ethical values among the major stakeholders in a country's news media system while promoting radical transparency with the producers, disseminators, and consumers of the news content.

For me, though, this work represented every one of the eight new categories of skills being promoted in this trust-building built environment: radical transparency, power dynamic accounting, mediation, reciprocity, media literacies, community offline work, needs/assets/solution analyses, and collaborative production. The work of the EJN required journalists to take on roles in addition to those they had traditionally, including the four new roles I describe in this book: *relationship builder, community collaborator, community conversation facilitator,* and *professional network builder.* Here was a prime example of how journalists worked with various entities from governments to community organizations in collaboration for a shared set of values around information exchange. All of this brings me to the topic of Chapter 4, exploring the *how* of our trust-building theory: How do we enact an identity-aware care through engagement practices so that we build trust in public information? Here I laser in on the final part of the theory: **Trust building happens through the nurturing of personal, organizational, and institutional relationships that people have with information, sources, news brands, journalists, and each other during what is commonly referred to as engagement. For trust building to occur, engagement needs to be practiced with identity-aware care** *and enacted through listening and learning.*

What does it mean to listen and learn in acts of journalism (that is, producing, disseminating, and consuming accurate, relevant information about public affairs) so that trust in the work is built and nurtured? To answer this question, I go back to the 30 trust initiatives my research team and I analyzed over the years. I included in this a couple projects that I myself had been working on in collaboration with different groups, one being the Citizens Agenda project that I highlighted in Chapter 2 and another an educational journalism video game news media literacy project for public middle school classrooms with the Wisconsin Field Day Lab. This latter example offered a way to further analyze the link between engagement and trust building through different modes of caring by looking at news media literacy as a promising mechanic. A few implicit understandings thread through all eight skill sets being encouraged in the built environment: *listening to learn*. The work of the EJN succeeded because stakeholders with different identities, histories, goals, and methods were forced to listen to each other's perspectives, learning how to reconcile these differences in order to establish consensual protocols and standards for information-exchange ethics. This had not been taught in journalism schools or in newsrooms traditionally.

Of course, as I talked about in the prologue to this book, journalism has always been about listening and learning; indeed, essential to any kind of trust building with any relationship must be some type of listening and learning. But here I focus specifically on the ways in which every person and entity playing some part in news exchange must intentionally and actively engage in listening-to-learn practices. This chapter lays out how actors in this built environment wanted people—journalists, yes, but the rest of us as well—to listen in order to learn about good content characteristics, to listen in order to learn with each other, to listen in order to learn about our own selves, and to listen in order to learn from different kinds of groups and communities.

One well-researched concept already encapsulated how we listen and learn, and that was media literacy, with its robust body of scholarship. This concept now serves as a grand example of how this trust-building theory has been playing out in journalism and other public information-exchange circles. Thus, this chapter is guided by these two questions about this built environment: **What kinds of news literacies are being promoted in the name of trust building? And how are these initiatives operationalizing trust building through listening-to-learn literacy work?** The answers to these questions came from the analyses that my research team and I did of the 30 case studies of trust initiatives, especially the interviews with the founders and directors.

It is one thing to call for new listening-to-learn literacy initiatives of various dimensions, and quite another to see them implemented with success, as those influencing the work in this built environment are pushing. Any initiative taking on a Herculean task such as getting an entire society to change how it thinks about, consumes, produces, shares, and vets news content must specify whose tasks are whose, bringing us to a third question for this chapter: **Who is responsible for listening to learn in order to restore trust in the public affairs information available to us?** This observation arose from a conundrum observed as we analyzed the cases: whereas traditional conceptions of "news literacy" have always relied on people willing to be taught how to critically interrogate mediated products, recent trends of polarization, airtight information bubbles, and widespread distrust of facts challenged these assumed norms.[2]

All of this helped nudge me toward a revelation of the connections between trust and engagement as operationalized through listening and learning. As part of appreciating the idea of listening-to-learn literacies as a viable solution for *trust building*, we must consider in this typology those with the power to make effective change and the means with which it might be done. This equation must incorporate contexts, histories, and identity constructs, and it must interrogate the intentionality of those involved. And so we come to a major statement for this chapter: how acts of identity-aware caring as demonstrated through *listening* are promoted to achieve the goals of *learning* for information exchange. A "listening-to-learn literacy" inputs the idea that all the stakeholders in any mediated news exchange must pay attention to all the dynamics of information exchange while producing, sharing, or consuming news. I take a broad view of listening, as something that happens intentionally and actively between two or more actors, which might also include the content itself. The idea of listening to learn as an important news literacy tactic unfolded organically and often unexpectedly as my research team and I analyzed these trust projects and then worked through the engagement ethnographies of Citizens Agenda and the Journalism Game. The trust-building initiatives studied here demand symbiotic relationships between communities, journalists, platforms, technologists, teachers, parents, and other stakeholders such that we transition from an institutional trust in which any listening and learning are done via elites and through problematic structures and the norms and routines associated with them to a more personal, individual, relational trust steeped in care. For each of these categories, we highlight the ways in which various information actors must "listen"—to constituents and audiences, to governments, to newsrooms, to technology companies, and to each other—and then develop continually informed strategies to combat the persistent information threats based on what is learned.

After delving into what "listening" means and how it works with trust, engagement, identity, and care, I present the idea of media literacy as a heuristic for the listening-to-learn part of the trust-building theory I am building in this book. Analyzing the trust initiatives for the ways they promote listening-to-learn as a response to distrust in journalism, I lay out the four realms in which listening-to-learn serves as a primary construct to improve trust: the civic space, the journalistic professional space, the social amateur sharing space, and of course the digital space. I call these techniques "listening-to-learn literacies" and, in the process, expand the scholarly definition of media literacy to match the palette proposed in our theory of trust building, the four new journalism roles with eight categories of new skills. This typology of sorts highlights *listening* to *learn* as a key element at work in our built environment. The identity-aware ethic of care undergirds this literacy work, which this evidence demonstrates was not only the domain of K–12 teachers and universities but also journalists, technology companies, parents and community members, you and me.

Listening to Learn

In October 2019, two people from the Field Day Lab at the University of Wisconsin–Madison[3] came to my office at the School of Journalism & Mass Communication. One was artist and university relations specialist (white-, female-, cis-identifying) Sarah Gagnon, who was bubbling over with enthusiasm about an idea she had to design an educational video game about journalism. Distraught over the rampant misinformation sullying public discourse, Gagnon proposed that we apply for a grant to create a game that would help kids understand the important role journalists play in collecting information so we can govern ourselves—and also know the world around us. She and her partner (white-, male-, cis-identifying) David Gagnon, who is the director of Field Day and a game designer with the same center, asked me to join them as the principal investigator on the project, a game that would ultimately be played in public middle school classrooms across the United States.

Was I interested? They asked. Um, yeah, I said. Count me in! I couldn't think of anything more important at that moment. Or more fun.

We spent the next few months developing the idea for a Baldwin Wisconsin Idea Endowment grant, which we secured in March 2020 and then plowed ahead even as the world around us fell apart because of the COVID-19 pandemic. Indeed, the pressing importance of what we were trying to do spurred us on.[4] Sarah Gagnon, the lead on the project, aggregated the stakeholders—teachers, journalists, game designers, artists, content producers, and me—and we started meeting virtually to figure out the content and narrative of the game. What did kids need to know about journalism and journalists? How might we incorporate elements about credible strategies for information seeking? How can this game make news media literacy fun? Will this game help build trust in journalism? In the resulting game, students would be taught how to engage with the facts in the world around them and how to consider and evaluate journalism and other information sources. In addition, Sarah Gagnon wanted to make the journalist character in the game collect information around a flood so that kids could also learn about natural disasters, water, and other science material in the course of playing.[5]

One day in February 2021, we were meeting virtually with teachers informing us about middle schoolers' needs regarding information, such as primary sources and the connection that journalism has to democracy. As we were going through these learning objectives, the teachers began underscoring something I had not expected for this fairly straightforward learning intervention: the game needed to highlight to students how to be self-reflexive about their own identities as they thought about information sources and pursued facts in the choose-your-own-adventure format.

"They need to be able to weigh their own personal bias, and where that is leading them," said one of the teachers, presenting as white and female.

"What kind of tools do you give them to think about their own bias?" asked Sarah Gagnon.

"I just ask them questions like 'Where are you coming from?'" the teacher replied. "Before they even start the story, they need to think about what is their opinion about the story already. 'How are you going to try to be honest in your reporting? How are you going to try to cover all the sides that are pertinent to this?' So it is more of a reflection question for me."

The other teachers started weighing in as well, each giving an example of how in their classes they needed students to consider how their positionality influenced how they act with information. In other words, these students had to *listen-to-learn* not only to the information in front of them—its sources, its authority—but also to themselves, to understand how their own biases might be influencing how they were interacting with their sources and the information they were gathering. It was a much different brand of news literacy than we were taught in the 1980s and 1990s. For one, we didn't have video games in schools, at least as part of the curriculum. And also, our news literacy was about not getting duped by advertisers and not turning into a serial killer because of too many violent video games. News literacy didn't mean listening: it meant *not listening*. But here was yet another example in this growing number of trust-building projects I was researching that centered listening as a major component of news literacy—listening to ourselves, listening to information content and its sources, listening to communities, listening to each other. This centering on *listening to learn* was being billed in this built environment as an essential element in saving our democratic souls by rebuilding trust in our public information-exchange system.

To *listen* is to engage in an intentional act that offers attention to something or someone. Much scholarly focus has been given to the idea of listening—of listening for language, of listening in organizations, of listening in speech communication, of listening for remembering, of listening in learning and education, of listening in biology (e.g., hearing), etc. Ethel Glenn in 1989[6] collected 50 definitions of listening, finding that to define listening merely as paying attention fails to adequately express its complexity as a concept. The definition changed according to the purpose of using the concept, but it most often incorporated the following dimensions: perception, attention, interpretation, response, and spoken and visual cues, according to Glenn. Through listening, we find meaning (as opposed to *hearing*, the physical act).[7] Many professions have prioritized listening as a valuable skill to have, especially in workplace and school settings, and yet it had been described as an underdiscussed competence with little associated training within these industries.[8] "Listening, however, is not automatic. To be better listeners we need to understand and work with the components of the listening process. For our purposes, whatever definition of listening we choose we must know that (1) listening can be learned, (2) that listening is an active process, involving mind and body, with verbal and nonverbal processes working together, and (3) that listening allows us to be receptive to the needs, concerns, and information of others, as well as the environment around us."[9] And, of course, many different kinds of listening exist, including active listening, empathetic listening, interpretive listening, and recall listening.[10]

Listening to learn about others, about complex problems, and about possible solutions has been taken up by deliberation, rhetoric, and other communication scholars as well, and has been acknowledged to be important for a democracy to thrive.[11] In Andrew Dobson's *Listening for Democracy: Recognition, Representation, Reconciliation*, listening as a democratic facilitation tool must be intentional and planned, and listeners must hear in as "apophatic" manner as possible—that is, in silence, without the cumbersome reflex to react according to one's ideological stances. Furthermore, the listening must be done empathetically, with meaning construction happening via the dialogue itself as much as possible. Journalists innately understand how to do apophatic (or silent) listening, or at least they think they do, as their entire career basically has depended upon proficiency of that skill. They may revolt against the second part under traditional training and protocols, but it is only through this second process that journalists can be truly effective in trust building. Listening can "enhance legitimacy claims, increase levels of trust, help deal with disagreements, improve representation and refine deliberation."[12]

Listening can also be a "solvent of power," especially as those with informational and other kinds of power, like journalists, who can authorize what information gets circulated in public discourse, remain silent and thus cede power.[13] Dobson noted that "being listened to is experienced as power, particularly by those who are generally not listened to," and further stated that "we cannot consider democracy's inclusionary work to be done once we claim simply to have allowed people to speak."[14] Michael Levin asserted that productive listening must overcome "auditory distortion, ideological deafness, institutional noise, the specific ways in which power channels hearing, and listening channels power."[15] Indeed, some democratic theory scholars have paid close attention to how *not listening* is also a kind of power at work in deliberation historically; Gideon Calder argued in fact that this "must entail an advance decision not to listen to certain kinds of voice,"[16] explicitly suggesting that not listening is often intentional on the part of dominant actors in the public sphere (e.g., white men).

It was in this deliberation and rhetoric field that I found the nuanced thinking about listening as a way to express and also to hear differences in identity related to public discourse. Nancy Fraser, writing about power in deliberation, pointed to identity as a key mitigating factor in listening, especially as different groups attempt to make claims for recognition and to be heard in community conversations.[17] And yet the very nature of listening as we have come to know it culturally has become both gendered[18] and racialized,[19] with dominant groups such as white men implicitly thinking of listening as a weak position; in such contexts, "listening" is really more about self-absorption and status conferral than about mutual understanding and relationship building. Jacqueline Jones Royston, writing on African American rhetoric, found that as a Black woman she could speak and could feel that she may have been listened to, but she was not believed.[20] To be heard, Royston evoked subjectivity, equating it with lived experience to bear witness in speaking with the aim of cross-cultural understanding. I liked this description because it prefaced subjectivity not as oppositional to objectivity but rather as a strategic concept on its own, a reflection of something authentic and representative of truths. This view that Black women in particular are rarely listened to has come up in other arenas as well. For example, Sydette Harry wrote a scathing accounting in *Wired* in 2021 about how Black female technologists remain invisible despite their presence in these worlds, such as their ignored warnings about the rise of the alt-right online well before 2016.[21] Furthermore, when women, and particularly women of color, speak up and call out, they are labeled "angry" and "unreasonable," as the feminist writer and scholar Sara Ahmed explained in 2010.[22] Their very speaking up and speaking out renders them into this constructed stereotype and ensures that no real listening can happen when some other dominant class (e.g., men) becomes so fixated on their identity rather than the words.

Krista Ratcliffe, an English professor, coined the term "rhetorical listening" as a way to highlight identification in public discourse, particularly for gender and race, and made the case that listening itself embodied an essential component to meaning construction in rhetorical practice.[23] Her definition of rhetorical listening was a "a trope for interpretive invention, that is, as a stance of openness that a person may choose to assume in relation to any person, text, or culture; its purpose is to cultivate conscious identifications in ways that promote productive communication, especially but not solely cross-culturally."[24] Particularly interesting for theory building around the concept of trust, Ratcliffe put forward a multidimensional process of listening with four "moves": "1. Promoting an *understanding* of self and other; 2. Proceeding within an *accountability* logic; 3. Locating identification across *commonalities* and *differences*; 4. Analyzing *claims* as well as the *cultural logics* within which these claims function."[25] Here I discerned the scent of engagement strategies being advocated in this trust-building environment, like self-introspection, like power dynamic appreciation, like collaboration and mediation (which you may remember were three of the eight categories of skills demanded in this new kind of trust building).

Thus, here is what I got out of my engagement with these texts. One, importantly, this kind of listening will not prove to be the ultimate resolution to polarization and renewed trust in public discourse involving news. Rather, as Ratcliffe underscored, listening embodies a process of relational exchange that not only seeks commonalities in deliberation but also celebrates difference and disagreement. Ratcliffe also argued that within discourse, people make claims based on a belief system or set of logics that are cultural but evoke the political, leading to people talking at each other: "By focusing on claims and cultural logics, listeners may still disagree with each other's claims, but they may better appreciate that the other person is not simply wrong but rather functioning from within a different logic,"[26] and she considered this a process of negotiation. Journalists, in my interpretation of how rhetorical listening might be applied to reporting, can frame news without the binaries of agreement-disagreement but instead focus on the reasoning behind the statements, providing the context and histories and helping to bridge logics or belief systems.

Two, in honoring identification within the reciprocal exchange of talking and listening, one can *learn*—about the person speaking, yes, but also about those contexts, cultures, and histories informing and shaping the dialogue through the identities present. In this process, we can undergo community learning, and with each dialogue or news piece, more knowledge is gained, and the needle is pushed forward toward resolutions. As such, people become accountable to the ways we are socialized to be part of certain cultural and political logics, often based on our identities. But those listening must also be aware that their biases against certain identities, such as women or women of color, will influence their instinctive response. That must be overridden. Being aware of this socialization is part of that accountability necessary for productive listening to others. Through this accountability, we become ethical, caring participants. The goal here is that through listening, one can learn, and then one can act.[27] Engagement journalism assimilated these components through its various techniques and modeled this work in many of the programs and initiatives aimed at trust building, as I will describe in the second half of this chapter.

One common and familiar heuristic through which we as a society have listened to learn has been news literacy, which has both a scholarly and a civic/educational history. In this chapter, I use news literacy as an analytic framework because it offered an intersection of actions and a logistical intervention for journalists as well as communities, politicians, technology companies, schools, and all stakeholders in the conditions of any public discourse. News literacy seemed embodied in not only many of the trust initiatives I was exploring and analyzing but also the projects that I myself was participating in, such as the Journalism Game with the Wisconsin Field Day Lab, where we were striving to teach kids how to engage with information, as well as the Citizens Agenda project, where we were teaching journalists how to engage with communities. In the next section I explore what we already know about news literacy and its relationship with trust building.

News Literacy as a Heuristic for Trust Building through Listening to Learn

The field of news literacy as a body of scholarship and as something to be desired emerged in the 1970s—though the practice itself dated to the early 1900s.[28] The desired outcome of news literacy has comprised an informed citizen that can act from a place of knowledge toward the improvement of democracy as well as toward the nurturing of productive interactions between individuals.[29] This definition from an oft-cited Aspen Institute report by Aufderheide was foundational: "The basic definition spelled out media literacy as the ability of a citizen to access, analyze, and produce information for specific outcomes" (e.g., democracy).[30] Twenty years later, UNESCO centered literacy on the ability to read and write critically and with understanding.[31] News literacy has taught people to constantly question the information they encounter.[32] The goal, then, has been to practice what Brown called "discriminating responsiveness" and a deconstruction of intention and influence.[33] James Potter presented a "typology of media literacy" that contained eight stages along a continuum for the development of media literacy. Young children were at the first stage, "acquiring fundamentals" in understanding what media were, and many adults were in the more advanced stages, such as "social responsibility," where the person was literate enough to "take a moral stand that certain messages are more constructive for society than others." No one, he emphasized, reached full media literacy.[34] We know that this continuum, this ebb and flow of literacy, has corresponded to trust as well in that the achieving of trust follows a nonlinear, stubborn, uncertain, and ephemeral process.

By 2022 the conversation around news literacy was made much more complex by the mass sharing of fake news, an ambivalence about truth or facts, machine-produced content, and the increasingly polemic press. The National Council of Teachers of English had included the internet as one of the components of literacy, and scholars were noting how "connectivity and digital engagement and expression are increasingly being equated with citizenship, vested participation or enfranchisement not only in local or national political systems, but in global communities."[35] News literacy was one possible answer to fake news and included the need to educate people about the social/emotional components of shared information in social platforms as well as to teach skepticism and rejection of misinformation.[36] Consider the addition of a kind of algorithmic news literacy as technology corporations such as Google and Facebook manipulate networks of information through codes that have privileged some content over others.[37] Van Dijk et al. observed that the once "human power" of selecting news content that involved a professional editor shifted to an "algorithmic power" deployed by platforms. Contemporary news distribution in the "platform ecosystem" was now shaped by the complex interplay between a wide variety of actors: "platforms, ad networks, news and fact-checking organizations, advertisers, and billions of users." Because platforms have sought to maximize user engagement through leveraging principles of "personalization" and "virality" rather than provide users with an "accurate and comprehensive news offering," this shifted the onus of responsibility onto platform users themselves to make value judgments of content. This essentially resulted in what van Dijk and colleagues saw as a "platform driven shift in editorial responsibility from professional editors to individual users."[38] This responsibility became further complicated with the entrance of algorithms hiding any latent biases that were programmed in, rendering any intentionality invisible.[39] Thus, Cohen called for "an immersive media literacy" for people to "incorporate new methods of reading and interpreting feeds by understanding the multiple ways user actions are converted into algorithmic tools."[40]

Of particular interest to the book at hand, scholars have long connected higher levels of news literacy with higher levels of trust in journalism.[41] Maksl et al. found a connection between how literate high school youth were and their desire to consume news; though they found that these highly literate individuals also had higher levels of skepticism, their trust in credible news sites was high.[42] But danah boyd in a *Data + Society* essay provocatively titled "Did Media Literacy Backfire?"[43] suggested that we had taught our youth *too well* to be skeptical of media; in encouraging independent research, we helped create a sharing culture around fake news. For boyd, the solution must move far beyond information transparency and toward a more cultural reconceptualization of what is good information, what is a good source, etc. Furthermore, literacy will not work if trust building around information is not present—and trust not merely between journalists and their audiences but also among community members. Chris Peters insists that "one cannot look at the notion of trust in isolation to judge the current state of audience-journalism relations; public trust must be considered alongside audience involvement and levels of media literacy as well."[44] Like boyd, Peters countered that we were actually in an age of very high literacy corresponding to lower levels of trust as people turned away from mainstream news and sought alternative sources they deemed trustworthy.[45] He and others argued that *The Daily Show* and other satirical news-oriented entertainment were serving as new media literacy tools that inculcated young people into savvy public affairs information consumption, yes, but also infused distrust of mainstream news.[46]

Where does that leave us, then, as we work to restore trust in a shared set of facts through mainstream journalism? Turning to the giant data set my research teams and I collected, I found the common assumption from these actors in this thriving trust-building built environment that news literacies would be one response to malevolent misrepresentation of facts from political and foreign entities as well as ubiquitous fake-news sharing. Certainly, this was one of our main goals in the Journalism Game for middle schoolers: show them the work of journalists, immerse them in the world of fact-finding. But the work I was seeing coming out of these trust initiatives was not calling for the same old news media literacy from days gone by—or at least, not *only* for these kinds of strategies. The literacies being suggested varied widely, and their responsibilities spanned not only schools but also technology companies, newsrooms, and communities. It struck me that all of us were going to need some intense retraining around our news habits to get to this place of shared facts. I say this after listening to Aiden White's story about the Turkish journalists and government officials' difficulties in creating a shared information policy via the EJN. I say this too after contemplating with teachers and the Wisconsin Field Day Lab how to make a reporting game that didn't antagonize conservatives. This task seemed daunting, and I decided to, first, break down what was really being suggested as a pathway to trust through literacies, and then to tease out how these literacies represented, really, a listening-to-learn vessel for how to operationalize an identity-aware ethic of care within engagement and other kinds of trust-building strategies.

Listening-to-Learn Literacies: Civic, Professional, Social-Amateur-Sharing, Technology

All the 30 trust initiatives that my research team analyzed as mini case studies assumed some level of news literacy needed to be jump-started or demanded that certain actors in public news discourse needed to step up around fact gathering and vetting. Four categories of news literacy emerged from the initiatives: civic consumption through schooling; amateur (co)production, such as social sharing; professional information production, such as what happens in newsrooms; and algorithmic and technological literacies.[47] I think of these not only as categories but also as spaces where this work can happen.

Civic Consumption

Civic consumption literacy (often referred to as "civic literacy" or just the umbrella terms "media literacy" or "news literacy") remained an essential ingredient in communities' education against fake news, hidden or toxic messaging, confirmation bias, and polarization in these projects. In other words, parents and teachers in K–12 schools, universities, and colleges were tasked with making sure people know how to get the information they need for democracy (or daily life). However, much of the discourse around trust building positioned news literacy at a grassroots-level (post-parents, post-school) responsibility as well. For example, the News Literacy Project, partnered with Facebook's Journalism Project,[48] offered modules, virtual guides, real-world examples, live conversations with journalists and experts, and assessments (with points and badges) as strategies to do this. This discourse argued that adults must continuously educate themselves to be not only consumer savvy but also citizen savvy. Charlie Firestone, executive director of the Aspen Institute and cofounder of the Knight Commission on Trust, Media and Democracy, said adults needed to be "lifelong learners," and in our interview, he highlighted for me a project led by the American Library Association wherein librarians developed a series of adult media literacy programs in public libraries.[49]

Journalists also had a role to play, according to these initiatives. For example, in June 2017, four news organizations in New Jersey—WNYC, WHYY, NJ Spotlight, and *The Record*—launched the collaborative Voting Block, bringing people together around controversial issues, with reporters moderating. More than 25 newsrooms participated, more than 24 forums were held, and more than 70 stories resulted. A report on the project documented that "Voting Block contributed to stronger ties among participating community members and news organizations," establishing a more trusting relationship between communities and these newsrooms than had been present previously.[50] The project taught people not only about this new facilitation role for journalists but also how to be engaged in heated dialogue, productively, through careful listening—and in this process, learning about the issue, about each other, about journalism.

Amateur (Co)Production (Sharing)

This metadiscourse around trust building circulating in journalism's professional circles also called on amateur coproducers—those who produced, manipulated, and shared public affairs content via digital social platforms—to be educated on everything from fake news to how to properly generate social media interaction.[51] For example, the international UNESCO EU-funded project Building Trust in Media in South East Europe and Turkey held a two-day training seminar "focused on . . . responsibilities and protection mechanisms for bloggers and civil society campaigners engaged in 'acts of journalism.' "[52] The Knight Commission formerly called on people to understand what they were sharing, from whom and to whom, as well as to understand what might happen to that information in the networked digital world. Knight commissioner and conservative radio host Charlie Sykes said in an interview with us, "I'm willing to spend a lot of time criticizing Facebook and Google and all those folks, but ultimately, this is on us." A number of the initiatives were collaborating with Google, Facebook, and other platforms to develop pop-up information boxes detailing sourcing (e.g., the U.S.-based Trust Project) or to deposit in public spaces all the documentation needed for reporting (e.g., the Transparency Project with *Frontline* as part of the

Knight Commission partnerships). A Knight Commission trade press article echoed this notion: "Technology may have been upgraded, but people have not been. Most of America shares articles before really reading them. Too often we believe information based on feelings about the person who shared it and not what it says. We are suckers for misinformation when we share without care."[53] Beyond passive consuming, these projects urged people to *listen with care* and to *learn* actively by asking platforms to demand or label content in the pursuit of transparency, attributing information, and analyzing content before sharing.

Professional Information Production

Some media trust projects identified newsrooms as important places for literacy to happen, with journalists as key facilitators in spotting and combating fake news and rebuilding trust in political facts. The EJN, comprising more than 60 groups of journalists and journalism organizations transnationally, listed "media and information literacy" among its six major foci. The network produced research reports and online courses in ethics as well as advised newsrooms on issues like hate speech and disinformation. One of its courses tells reporters, "By the end of the course: You will have developed your own 'ethical toolkit' that will help you make the correct judgement for every story. You will feel more confident in maintaining your independence and sticking to your principles when dealing with false information, sensitive material or attempts from vested interests to influence your work. You will understand the connection between applying your ethical toolkit and the trust which your audience places in your journalism."[54] Projects like the EJN retrained reporters in a production literacy that reestablished common standards for an increasingly complicated information world.

Some of these projects retrained journalists to help publics be their own information agents, such as in the nonprofit Journalism That Matters,[55] which convened journalists with technologists, librarians, engaged community members, educators, policymakers, students, and others in places where *listening to learn* was the main objective. Through collaboration and conversation facilitation, retrained journalists then taught these same literacies to communities. In other words, for the public to achieve a high level of news literacy, journalists themselves become agents in that education, according to these projects. Journalists deployed a variety of listening techniques that integrate sources and audience members into the production of the story itself. Journalists were taught new workflows to emphasize community-driven practices—to put the public at the center, as EJN's White said in our interview and which the Hearken engagement company also touted. The project Your Voice Ohio hosted community forums with journalists connecting with stakeholders in solution-driven projects around intractable problems, such as the opioid crisis.[56] Seattle's KOUW radio station hosted a series of discussion-based events called "Ask a . . . ," where journalists helped people engage in civic dialogue across difference; the executive producer of the program, Ross Reynolds, said in our interview, "Part of the idea is also putting an average citizen into the role we often get to have as journalists of having permission to ask questions."[57] Ultimately, this kind of literacy invigorated a shared sense of responsibility between newsrooms and their communities, foundationally, around public information exchange.

Algorithms/Technology

Finally, many of these projects emphasized that technological literacies must be taught to us all. According to the Knight Commission on Trust, Media & Democracy, these "digital literacies" included how algorithms worked, how search engine optimization played out, and what networked infrastructures could do to content.[58] In this category, technology was both the problem (information manipulation, privacy loss, viral spread of misinformation) and part of the literacy solution (training about algorithms, platform content/sharing transparency, platform safeguards against spreading fake news, government regulation embedded in technology).

According to the Knight Commission, technology platforms like Google and Facebook were an essential player in developing this literacy, creating new products to increase people's technical skills as well as apps and programs. As one example, the Trust Project received funding through Craig Newmark of Craigslist and Google to connect newsrooms with technology companies for new tools, apps, and plug-ins to build transparency in online content. In another effort, the director of Google News Lab, Steve Grove, explained in a news article that Google's organizations were creating "collaborative newsrooms around elections . . . [bringing] together a group of journalists, empowering them with our technology and tools through training, and build a sort of collaborative workflow around identifying the rising fake news memes around that election to be debunked—and to be corrected."[59] Facebook's News Feed vice president Adam Mosseri declared in a trade press article about the News Integrity Initiative (NII) (funded in part by Facebook) that tech companies had an important role to play in building trust in a shared set of facts.[60] In this work, the listening-to-learn component asked content producers, sharers, and stakeholders to pay attention to the technological aspects of the information exchange. The correlation between social media posts and advertisements, as regular users experience, displayed how the technology was "listening" to us.

In consideration of this typology of diverse literacies, the problems they solve, the agents responsible for implementation, and the strategies that can be used, a fuller definition of news literacy was needed. Using Aufderheide's 1993 definition cited earlier, my research team submitted a contribution to that body of scholarship, linking it to the work being done on engagement journalism.[61] The italics represents my expansion of the definition to incorporate the listening-to-learn heuristic as a core scaffolding for the concept of news literacy:

> News literacy is the ability of citizens to access, analyze, *modify, share, co-create*, evaluate and produce accurate and true information as well as to understand how and why that information exists and circulates, and the consequences of using that information as is for specific outcomes such as self-governing. *The emerging actors responsible for news literacy include not only students, consumers and teachers, but also journalists, technology companies such as Facebook or Google, and anyone who engages on social media platforms to mass (re-)produce information. Literacies entail the understanding of content production and consumption and insist on pro-active learning and teaching through interactive and collaborative listening on the part of all participants.*

This news literacy definition offered not only an updated version for scholarship but also a more holistic understanding of the goals of literacy initiatives with building trust in mainstream information. Further, the definition expanded who was responsible for accurate information in public discourses as well as extended the spaces where this work must occur, such as:

- In advertising board rooms. For example, the Building Trust in Media in South East Europe and Turkey project focused on convincing advertisers and publishers to respect independence between their special interests and journalists, helping them listen to learn about how journalists work: "Editorial independence is key to credibility and the only route to news media gaining trust, respect, influence and business success."[62]
- At home on our computers. Craig Newmark,[63] the Craigslist founder working with NII, saw any news literacy solution as an individual effort: "As news consumers, we need to be smarter about the news we read. Clickbait is not clickbait when users ignore it. Also, we need to ignore trolls when they post disinformation."[64]
- Out in communities. Andrew Losowsky, head of The Coral by Vox Media (formerly the Coral Project), suggested to us in an interview that "listening" was a key action that journalists can implement in communities: "If they want to reach new populations, it's vital that journalists begin by listening to people in communities outside of their normal reach, and learn their information needs."

In the "listening literacy" exercises being put forward by many of these initiatives and projects, we can understand how information connects communities and can be networked with journalists, policymakers, etc. With listening to learn, collaborations often happened, creating conciliatory positions between audiences and news production, according to some of these projects. News outlets "should explore collaborations with community partners to conduct outreach. Even low-tech, low-budget strategies such as basic flyers, street signs, hosting, and/or advertising community events may be useful to build ties with residents," suggested a report inspired by the Curious City radio series from Chicago's WBEZ Public Media, which developed a strong interactive relationship with underrepresented listeners. These strategies "explore pathways that could help them listen to audiences, integrate input into reporting, and offer shared spaces for community members to discuss with each other."[65] These advancements in news literacy emphasized listening as a core component for trust building: journalists listening to audiences, community members listening to each other, and community members listening to journalists and other information producers to appreciate when and how information comes about.

Identity-Aware Care through Listening-to-Learn Literacies: Some Conclusions about Trust Building

After 11 years at the Geraldine R. Dodge Foundation in New Jersey, Molly de Aguiar was asked by Jeff Jarvis at the CUNY Graduate School of Journalism to lead an initiative to stem the hemorrhaging of trust in mainstream journalism in the wake of the election of Donald Trump and his acceleration of the sharp freefall of the press's relevance. It was July 2017, and before she was done, in February 2019, she would give more than $12 million to 30 projects aimed at a "vision for local journalism that serves as a force for building trust, empathy and solutions in communities around the world," called the News Integrity Initiative. But in an interview with us, de Aguiar remembered she almost refused the gig, primarily because the mission seemed so impossible.

"It was sort of holy-crap-what-do-we-do initiative," she told me and my research partner Kelly Jensen[66] in our interview in June 2018, a year after she said yes. There was "this general sense that this is a trust building initiative. However . . . it was also about civic dialogue and polarization, and also about in some ways mis- and disinformation. . . . And I actually almost didn't take the job because it seemed like tackling too much with not enough resources, and I didn't know where to start. And then I realized that I can make it what I want it to be. So the first thing I did when I came on board was to try to refine what we meant by that."

A few weeks in, and that refinement showed up as engagement journalism practices. Indeed, de Aguiar, with the NII's deep pockets from funders like Facebook and Newmark, became a key influencer in this developed built environment designed to build trust in mainstream journalism through engagement practices. In the course of networking, researching, promoting, and funding projects big and small throughout the United States[67] between 2017 and 2019, the NII was instrumental in helping to retrain the industry and communities touching on all eight of the categories of skills: collaboration, conversation mediation, radical transparency, solutions-based journalism, community offline work, power dynamic appreciation, feedback loops, and, of course, news literacies—all of which had as their fundamental paradigm the listening-to-learn motif. And *that* listening-to-learn motif became the scaffolding upon which NII based much of its funding; de Aguiar, though, described this using different phrasing, as projects that were "close to the ground" and "trying to build relationships in a genuine way" and "in an authentic way" that also included "newsroom cultural shifts toward a more participatory model" with "feedback mechanisms into the work."

Ultimately, she added, a lot of this new kind of labor NII was pushing the profession toward looked like community organizing, "where they bring journalists, local journalists, and community members together in person to talk about issues happening in a particular community, and they're trying to build those relationships. And then helping journalists . . . hear directly from the public, see how many stories they're actually missing that the public is hungry for, and hopefully building some collaborative projects with the public over time through that model."

But, she continued, none of these projects worked without a focus on representation and identity, without a commitment on the part of journalists to reach out to and listen to learn from *all* their communities. *And* none of these projects worked without a commitment on the part of communities to be engaged *back* with journalism. In a Medium post, de Aguiar recounted an anecdote from one of their projects, a newsroom hosting listening sessions with incarcerated people. The story was about "Anne,"

> a journalist who received several letters from incarcerated men and women, thanking her for hosting a community meeting inside the prison to discuss issues of mass incarceration and re-entry into society. In these letters, the people described feeling like human beings again, valued for their input, and not, for a precious few hours, like someone society has thrown away. One of the letters in particular had moved her, and she carried it in her bag until she found time to write back and let the person know how much it had meant to her. Journalists like Anne, who put community at the center of their work, perform these countless, unsung acts of kindness every day, often in workplaces that don't value it. They go out of their way to help people feel visible, to help them feel like *someone* is listening to them—not to win awards or recognition, but because it is the right thing to do.[68]

The underlying message in many of these initiatives to reporters, technology companies, and others was not to merely check the box of listening through mechanisms that allow for only superficial engagement. Rather, the point was that in *listening* with the intended commitment to *learn* within and around our information exchanges, we fundamentally incorporate an ethic of care for communities. As such, the concept of listening broadens into something more substantial, along the lines of Rinaldi's definition: "Sensitivity to the patterns that connect, to that which connects us to others; abandoning ourselves to the conviction that our understanding and our own being are but small parts of a broader integrated knowledge that holds the universe together."[69] The kind of listening to learn that this built environment's paradigm, that these NII projects, that the journalist Anne adopted reflected the fundamental intent behind an ethical practice of care that feminist philosophers and developmental psychologists have long considered. All individuals engaged in the process of public discourse around news—not just journalists and audiences but also community organizations, governments, technology companies, etc.—actively listen and, in listening, learn and, in learning, care for and with.[70] Just as care theorist Joan Tronto postulated that an ethic of care worked as a mediator between democracy and justice as a way to stave off abuses of power because it provided "a concrete basis for making judgements,"[71] this work suggests that an identity-aware caring approach to these various trust-building strategies through listening to learn can be encouraged and enacted through news literacies.

I believe that this way of thinking leads us into a kind of "caring citizenship"—that is, the "practices in which people can manifest themselves as givers and receivers of care and where they, in dialogue with each other, can contribute to the quality of social care"—that Selma Sevenhuijsen theorized.[72] Listening-to-learn literacies, according to this theory of trust building, should become a part of democratic practice, perhaps in the way that Tronto envisioned in her many writings[73] and certainly in the way the projects that de Aguiar's NII funded between 2017 and 2019. As we see from these trust-building projects, information in public spheres must be approached, modified, and exchanged intentionally and with care so that we may apply it to our governing practices. Mirroring the relocation—or, rather, an expansion—of care from private to public realms, news literacy must occupy all of our information-laden spaces, which are every space in which we exist, tethered to our devices as we are. Thus, listening and learning become integrated into our everyday lives—professional, civic, cultural, and personal. As Sevenhuijsen declared, "An ethic of care in fact presupposes an ethic of trust."[74]

In addition, in the education of these literacies, we must input the notion of power dynamic accounting; trusting an information source begets vulnerability and dependence at a source's intentions and competence:

Just as in other areas of human society, power is a significant factor here. Trust is always interwoven with power and responsibility. If one entrusts to another goods that one cares about, one does indeed make oneself dependent on the benevolence, the competence and the judgmental capacities of the other person. The "trusted" is confronted with her responsibility to handle the dependence of the "trustor" with care. It thus concerns a willingness to use this power in a positive and creative manner; in other words, by keeping an eye on the well-being of the dependent party and not abusing their vulnerability. The ethical moment for the development of trust thus lies in the adage that, wherever possible, one must be trustworthy for others and place trust in others. Reliability would thus be an important value in the ethic of care.[75]

Sevenhuijsen evoked Iris Young's work on "asymmetrical reciprocity"[76] as an important characteristic of any information exchange, entailing close listening to all the perspectives in the communication sphere and establishing a morality for an ethic of care. In asymmetrical reciprocity, Young argued, individuals bring their holistic selves to any communicative exchange, which is never egalitarian because of the varying levels of privilege and power located in the room. In dialogue, individuals must be aware that these different perspectives exist and, further, that they can never be assumed or known, at least not completely. As such, the communication happens through a caring kind of trust that does not force or expect a response; in other words, the information exchange must happen without strings.

I noted the expansion of roles implied with this work and, thinking about the journalist Anne in the prison forum, considered that all four expanded roles were in play for her and the newsroom: relationship builder to gain trust with the people incarcerated, professional network builder in getting journalists to the meeting, conversation facilitator in mediating that dialogue, and community collaborator in co-organizing the event. In addition, I observed the many layers of power accounting at work in such a session. How might that conversation go? Certainly, care must be given in the forming of questions and in managing that dialogue. Story ideas surely would abound, but note Anne's commitment to following through with the letters and her care to engage beyond the production.

The act of listening is an ethical decision that must be made repeatedly and deliberately. This of course poses a major limitation. The entire built environment undergirded by this listening-to-learn heuristic toward building trust in a shared set of facts rested on voluntary actions—to act rationally, to act ethically, to act in care. One unknown is the validity of the assumption that the majority of people *want* to trust information and *are willing* to undertake the listening and learning required. The spreading of fake news has not always been a rational decision. Reporters rejecting engagement practices because they conflict with other traditional journalism tenets can also be deliberate. Vraga and Tully found that "people with higher [news literacy] are *not* supplying high-quality content to social media environments, where many get news and political information."[77] Another impediment repeated by several of our media trust project directors was the continuing attitude—one trust-initiative director called it "arrogance"—from traditional, mainstream journalists that they did not have to change, did not have to engage, did not have to listen and learn in new ways. Many journalists who grew up in a different age of production consumption do not accept the responsibility of improved dialogues or that public relationships and community building might be more important than getting the information fast. Meanwhile, community members have shown themselves to be fickle when it comes to sustained engagement. Should the proper attitudes be present, there remains a number of other logistical challenges to better literacy in hopes for more trust. These include intimidation of public spaces, inadequate training in technology, and little time to devote to such engagement.

These projects ask all of us as teachers, consumers, journalists, social media users, algorithm developers, community members, students, immigrants, parents, policymakers, community leaders, and other active agents to develop our listening skills for many contexts, but always being appreciative of the varying positionalities innate in the exchange: understanding perspective in information sourcing; appreciating political ideologies; hearing what marginalized audiences need without making assumptions or being defensive; listening to the content itself for bias framings and credibility.[78] To listen as an ethic of care in the building of trust, information-seeking actors must be attentive, responsible, competent, and responsive[79] in their moral orientation toward news. Most important, we must listen intentionally, with the aim to learn.

Clearly, de Aguilar chose NII projects based, in part, on this journalism steeped in care, one that helped people identify with the news content, to identify with the journalists themselves. The projects of NII worked to make people feel as if they were heard, that their voices mattered, and that they were empowered to move forward collectively and collaboratively to act. In a Medium post about the NII work, de Aguiar articulated this vision: "What if the public always felt a deep and abiding sense of gratitude for journalists, because journalists were listening and genuinely responding to their needs? What if people from all backgrounds felt powerful because they got to tell their own stories, and collaborate with journalists around important, complex topics? What if everyone had easy access to all of the news and information they needed to make informed decisions in their daily lives and actively participate in civic life? What if, together, we made this vision a reality?"[80] Just as the world descended into COVID Times in 2020, Molly de Aguiar put the NII to bed and went on to be president of another foundation,[81] this one in Philadelphia but also focused on community-centered media, continuing the work toward her vision. By 2022, that foundation had developed some $30 million in grassroots journalism projects in the greater Philadelphia area. In a letter posted to the organization's website, de Aguiar reasserted this commitment to equity and justice through public communication practices "so that we can effectively, with integrity and care, build power with communities by supporting community-led and community-owned media making in our region."[82] This vision that defined and motivated de Aguiar in this work mirrored that of this built environment I have documented in these pages. In the next chapter, I lay out what happened with the few trust projects I was involved in—what worked and what did not—in trying to make this vision a reality.

5

How Journalists Can Listen to Learn and Learn to Listen

Two Interventions in Newsrooms and J-Schools

Since 2010 Joy Mayer had been convincing newsrooms that trust building with audiences must incorporate engagement of some kind. In 2016, she felt so strongly about this mission that she founded Trusting News, a program that trained journalists throughout the world for free on how to build trust with audiences. When Jennifer Brandel with Hearken and New York University (NYU) professor Jay Rosen of the Membership Puzzle Project invited her to be a partner on the Citizens Agenda project, she saw it as a chance to scale up her mantra, which she described in an interview:

> Engagement is a practice within journalism that keeps the journalism responsive to the needs of the people they aim to serve. Engagement is a set of tools and a mindset that relies on a continual feedback loop and continual conversation with the public that journalism intends to serve. So for me, the Citizens Agenda is a system by which newsrooms can base some of their most important coverage, election coverage, on the actual needs of their actual community, rather than on assumptions that journalists make about what their community needs. I would say that the Citizens Agenda is consistent with other engagement strategies and for sure falls under the umbrella of engagement . . . strategies that also involve that continual conversation and feedback loop.

Citizens Agenda,[1] mentioned in previous chapters, was the name of a 44-page guide that Rosen penned as the next iteration of a public journalism movement from the 1990s for which he was a proponent and orchestrator. Hearken, an engagement consultant firm, worked with him to present it in guide form, hired Trusting News, and started to find funders to take

How Journalists Engage. Sue Robinson, Oxford University Press. © Oxford University Press 2023.
DOI: 10.1093/oso/9780197667118.003.0005

it to newsrooms. In the middle of the pandemic in spring and summer 2020, the group, with the help of Democracy Fund, was able to train more than 100 journalists ahead of the fall U.S. presidential election of Donald Trump on revising their political coverage, using the Citizens Agenda as a framework.

Mayer saw Citizens Agenda as an important and potentially effective tool to help newsrooms immerse themselves into engagement. She and Trusting News serve as a bridge between the active role that journalists actually want to play and the more passive roles that journalists have been taught to play or forced to because of budget cuts and limited resources:

> So I think when you describe the idea, "Don't you want your election coverage to be based on what people actually want to know and actually what candidates want to be talking about?," a lot of journalists don't argue with that. It's just really hard to picture. Our routines are so firmly entrenched and it's hard to go into a newsroom and translate that big idea to What does that mean I do right now? How do I know what my community wants? And what stories does that actually mean that I would write and not write? So I think the beauty of the Citizens Agenda is that it lays out a plan and a path for that.

For Mayer, radical transparency around content production is essential to trust building, and her job in the Citizens Agenda trainings was to show journalists how to do that: engage relationally with transparency and intentionality. In the interview with my research team member, Steven Wang,[2] she described what this looked like:

MAYER: So for us, what we contribute specifically to the project, I think, is that reminder for [newsrooms,] making sure that if you make this investment in a more audience-focused type of election coverage, that your audience notices it.

WANG: Can you give me one or two specific examples of [what] that reminder would look like?

MAYER: So not just asking people "What do you want the candidates to be talking about?" but saying, "Here's why we're asking" and "Here's why that's consistent with our goals." And when you do stories that are based on the Citizens Agenda, including language that says, "As a reminder our approach is based entirely on what you told us you want to know, [and] here's how you can get involved in that process." That sort of transparency around motivation is important because, if you think about the basic complaints that people have about journalism and about the media, especially during an election year, the assumption is that coverage decisions are based on personal and political agendas and financial agendas, that they're based on making certain candidates or parties look good, that journalists have an ax to grind with certain candidates or parties. All of the sort of worst assumptions people make about journalism, this is a direct counter to that. And yet journalists wish that they could just do good journalism and that people would notice it and give them credit for it.

Citizens Agenda—and the umbrella program Elections SOS[3] that Citizens Agenda was a part of—mixed engagement work with the already newsroom-approved transparency work by amplifying community members. As Mayer implied, Citizens Agenda worked actively to counter some of the newsroom obstacles that have kept election coverage stagnant and one-dimensional, which had been perceived as untrustworthy with its game frames and focus on competition rather than issues. Part of what we see in this explanation by Mayer is the tension the industry is navigating between 100 years of norms and practice and the reality that a radical transformation in thinking and producing must happen for the profession's survival. Teaching about communication and feedback loops, teaching about expressed motivations, teaching about *listening* and then acting on what is *learned* all help journalists restructure their routines to encompass the basic components of what goes into successful relationship building. Citizens Agenda offered a media literacy approach that asked *journalists* as listening-to-learn agents to invite people into previously closed processes of reporting, as we discussed in Chapter 4. In that chapter, I explored what the trust-building paradigm was proposing as part of a new value system, bringing with it new roles and skill sets as part of a deluge of engagement and other kinds of initiatives. That analysis surfaced how different categories (and spaces) of news literacies—including civic, amateur sharing, professional, and digital—served as mechanisms for the identity-aware caring to listen to learn anew.

For this chapter, though, I embarked on the third and final phase of the data collection: the implementation of all that learning from 2018 to 2020 into two initiatives that I helped organize and also participated in during

2020. One was the Citizens Agenda, for which I was the research lead and also a participant observer in the trainings during most of 2020. I have already introduced the Citizens Agenda work, for it has threaded through all of the chapters thus far. The second project was a journalism curriculum disruption program I started in 2020, developing four classroom modules: Power & Privilege, Content Collaboration, Community Conversation Facilitation, and Basic Engagement Strategies. I created a network of about 100 journalism instructors around the world and invited them to use what they wanted of the modules, which had PowerPoint presentations, readings, class exercises, and discussion prompts. I named the group the Journalism Educator Collaborative, and we began meeting regularly during 2020 and in subsequent years to compare notes, share work, troubleshoot, and brainstorm about how to incorporate engagement and other kinds of trust-building practices into our classes. Fourteen of the professors[4] agreed to adopt some part of the modules into their fall 2020 reporting skills courses. My research team helped me evaluate how it went[5] via interviews with 12 of the professors and surveys with 165 of the students. My fall 2020 advanced reporting class also committed, though we dedicated the entire class to the community conversation facilitation skill set specifically.[6] I will describe this project more in detail later in the chapter.

The ethnographic participant observations of these two projects offered a glimpse into how this trust-building theory could be intentionally initiated on the ground in newsrooms and in journalism schools. To remind you, here is the working theory of trust building developed in the first three chapters of the book: *Trust building* **happens through the nurturing of personal, organizational, and institutional relationships that people have with information, sources, news brands, journalists, and each other during what is commonly referred to as** *engagement.* **For trust building to occur, engagement needs to be practiced with** *identity-aware care* **and enacted through** *listening* **and** *learning.* Once a theory is conceptualized, it must be tested. I wanted to see how these strategies unfolded in real-world settings with actual journalists in working newsrooms, amid all the constraints, resource issues, audience disengagement, editor and co-worker disdain, and other obstacles to building trust. The eight skill sets that I have described in this book privileged identity-aware caring in the listening-to-learn paradigm, and their uneven but prolific adoption nurtured a transformation in the industry within this established built environment. I personally worked to make the environment's paradigm as robust as possible because I believed it to be essential to saving journalism and also public, authentic information exchange. This chapter is guided by a few very pragmatic questions. First, when we set out to intentionally implement this robust understanding of how to build trust as journalists and journalism students, what happens? Second, what are the challenges and the strategies to overcome them in these projects? Third, in what ways, if any, can an identity-aware ethic of care be applied in the training and teaching of how to nurture community relationships toward the boosting of trust in authentic information?

A Citizens Agenda to Build Trust

Jay Rosen wrote his dissertation in 1986 at NYU trying to define the public, dedicating an entire chapter to John Dewey's notion of the public[7] as something much more nuanced than audience or consumers. He told us decades later in an interview that, "Dewey's point was that in modern society, we have all kinds of problems arise where action in one area affects people in another area. And a public is a group of people who share those problems and have to decide what to do about them. So I have always thought this is the heart of journalism. The heart of journalism is not making content; it's informing and engaging publics. And publics don't just consume information; they have jobs to do [with that information]."

In 1991, a few years after he defended his dissertation, Rosen made the decision to spend his career not on researching journalism and the public—the path most academics take—but to instead apply his growing theory about the public within newsrooms themselves. Rosen, who was a professor at NYU's Arthur L. Carter Journalism Institute at the time of this writing, started experimenting; this was pre-internet, pre–newsroom financial collapse, but post–cable news and after political officials and their publics had begun disconnecting.

And then in 1999 he wrote *What Are Journalists For?*, a book that is still widely cited and considered one of the anchoring statements about the connection between journalism and the public and how journalists might reposition community members as collaborators rather than merely as audiences consuming a product. I believe the book, with its establishment of the "public journalism movement," was the first work that was done in what would much later morph into "engagement journalism." The public journalism movement fizzled out in the early 2000s as newsrooms began contracting, but Rosen never let go of the idea that journalism could become more participatory for publics. He continued writing about the concept in his popular ThinkPress blog and other publications.

Rosen watched with interest as the engagement consultant firm Hearken used the very concepts he had been proselytizing for decades as its business model, with the motto "Public-powered journalism." When the 2016 election of Trump showed just how distant and disengaged journalists— both local and national—were from their publics, he started plotting with renewed enthusiasm and reached out to Hearken, setting up a meeting with them in Chicago on a blistery January 10, 2019, at Hearken Headquarters. Five people—Rosen with Hearken cofounder and CEO Jennifer Brandel, Hearken engagement specialists Bridget Thoreson and Stephanie Snyder, as well as Mara Zapeda from Switchboard—sat around the table, taking notes on a whiteboard and launching an idea that Rosen had been thinking and writing about for a few years on how to make political reporting more public-based. He called it The Citizens Agenda for the U.S. Presidential Election in November 2020.[8]

An opportunity exists here, he said to the group, to synthesize a different kind of election coverage. To reject horserace coverage. To ask newsrooms to start coverage with their communities, asking them what they want candidates to talk about. He elaborated in an interview with my research team member, Steven Wang:

> I think election coverage is far too frozen in place. It's dominated by a single cluster of ideas, and there are different names for these ideas. You can call it horserace journalism or insider journalism or just campaign coverage, the way it's been done. . . . And so I just wanted to let it be known within journalism and larger spaces that there is an alternative and that in the 2020 campaign and the 2020 elections, it would be viable. And then if we were able to get that word out to in some ways support or encourage newsrooms that wanted to experiment with this alternative. So that's the whole idea, is let the word go out. That there's an alternative to the campaign coverage as usual and that there are support systems for those who want to experiment with that alternative.

As Brandel listened to the pitch, she became more enamored with the idea. She recalled that meeting in an interview with me:

Jay had been on my radar for a while. Over the years we got to run into each other at conferences and whatnot. And every time I heard him speak, I was just like, "Yes, we're on the same wavelength." And so he became someone that I followed and really admired and was lucky enough to get to a point where he would take my phone calls and questions and emails to get out some of this stuff. And when I heard him talking about the Citizens Agenda . . . I was like, "Oh, this is the public-powered model. It's just applied to political coverage."

Everyone around the table agreed that the nation could not sustain another 2016 political journalism fiasco.[9] But what would this look like in practice? The group started brainstorming, furiously scribbling on the whiteboard walls of the room, as Brandel described to me: "Is there a way to create a guide? Can we take this theory and just break it up into the steps we know [are] needed for public power journalism, with the Citizen's Agenda veneer on it and do that? And so that's kind of where that idea began. And then we got some funding, thank goodness, from the Democracy Fund, to print those, to distribute them, to speak at some conferences, et cetera. And that's kind of what started snowballing." About nine months later, the group had a guide, website, and protocol for changing how political journalism could be done, and held a series of workshops to introduce Citizens Agenda to the world. In May 2020, they had created a working consortium of trainers such as Joy Mayer from Trusting News and Malii Watts Witten from Engage Between—both of whom appeared in earlier chapters—to take journalists through the concept of engagement with communities. They did five cohorts of 104 journalists total between May and October in groups attending eight sessions of one and a half hours each.[10] In these sessions, Hearken and the partners trained journalists in the guide's protocols: "Setting the vision; Map your network of stakeholders; Outreach; Ask the question 'what do you want the candidates to be talking about as they compete for votes?'[11]; Use the agenda in coverage." Rosen emphasized that three activities were necessary in the implementation of the guide if newsrooms wanted it to be a scaffolding for building trust: (1) outreach must be robust and extensive, beyond existing audiences; (2) journalists needed to use the input to actually change political discourse and election coverage; and (3) journalists must go back to communities after the election and keep politicians focused on that agenda. I now detail each of these three essential tasks for newsrooms, according to the Citizens Agenda.

Outreach

First, the outreach for the collection of answers must go way beyond the existing audiences and into as many corners of as many communities in the city as possible. It should all begin, Rosen told the groups, with a "listening plan." The plan needed to be realistic and also direct about the newsroom's community connections:

> I would begin by breaking the public up into "easily reached," "modest effort," "going to be really difficult." And maybe there's a fourth category, if you're being really honest, which is "We don't actually have any chance of talking to those people or we're so distant from them or they are so alienated from us that we have to try something completely out of the box for that group." . . . You have to use every eliciting method you have. And that includes in-person meetings. It includes calls. It includes meetings face to face. It includes interviews. It means email. It means WhatsApp. It means every application we have and every method that we can think of.

He recommended that the journalists make use of their existing networks to extend the ask for agenda items into groups the news brand was not yet connected with.

Some of the newsrooms set metrics around this outreach, such as "Get 500 responses to the question on what you want the candidates to be talking

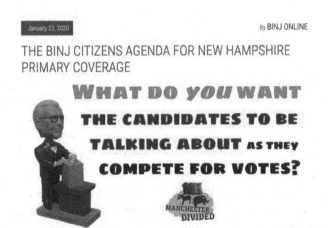

Figure 5.1 Boston Institute for Nonprofit Journalism's website for Citizens Agenda.

about," "Get at least 50 different voices to include in our coverage," and "Get at least 75% of responses from people who aren't within our current circles."[12] To solicit input for the political agenda, newsrooms got creative (e.g., moving beyond their traditional social media platforms and email listservs), including the following outreach: initiated texting campaigns, placed a collection box in grocery stores and other community places, staffed tables at food pantries, ran advertisements throughout the community infrastructure, submitted Google Forms, sent out reward-incentive surveys, networked with community nonprofits to relay surveys or forms, set up pop-up newsrooms, canvassed neighborhoods, printed flyers, partnered with bookstores and libraries, held virtual Town Halls and other forums, sometimes as part of a popular event already ongoing, sometimes as part of membership meetings with community organizations.[13] Journalists also translated much of this outreach into Spanish and other languages. See Figure 5.1 for an example of one outlet's call.

Key to collecting plenty of agenda items from as many different kinds of people as possible, said reporters, was making it feel safe and nonjudgmental. One cohort participant told Hearken, "So at this point, we have established ourselves as the station in town in which you send us questions, engage with us. . . . We are getting quite a lot of people. . . . It gives us a better idea of which communities care about which issues." Almost all the participants in the trainings did something with the Guide, though many used it internally to think about coverage rather than embracing the full public accounting that Rosen had hoped for.

The Agenda Enters Public Discourse

The second major component that Rosen underscored was that the resulting agenda must be brought to politicians directly and offered as an actual agenda for the political discourse with direct engagement from the politicians. Many of the newsrooms published their complete agendas, such as the Boston Institute for Non-Profit Journalism (BINJ) (see Figure 5.2), whose stories ran in dozens of dailies and weeklies in New England. New Hampshire residents during the primary told BINJ that they wanted to hear from politicians about disability rights, income inequality, gun control, and the opioid crisis, "pared down from dozens and dozens" of issues, the editorial director Chris Faraone told us in an interview.[14] Further, the agenda

- income equality
- government transparency/FOIA
- leadership style
- disability rights
- voter rights
- climate change
- student loan debt
- the opioid crisis
- infrastructure/ transportation
- labor
- money in politics
- death penalty
- surveillance
- gun control
- caregiving/caregivers
- police brutality
- SCOTUS
- cannabis
- immigration
- religion

Figure 5.2 BINJ's Citizens Agenda.

items were much more specific than the more general topics reporters often cover, asking for topics like "nuclear regulatory commission policies," and "wind farms." Faraone said most of the coverage his crew of reporters published during the primary stemmed from the Citizens Agenda, and not from the preconceptions that he had had going into the race. For example, at the Taproot Edmonton in Canada, participants wanted to know "Will we build our city intelligently? The people want candidates to think about various infrastructure-related issues. Many have concerns about projects being late and over-budget; others are concerned about the costs of urban sprawl." Or in Chicago with WBEZ's initiative: "Bruce Mabee from Downers Grove asked for you to give a specific example of a time you worked to compromise with someone you disagree with in a political or professional setting. If you have an example from your work in policy or public life, please share that example." Over at Northern Public Radio in Illinois, community members asked, "How do you propose to incorporate mental health professionals into the way we police our communities?" Other newsrooms also used the Guide as a major approach to their coverage. One California radio station sent the agenda to city council candidates and then did 45-minute podcasts with each one to hear their positions on each item. At a news outlet in Ireland, the staff asked readers for help distributing the guide, received 11 offers (all but two declined the small stipend offered), and each volunteer vowed to spread the Guide through their networks.

The agenda changed how the participating newsrooms would have covered the races, according to the post-project interviews.

> For example, in response to one of the surveys put out by a local newsroom, readers wrote back with a lot of questions about one government action affecting health care coverage. "So we ended up pivoting and writing about that. And I think it was really meaningful. And we were able to get to the bottom of what the government was unclear about cutting. They kept saying they were not cutting, but there actually were drastic cuts. So we were finally able to explain the small print of why this actually made a difference. And that was only because we cast this big net, and people came forward to us in this safe space to tell us what happened."[15]

Several of the journalists remarked both during the trainings and in our post-project interviews and survey that the Citizens Agenda approach, while seemingly basic in terms of its philosophy of centering the public, revolutionized their way of thinking about election coverage. In the course of the outreach, news organizations heard from community members a great need for logistical, procedural, and other basic government and voting information. Many newsrooms published the typical guides on where and how to vote, but also explaining how the election worked, the jargon used on ballots, and electoral mechanisms such as when and why a recount might be triggered. Some editors vowed to produce year-round information to provide background on topics in the news. "I think what our audience really needs from us is basic civic education," said one participating reporter.

Follow-Through

Journalists must both publish the agenda itself and also circle back around to community members to let them know how their words were used and what candidates promised. Rosen urged newsrooms to keep tabs on the politicians after the elections to hold them accountable for their promises. Several of our publications took this urging to heart, especially in presenting the agenda to the candidates and asking them to respond, as in a California public radio CapRadio piece headlined "Bloomberg Stumped in Sacramento, So We Asked Him Your Questions on Climate Change, Homelessness." A small midwestern online news outlet used the Citizens Agenda to guide conversations around the city in collaboration with a national program run by the nonprofit Cortical and called the Local Voices Network (LVN).[16] That political reporter told me, "During one debate over the summer, I played a snippet of an LVN participant's view on K–12 education before asking a legislative candidate a question about the topic. It was really powerful to have that commentary lead-in to the candidate's answer, especially during an entirely virtual debate that didn't allow for audience interaction."

The coverage that resulted from Citizens Agenda efforts illuminated those candidates with more developed platforms compared to those politicians who could talk in forceful sound bites but little substance. As one example, BINJ offered an eclectic collection of stories, most of which stemmed from the long list of agenda items they had gathered via Google Forms and pop-up newsrooms at bars and other places. Although the hyperlocal site had always shunned game-frame coverage and put forward more alternative perspectives, the January–February 2020 group of stories highlighted community members' voices more than in the past.[17] The agenda, for example, prompted a first-person piece by a disabled freelancer trying to attend campaign events during the primary season.[18] When asked if their coverage changed, participants reported the affirmative, that they threw away their planned story budget and replaced it with the agenda items.

However, it was at this stage that we saw the Citizens Agenda effort significantly start to falter. The relentless news cycle, the pandemic, ever-decreasing resources, fatigue, and inertia prevented a more robust follow-through. The challenges for newsrooms in summer and fall 2020 rose up in unique and daunting ways, from the COVID-19 pandemic that made trust building in local communities particularly difficult to the unending news cycle of the Trump presidency and the increased financial pressures that constrained resources. Some newsrooms had more capacity than others to run with Citizens Agenda, but most cited the need for more people as a reason follow-through went flat. Others had difficulty convincing newsroom managers to change coverage or they could not get buy-in from others. One said, "For the next election, I want it to be more inclusive of the staff. I want everybody to have some sort of training. . . . I wish I would have incorporated our reporters a little bit more into that coverage." Another reported, "We tried to get surveys on air, but broadcast reporters declined. Digital staffs were more receptive." Although 41% of the newsrooms felt they had enough support for the Guide, about 40% of them said they did not have adequate support or were neutral on the matter. "There wasn't the space or bandwidth to bring our ideas to the larger newsroom," wrote one reporter in our postelection survey.

Overall, all those who participated in the cohorts as well as the organizers and trainers declared the intervention a success because Citizens Agenda prompted dozens of newsrooms to reconsider election coverage and intentionally incorporate more voices into the public elections dis-course: the end goal. An industry report by Thoreson and others at Hearken and Trusting News documented the following wins, as told to them by the newsrooms: service journalism did in fact serve audiences and drove up engagement; engaging audiences led to stronger reporting and furthered reach; reaching underserved communities required making that a priority; listening to audiences built trust and in turn drove impact. Many of the participants reported increased subscribers, memberships, comments, and other kinds of engagement. In addition to the Guide itself and the trainings in engagement and outreach, cohort participants reported that the network of professionals ranked high as an unexpected benefit: "Talking to people from different newsrooms, being able to share your experience and have somebody to bounce ideas off of that is also working on similar projects was really cool." And this: "I loved that we felt part of a team." According to the data analysis of the work, the intentionally collaborative nature of the project decreased feelings of newsroom isolation in this innovative engage-ment work and, as such, spurred creation, experimentation, and more robust outcomes for content and relationship building—at least on the production end.[19] Yet I must also point out that this was self-reporting by the journalists; we do not actually know if the trainings resulted in different coverage or if the experiences meant audiences trusted these journalists more because of this approach.[20]

Trust-Building Modules

Right around the time the Citizens Agenda project was being launched in 2019, I started thinking about how to incorporate more engagement work—not just the associated skill sets but the entire paradigm—into journalism school curricula. I made the argument with the Citizens Agenda team and funders that we should tag onto the endeavor a J-school piece, that until we changed the primary training grounds for journalists in the United States, the industry would continue to falter. However, even though its genius lay in its simplicity, the project already contained a lot of moving parts and the J-school component I envisioned (e.g., supplying newsroom interns to help collect agenda items or partnering with reporting classes to produce agenda-specific content) was not to be at that time. So I decided to start the process of blowing up J-school curricula and replacing them with an engagement mindset on my own.

Generally speaking, J-schools have never really fostered the innovative work of the journalism profession for they tend to be mired in institutional baggage, professors who have little to no contact with the industry, and rigid curriculum standards and learning objectives that reflect the status quo more often than not. Furthermore, J-schools have a hard time changing quickly. Usually there are committees and subcommittees that must pontificate upon every significant addition or modification. For example, at my institution, any new class or sets of classes (as I was envisioning) would need to go through at least two clunky approval processes—with my school's curriculum committee (and ultimately our full faculty) and also with a university curriculum committee. And then you have to finagle getting assigned to teach the class given that your schedule in any given semester must abide primarily by department needs.

Lucky for me, I was not reinventing the wheel here. A lot of my fellow journalism instructors across the world were already inserting more engagement work into their reporting classes. Some were inventing entirely new programs, such as the Engagement Journalism MA program run by Carrie Brown, director of CUNY's Craig Newmark Graduate School of Journalism.[21] Many others were creating partnerships with news outlets or community organizations to teach engagement on the ground, such as the Germantown Info Hub[22] site that Andrea Wenzel[23] of Temple University began as a result of a research study and that is powered in part by her journalism students heading out into Germantown in Philadelphia to report on neighborhoods. This kind of work had been around for decades, of course; professors had long urged their journalism students to get off campus and into the surrounding communities. Yet as the profession moved farther and farther away from objectivity as a norm and expanded the skill sets required for its employees (e.g., forum hosting, event planning, town meetings, and community conversations), J-school teachers were starting to realize we needed to transform as well. Nonetheless, when I sent out a call to let professors know I would have a bunch of modules centered on trust building and wanted to create a vibrant network of folx interested in brainstorming exercises, readings, and assignments, I hoped for five or 10 people. As of 2023, I have more than a 125 in the network and 20 to 25 who show up regularly at Zoom brainstorming sessions I hold throughout the year.

The four modules were created using the data my research teams and I had collected over the previous four years, thinking not only about the tried-and-true trust-building strategies that had been researched and proven (as aggregated in Phase 1 of this project) but also about the realities of implementing them on the ground (as queried in Phase 2). This was part of Phase 3: trying it all out (albeit without much money or resources). The modules—Power & Privilege, Content Collaboration, Basic Engagement Strategies, and Community Conversation Facilitation—represented the four trust-building categories to come out of this research that translated into tactical skills for the classroom. The modules comprised 10 PowerPoint presentations, 18 handouts and in-class exercises, 14 assignments, and dozens of readings and discussion prompts for all of them. The network of journalism instructors—named the Journalism Educator Collaborative—helped me crowdsource the modules as well.[24] We also uploaded our syllabi so we could share wording and scheduling examples. In fall 2020, despite the pandemic that was still raging, 15 of us implemented some parts of the modules in reporting skills classes. The professors[25] allowed me (and the team) to interview them and to survey their students to find out how it went.[26] We wanted to know how the professors and students thought about engagement after the course, what they did and why, the challenges of what they did, and suggestions for improving the modules.

In both the professor interviews and the surveys with the students we noted not only the traditional teachings of trust building in reporting classes—respect, empathy, and transparency—but also a deeper level of commitment to the idea of relationship building, moving past outreach for the sake of the story, to get the good quotes: being involved, displaying humanity and compassion, finding common ground, not only hearing but *listening* by monitoring language (i.e., not using jargon), working for the greater good, and acknowledging privileges and bias. For both the students and the professors, teaching trust-building skills with an engagement focus must underscore that the relationship between journalists and their communities was not transactional but "reciprocal"—a word that showed up repeatedly, as Perry Parks, an assistant professor of journalism at Michigan State University and one of the participants in the engagement curriculum, said in an interview: "I would define engagement as a process of reporting in a way that takes input from communities and then sort of works reciprocally with communities to develop storytelling and present results in ways that are meaningful to the community." Long-time trust-building techniques like transparency (e.g., an information box alongside a story) took on more robust (I call it "radical") dimensions. As Amara Aguilar, a professor of professional practice at the University of Southern California Annenberg's School for Communication & Journalism told us:

> Some of the students did final projects related to trust. One of them built a toolkit that would go with political stories to help people learn more about how the story was put together and give them more resources for balance. Another group did a final project called Meet the Editors so that readers could have a more personal bio of editors. They actually made an Instagram account and had all of their portraits and their bios from their interviews so that people could better get to know who the editors were and see their photo and see more personal details about them just to get to know them on a human level and not just a name in a staff list.

The professors used the modules provided in unique ways that made a much bigger commitment to transparency, helping audiences get to know the journalists at work on the stories.

Similar to the journalists trying to implement these practices in 2020, professors also reported that the COVID-19 pandemic made the semester particularly fraught. Students were frequently in crisis, all the schools were either virtual or a hybrid with restrictions on public interaction, and professors themselves were taxed trying to learn online teaching techniques and still meet the learning outcomes for the class. The idea of engaging with communities proved daunting. In addition, being online meant identifying privilege and bias became more difficult in a two-dimensional setting without being able to "feel the room." Many of the professors elected not to do the recommended Power & Privilege training because of these issues.

Another big challenge for the professors—and the students in the surveys—was the nebulous identity of engagement work itself, especially within the confines of the class, as Joy Jenkins of the University of Tennessee–Knoxville's School of Journalism & Electronic Media told us:

> I think the biggest thing for me . . . is trying to help students who were very, very new to journalism understand what engagement is. I didn't really introduce it fully until toward the end of the semester, and by that point it was hard to figure out how to introduce them to it. Like when they think engagement, they don't think of the things that journalists are thinking of. And so, trying to get beyond that to explain it in a way that makes sense to them. And I only had a couple class periods to do it. At that point I wasn't super confident they were watching any of my video lectures or doing any of the readings. And so it was tough trying to figure out how to get these new concepts across to them when there's already so much else going on.

Instead, Jenkins had them look over a set of engagement strategies and consider the logistics that would be necessary. "I had them find an example of a news outlet who was doing something like that and reflect on it." But by the end of the semester, Jenkins said, she was not fully convinced the students understood engagement journalism.

The end-of-semester surveys from the students, though, indicated a clear understanding of the term. Although some variance appeared, with some students defining engagement journalism as "interviewing" or "transparency," the majority of the 160 surveys, including in Jenkins's class, mentioned "connections," "community work," or "relationships." Here are a few:

- "Engagement means 2-way communication or interaction between the audience and the writer or creator."
- "A good journalist should be involved with their community to understand what issues most interest and affect them."
- "Engagement means connection. With journalists and journalism, it's about connecting with the audience in various ways to create a more open and trusting relationship between the journalists and the public."
- "To form relationships."
- "It means interacting with and being a part of a community (national or local)."

Further, most of the students had integrated the professors' own definition of engagement (as relayed to us in interviews), suggesting that teaching this work in J-schools was essential to changing the mindset of trust building during the building blocks of the journalistic industry paradigm.

The reporting instructors agreed that J-schools had generally not been at the forefront of this kind of work. Associate Professor Lisa Miller[27] from the University of New Hampshire told us, "I think we've neglected this for a long time and taught students how to do interviews, how to conduct interviews, how to find sources, but not necessarily how to build relationships in communities. And I think that's the important thing that we need to teach them how to do. So I think that journalism schools need to take a bigger role in doing that."

J-schools were absolutely essential to making sure this paradigm shift takes hold for good in the industry, according to Professor of Practice Lori Shontz of the University of Oregon's School of Journalism and Communication. She began every reporting class she taught with trust-building principles, centered on engagement practices: "This generation of students is very open to this. At the professional level, people need to unlearn what they've been doing for quite a while. So I think that giving people a place to start with this and building it into the curriculum from the very first moment is key because when those students go on into the industry, they're just going to bring their work habits with them. And I think that that can help to make change in newsrooms. . . . This is core to where the industry needs to go." But, she added, "change comes slowly." This corresponded to what had always been known about J-schools lagging behind, according to this research: "This exploratory study finds that most departments/schools are not offering classes that reflect pedagogical approaches recently promoted in professional literature (e.g., hospital model, entrepreneurship, apprenticeship) nor are they responding to calls for greater integration between the classroom and industry via quasi-professional experiences."[28] J-schools needed more classes in writing basics,[29] coding, and more.[30] However, this research demonstrated that there was a core group of reporting instructors actively adopting new skill sets and teaching engagement as relational journalism in addition to entrepreneurship, web skills, podcast technology, solutions journalism, and even social-justice reporting.[31]

Learning about Relational Engagement

Before the training—either on their own, through the Citizens Agenda or because of the curriculum modules taught in fall 2020 classrooms—many of the journalists and journalism professors we talked to considered engagement to be an add-on to traditional journalism. Kara Meyberg Guzman, CEO and cofounder of Santa Cruz Local, said, "I guess before the training [with a public radio engagement specialist in 2019], I didn't know exactly what community engagement was. I had a very different idea. I thought it was more outreach." Engagement in traditional journalism mantras was something they did or taught if they had time, like responding to questions in comment sections or asking for help crowdsourcing a story. By 2020, though, these journalists and educators who had self-selected to try something new had fundamentally shifted their paradigm governing the very role of journalism. Guzman continued in her interview with us: "And now I understand that it's more of a relationship building and listening." She read us her site's new community engagement statement: "For Santa Cruz local community engagement means building a trust-based relationship with you. We want to understand your needs to guide our reporting, then connect you with information to strengthen our community."

Assistant Professor John-Erik Koslosky at Bloomsburg University's Department of Media and Journalism spent more than two decades in newsrooms before teaching reporting classes. In fall 2020, he went all in with the modules for his Journalism Workshop, an upper-level skills class of 11 students, nine of whom visibly identified as white. In his survey, he "strongly agreed" or "agreed" that his students had "engaged more with community members," "created new opportunities for community members to participate in journalism," "had made progress in assuring that their sources/ participants are broadly representative," "learned better what it meant to listen and respond to their sources/participants or community members," and "seemed to connect this engagement work with building trust in communities." In our interview, Koslosky told us about his own mindset shift as he worked more with engagement as a pedagogical tool for his reporting students:

> In our minds, we had the idea that engagement really was drawing people into your [site]. . . . As consumers, we want to engage the audience. And really what you were saying is we want to make efforts to have them consume

our work. To kind of turn that around now and say, "Well, we want to engage the audiences. We want to bring them in and make them part of our
work. We want their ideas to drive what we do. We want their agenda to
become our agenda and not our agenda to become their agenda." In some
ways it really kind of turned that onto its head. In the ways we, I think, define engagement has changed a lot in just a short amount of time.

Note here the conceptualization movement from a focus on product consumption to a focus on relationship building with audiences. In this enactment of trust building for this built environment, product consumption
became more of a process outcome than the end goal.

Students[32] of not only Koslosky but the other professors reported that
the strategies taught in the class had significantly changed their understanding of both trust-building practices and also the very role of journalists
and their relationship with audiences. Here are some of the statements student participants made about the role of journalists today, their jobs with
audiences, and their definitions of engagement—after they had finished the
classes:

- "Really listen to what they are saying, make them feel that they ARE
  being heard. Engage with them, and learn from them."
- "Before this class, I thought that engagement was limited to people
  reaching out to journalists/news organizations. Now, I have come to realize that it is the journalists who need to take the initiative, and reach
  out to readers."
- "In relation to journalism, engagement means being involved in one's
  community to the fullest extent. It does not mean simply being present,
  but fully engaged in the moments the journalist spends with the
  community's people."

In these responses we see the following terms that indicated a more animated
and committed journalist role: "*immersing* oneself," to *collaborate*," "to really
listen," "*actively* interacting," and "*connecting* with communities." For these
students—the majority of the respondents—journalism had become "not a
one-way dynamic" but a way to "form trusting relationships with community members."[33] In these conceptualizations we can start to see a different
kind of relationship being envisioned between reporters and communities,
one that moves away from amorphous audiences and product-attention and

toward an approach that privileges personal connections and, particularly, an ethos of care. To *really listen* or to *immerse oneself,* a journalist must be reflexive and fully present, attuned to the process of reporting as it is being experienced by someone else. In this kind of empathy, journalists create new job tasks based on the forging of attachments within community.

The participating journalists also reported to us and to the Citizens Agenda team that the trainings had forced a major rethinking for them about their obligations to the people they cover. The relational engagement tended to be more successful because the Citizens Agenda Guide and other strategies were more concrete, with explicit tasks. One participant said:

> Citizens Agenda led to us using engagement as a comprehensive, multi-faceted, open-ended ongoing approach to an editorial focus. Though we've done engagement work with great success in the past, it's often been either too open-ended, without clear goals and strong follow through on what we're doing with community response, or limited/static, like doing a callout to crowdsource ideas for one story. Asking people for their questions (in general, and for particular officials) was also somewhat new and really important to the success. We also for the first time directly responded individually to respondents in a systematic way to answer their questions and share pertinent coverage.

It was this formalizing of the process of engagement that seemed to click for these reporters, showing them how to begin working with people and their communities as opposed to the newsroom-led story ideas. The guide and other strategies created a "journey" of collaboration, as one journalist told us, and through that journey, audiences could be built around and through the content. The public-powered[34] content then became knitted into public discourse. "We would never have thought to invite candidates to a 'candidate forum' but ask them to listen and not speak. I think that was a game changer," one reporter told us. And in this rhetoric transposition, we noted that journalists also discussed a more active responsibility, beyond merely providing true and accurate information. Consider this reporter's comments: "We set a goal to do more audience listening as a general course of practice and the Citizens Agenda really helped to solidify what can come from listening. We don't want to listen just for the sake of listening, but to let the audience be our guide in determining what problems we can solve for them." *What problems we can solve for them* struck me as a very different obligation from the more passive goal of making sure accurate and thorough information abounded so communities could solve their own problem.

Identity Work in Journalistic Spaces

It was fall 2020, one of the worst semesters in terms of logistics and student crises that Professor Lori Shontz had ever seen during her time at the University of Oregon's School of Journalism and Communication. Having redesigned her reporting courses a few years before, Shontz in fall 2020 used two of the modules, Power & Privilege and Basic Engagement, to supplement what she had already built. Her Reporting 1 class had 16 students, all but four of whom visibly identified as white. She started off right away with a discussion about identity, especially personal privileges and biases that would influence everything they did in the classroom and the world beyond. Having the class online meant she could also use the chat function in real time to help those introverted or more reticent because of the topic. A few students of color, including a Palestinian woman, felt comfortable sharing their experiences, "and that made a big difference in getting the other students to open up," Shontz told us, adding, "I noticed that many of the white women in particular were so careful, so afraid of offending somebody and making a mistake. That was very evident."

Across the country, another professor, who identified as a white woman, had had little experience thinking or talking about race on her own, never mind with the all-white classes she taught. She rejected the Power & Privilege modules because trying to tackle something so fraught seemed unwise when the university was virtual and the students behind blacked-out screens. Another professor[35] understood this hesitancy as well, telling us in an interview, "Just the fact that I wasn't comfortable teaching. I didn't feel like an expert in the material. And when I don't feel like I'm an expert in the material, sometimes I shy away from talking about it or engaging in it." As I heard these professors grapple with these challenges, I admitted to myself that even though I had trained in social justice techniques as well as conversation facilitation around identities, I was still making a lot of mistakes and was still often uncomfortable and afraid I was going to cause someone trauma inadvertently. Indeed, at the time of this writing I was still lamenting using the wrong pronoun with a spring 2022 class speaker who identified as trans. In the age of YouTube and an environment of attacks[36] on any pedagogy having to do with race, this classroom work required constant vigilance, careful prodding, and complete self-awareness.

Nonetheless, many of our participating students, especially those from marginalized communities, in that fall 2020 talked very explicitly about how their identities influenced their reporting, including what their identities meant for their new conceptualizations about journalism. "I didn't know that my identity as an Asian American could be part of what I do as a journalist, and I get that now." And this comment: "I'm Black and I don't see enough Black reporters, and that's why I want to be a journalist. This is my mission." Connecting the students' identities with engagement practices "helped them realize how important it is to connect with the community directly," one professor told us. Yet, white-identifying students had a more difficult time seeing how their race affected their work; one professor pointed out that many did not really understand that they had a race. These professors told us they became vulnerable themselves as a way to help students work through their blocks around the importance of identity acknowledgment in journalism. Said one of our white male professors, "It's always uncomfortable talking about issues of race and gender and that sort of thing. I've only just in the past couple of years really attempted it in this sort of more progressive way. The challenge is first being able to discuss this comfortably yourself. Then the second is to try to encourage students to discuss it in constructive ways among themselves." As one journalist mentioned and several students reported in their surveys, "We were always taught you don't mention race."

Adopting an Ethic of Care in Engagement Work

In every class session during fall 2020 with my advanced reporting class, I started with some kind of caring work: a few minutes of meditation and breathing, a show-and-tell of favorite creations, story sharing of happy places or moments, etc. I instituted these based on some training our faculty did about the pandemic to help students make the leap to virtual and to still be able to get to know the students without the typical time we get in the classroom. I made myself available 24/7 and urged students to communicate with me if crises hit—and they did; at least half my students in this class were in major crisis at some point in the semester (COVID positives, parental deaths, sick grandparents, lost jobs, you name it). I broke up engagement work into group work so students not in crisis could pick up the ball for those incapacitated. Despite teaching virtually, I became closer to these students than I had in many other classes, and as a result, I developed a caring for them much more intense than was typical for me during in-person semesters.

As first a reporter and then a new professor, I had never been taught to care in these ways. It sounds crass and wrong as I write these words, but in fact, caring was not really something we were supposed to do. Maintain critical distance—from sources, from students—and you were a better analyzer and evaluator of facts, of work, etc. I took that mandate to heart and became known as a very hard-nosed reporter, grader, professor, person. I felt this was what my job and my students needed. By fall 2020, though, my thinking had pivoted. I still believed, of course, that rigor and high expectations were essential in all that we do. But I elevated compassion and explicit caring as part of my professor toolkit. And one unexpected outcome from that semester in crisis surprised me: despite all of the chaos of the semester, the quality of completed assignments surpassed any I had had before.

And I realized, startlingly, I enjoyed caring. I felt a much stronger sense of accomplishment and satisfaction with my relationships with these students than at any other point in my careers. The more I read about the ethic of care as a significant component for thriving democracies, institutions, and relationships, the more I started looking for evidence of caring in my data and in my own teaching and other kinds of work. What does caring look like in practice within trust-building strategies, particularly those involving engagement practices? In past chapters, I delved into how caring in practice could be thought of as having the following characteristics, as devised by Joan Tronto:[37] attentiveness (knowing the needs of others by attending to others), responsibility (feeling responsible for others' care), competence (adopting an ethic of care requires action with appropriate resources and effort), responsiveness (adjusting our caregiving specifically for the person or entity at hand and not by simply imagining what needs we ourselves might have), and solidarity (collectively understanding and accepting that care is essential to a working democracy and a thriving humanity). I bring these up again because in my own revelations during this fall 2020 coursework and in the interviews, surveys, and training observations, this ethic of care with these dimensions clearly was playing out, manifesting in intentionality, empathy, reciprocity, and a desire for the feelings of community cohesion. Thus, I was well primed to be receptive when my new advisee introduced me to the body of scholarship known as the ethic of care, mentioned in Chapter 3.

Caring meant being intentional and deliberate, especially in outreach, which needed to be an active and ongoing process based in empathy. For these participants training in trust building, the new protocols and strategies prioritized constant self-reflexivity as well as committed sensitivity to others' experiences. For J-school instructors, this meant the active creation of a classroom environment to spur trust building between students and the instructor as well as between students and community members they were reporting on. The J-school instructors intentionally integrated nuggets of care into the coursework, caring for themselves and the students in a tough semester (especially self-caring), but also into the teachings of journalistic values for students to take with them out into the world, to guide their professional practice. Consider this anecdote from Daniela Gerson, an assistant professor at California State University–Northridge's Department of Journalism, who participated in the fall 2020 engagement modules with her reporting class: "One of the things I felt like was a real success, was one student who came out, talking about her DACA status[38]. . . . [W]e did the story in collaboration with Southern California Public Radio, and she felt comfortable talking about her status. I didn't realize that she'd never talked about it before. She said that the class created a comfortable space to talk about these issues." For this student, the instructor had worked deliberately to create an empathetic environment such that she could be vulnerable because she felt attended to and a sense of solidarity with the class and the instructor. When students felt cared for, they expressed more connection—to the instructor, to the material, to journalism.

One of the students from my fall class was a supervisor for a dormitory that kept getting quarantined because of COVID outbreaks. I brought her and her dorm mates a giant pile of homemade cookies—a simple effort. Months later, in May 2021, she mentioned this moment in a public graduation forum as her happiest J-school memory and that it was key to her engagement in the class and the semester, despite the trauma she was experiencing: "I began my senior year taking a class with Sue Robinson. She had never met me, but after having only two small short chats before class, Sue decided to come visit me. Sue found out I was a house fellow living in the dorms during this pandemic. Without knowing anything about me, she took it upon herself to make me and my coworkers cookies. It was such a kind and heartfelt gesture. After being so isolated, her small act made me very connected to our school and helped me to remember we were all going to get through this together." The student became a skilled facilitator in community conversations, in part because she saw caring being modeled and replicated that ethos with the participants.

Other professors reported better-quality projects from students as well, also attributing it to different approaches to teaching prompted by engagement during a pandemic. When she was a younger professor, Lori Shontz of the University of Oregon believed "everybody needs to write a whole bunch of stories because that's how I learned how to write. . . . Just going to throw you into the deep end," she recounted to us in an interview. "And the longer I do this, the more I think that the more important thing is taking time to think about what you do and why you do it and slowing down the process." "Slowing down the process" was a common theme across both these classes and also the engaged news work by journalists. This work allowed these reporters (both student and professional) the chance to be responsive while demonstrating that a responsibility for others' care was present.[39]

Aguliar reported her experience with teaching empathy during that difficult fall 2020: "We did an assignment with KPCC [public radio] on community listening and how to interview people based on human-centered design. And they found that really helpful because it was different than the way they had interviewed people in the past for getting quotes or sound bites. They focused on taking it slower with the interviews. They focused on asking people what their information needs are and what would help them." These professors were explicit with their students, letting them know all the ways in which they could engage with professors, each other, the newsroom partners, sources, and community members, showing responsiveness and instilling a competence in this kind of teaching. They believed this promoted intentional empathy. Said Shontz, "Not everybody reacts to a reporter the same way. Not everybody processes information or wants to engage in the same way. So as you think about the different ways people in the class engage, how do your sources engage differently? What might stop them from doing this? So again . . . I'm really consciously trying to model that. That I'm trying to be an engaged educator."

Caring meant following through and checking in after the reporting, the story, the assignment, the class, etc., be it professors consistently checking in with students, journalists with sources, newsrooms with audiences, or students with community members. "When you do an engagement, you need to have a very clear plan of what you're going to do with that information so that you really value people's participation," a reporter told us in an interview about the Citizens Agenda implementation. Another said it this way: "Especially around elections you need to have [engagement] be continuous. . . . [I]t's important that once you have that base of people that are engaging with you, just continuing to engage with them and grow on that. . . . I think we want to continue checking in regularly instead of waiting until the next election cycle."

And caring, finally, meant *creating* community in all of these spaces— where students, audiences, and sources exist, but also in the trainings for both journalists and professors. In participating in professional networks, in sharing what was once thought of as proprietary information, journalists showed caring. In taking time to help colleagues teach engagement practices, in sharing what went well and what went wrong, instructors found caring as well: "Honestly, engaging with these modules and hearing the other professors talk about what they do has really taught me a lot as well. So I'm still learning and trying to recognize what it means and how it's changing. But yeah, it's new." The Citizens Agenda trainings in summer 2020 prompted journalists who adopted engagement practices during the election period to reject typical territorialism and to embrace collaboration, according to the postelection report: "This idea of working in partnership, and the value of that is a really good one that came from the workshops—this idea that it's better to connect with somebody and support the project that they're also working on, than to try and do it on your own. Because why would you do this on your own? They can reach more of a different audience, and working together creates a stronger community, right?"[40] In this collaborative work, journalists and students alike produced more solutions-oriented products that served to connect stakeholders in communities. It also provided deeper feelings of belonging within the covered communities: "It really helped give us a better profile of our audiences and how to serve them. And it just continues this stream of engagement with our communities, I think that's really important. I don't want there to be this division. . . . We're part of your community and having a constant mode of communication keeps that up."

Conclusions: Trust Building with an Identity-Aware Care via Engagement

Kirsten Johnson, an associate professor in Elizabethtown College's Department of Communications, remembered going through J-school without having a single conversation about how to build trust with audiences.

"It was just assumed that people trusted the media. And when I worked in TV news, I always just assumed that people trusted the content that we put out there." But in the reporting class she taught as a professor in fall 2020, she brought up "trust and credibility in just about every class period . . . whether we're looking at something that was reported that week and did the media do it in a way that was building trust with the audience or not, or disengaging the audience?" The reporters we talked to and surveyed also reported a primary commitment to building trust in their communities, very conscious of the changing cultural and political dynamics threatening the press's relevancy as a political institution in Western democracies.[41] I asked Citizens Agenda participating reporters about this explicitly, as in this interview with Chris Faraone of BINJ about his decision to go all in on the Citizens Agenda implementation during the January 2020 primaries in New Hampshire:

RESEARCHER: Do you feel like you were able to build trust even with those limited interactions?

CHRIS: Oh, totally. I mean to the point where [my reporters] Max and Jess were up there with us and like you should have seen the people [engaging with them]. . . . That's trust. Somebody was just in there for a beer, next thing you know they're talking to one of my reporters. They're sitting down with Max and Jess for a forty-five-minute conversation around the digital hearth. And it's all because of [Citizens Agenda and Hearken]. It's like what we were doing is obviously a little different. They were just kind of there with us and we shared some resources. But basically, that's the idea. We actually are listening and doing stuff with it.

And in that trust building, they reported that the news content became more audience-driven as a direct result of "listening and doing stuff with it":

RESEARCHER: And do you feel like your coverage changed?

CHRIS: Oh yeah. Yeah.

RESEARCHER: In what ways?

CHRIS: Of the twenty-five contributors, let's say twenty are writers. Half of them, ballpark, are not like brand new, but young. And certainly haven't covered something like the presidential primary before. I obviously have not just bias, but things that I think are important and all that. So if I'm the guy primarily guiding all these reporters with their ideas and everything, as opposed to a Citizens Agenda guiding them. You know, you get a lot of the same. You get a lot of my perspective, in a certain way. But that's not what we got. . . . I acted more as a middle man than an idea man.

In being more engaged with communities, journalists took themselves out of the reporting and privileged citizen information work. Here, the editor demonstrated a felt responsibility for whose voices could be amplified and generated competence to make that effort happen. In doing so, the journalism allowed for new ways of learning through a new kind of listening. For Jennifer Brandel and Hearken as well as the rest of the Citizens Agenda team, "instead of seeing engagement as a sidetrack to reporting, it needs to be closely tied to everyday coverage to sustain trust with the audience, to expand the community served, and show that the community's participation is valued."[42]

In this chapter, I have described the outcome of two major experiments, one in the U.S. journalism industry over the course of 2020 called Citizens Agenda and the other with J-schools called the Journalism Educator Collaborative, implementing engagement practices in reporting skills classes in fall 2020. Although this data could not allow evaluation of whether or not a discernible change in content or audience attitudes followed these experiments, the data did provide evidence of a distinctive mindset shift into the trust-focused built environment this book documents. This mindset shift foregrounded a desire to develop new relationships with both audiences and students, as well as between news brands and community members. It centered on identity introspection and emphasized work guided by an ethic of care. We know from scholarship and also from our own practice that both journalism and journalism pedagogy were born from processes that involved contestations over cultures and politics and that evoke, perpetuate, or snuff out power.[43] To build trust in these spaces, we must embrace experimentation more robustly, determined to learn from the inevitable failure. Were these projects complete successes? Of course not. We did not see the kind of consistent follow-through, for example, that our trainings mandated for trust to occur. Through these challenges of time, resources, cultural inertia, and the pandemic, we take to heart the lessons to try again, and again—always listening to learn ourselves.

As of early 2023, it cannot be known if the needle on mainstream news's imminent demise through widespread distrust moved at all because of these broad engagement efforts. However, this was the direction the industry began taking around 2010 and accelerated in 2016, and as such, there was value in documenting it. At the end of our interview about how her fall 2020 reporting skills class went, Shontz at Oregon added this: "I don't want to teach this like it's something special or something extra. I want to teach it like it's core. I don't call it engaged journalism. . . . I just call it journalism." Yes! Right there with you, and so are a lot of other people.

Several new journalism textbooks came out in this time period, formalizing this new paradigm and becoming part of the built environment that had emerged.[44] For example, the 2021 *Teaching Race: Struggles, Strategies, and Scholarship for the Mass Communication Classroom* edited by George Daniels and Robin Blom offers a blueprint for how to disrupt journalism and mass communication education. The very first chapter argues that to change the industry, we must teach identity and reject objectivity, replacing it with our positionality. We must change curricula to "place the discussion of systemic oppression in all your reading and lesson plans."[45] In the concluding chapter we draw from these learnings to fill out a theory of trust building around engagement practices and using an identity-aware care for a multicultural world.

6

A Theory of Trust Building

Framing Journalistic Practice with an Identity-Aware Care through Engagement

In late April 2021, after the 2020 election and after we finished our learning from the Citizens Agenda trainings, Bridget Thoreson, our "dream wrangler," left Hearken and became the first full-time Member Collaborations editor at the Institute for Nonprofit News.[1] Meanwhile, Jennifer Brandel, Hearken's cofounder, stepped down from CEO activities to lead strategic global partnerships at the company and chair the board.[2] This freed her to pursue some of the big-idea work she yearned to do around creating power networks of change. And by spring 2022, Brandel had embarked on a couple different projects, including one she called "Democracy SOS" in coordination with the Solutions Journalism Network. For this, 22 newsrooms accepted paid fellowships to train in the eight new skill sets I have described in this book, combining several of the movements that make up this trust-building theory, such as engagement journalism, radical transparency, solutions journalism, and community-based reporting.[3]

Almost a year after the Citizens Agenda trainings, Joy Mayer of Trusting News reflected on her time with the project, emphasizing the importance of the collaborative network of engagement-minded people and entities necessary to effect this paradigm shift:

The project has brought together similarly like-minded organizations researchers like you and Regina and Hearken, and the Membership Puzzle Project and Trusting News. But I can say our work has overlapped informally for a long time. And so it's really wonderful to have a chance to work together more directly. . . . The collaboration is really important. Because it can seem like it's hard to get journalists to stop and take advantage of a lot of the support that's out there that can help them do better work. There's a real power in this, not just saying, "Hey, look over here,

How Journalists Engage. Sue Robinson, Oxford University Press. © Oxford University Press 2023.
DOI: 10.1093/oso/9780197667118.003.0006

this shiny thing, and take my class," but to come together and say, "Look, here's the plan that incorporates what we're all working toward, that we think can really help."

Here Mayer articulated the existence of this built environment and our attempts to appeal to working newsrooms to change behavior with concrete strategies.

After the November 2020 presidential election, Mayer was struck by how many people's decisions at the polls were based in divergent understandings of the realities of issues like COVID-19, immigration at the border, and other devastating issues. On January 6, 2021, she watched with the rest of the nation in disbelief as extremists stormed the Capitol prompted by the lie that the election had been stolen by President Joe Biden. Polling numbers showed that, though most Americans didn't agree with the violent attempt to subvert democracy, the majority of conservatives had doubts about the integrity of the election. That means that, in many cases, fact-based journalism was failing to inform people about their shared civic life in a way that felt credible. Indeed, providing evidence for all of our fears, in March 2021 the U.S. Department of Homeland Security issued a National Terrorism Advisory Bulletin against the rampant false narratives inciting people to violence in their own country.[4]

By summer 2021, Mayer was formulating a trust-building collaboration she called the Road to Pluralism, to help "journalists strengthen trust across diverse values, experiences and political views to bridge divides, foster productive conversations and fuel open-mindedness." By fall 2021, Trusting News had convinced 25 newsrooms to adopt one or more of five implementations that included things like "building listening into routines" and auditing their opinion pages for partisan polarizing content. And by spring 2022, Trusting News had embarked on a second phase of the study, honing the methods of interventions and figuring out what might work in a busy newsroom.[5]

These new projects going into 2022 demonstrated how the work regenerates as this emergent built environment entrenches into Western media landscapes. How can we think about "trust" as it manifests and appreciate that we may be going about information exchange all wrong? What are we learning from this trust-focused built environment about journalism and, in the process, ourselves as journalists, journalism educators, and community members interested in seeing journalism survive? In these pages, I have argued for the following theory of trust building that has emerged as the most significant paradigm shift for the profession of journalism in the past century: *Trust building* **happens through the nurturing of personal, organizational, and institutional relationships that people have with information, sources, news brands, journalists and each other during what is commonly referred to as** *engagement.* **For trust building to occur, engagement needs to be practiced with** *identity-aware care* **and enacted through** *listening* **and** *learning.*

This trust building will be in constant flux in terms of how it is practiced, what defines success, and who is responsible for the trusting work. In the next section, I lay out the theory as it has developed in the preceding pages, supported by the evidence of the built environment and evolving even as I write these words. The intentionality behind these revolutionary efforts resulted in four new roles for journalists: relationship builder, community collaborator, conversation facilitator, and professional network builder. In these roles, journalists were being trained in eight new (or newly emphasized) skills: radical transparency, power dynamic accounting, mediation, reciprocity, media literacies, community offline work, needs/assets/solution analyses, and collaborative production, as laid in the preceding chapters and in Figure 6.1. In practice, these skills necessitated deep listening (such as listening to content or mediating in communities around polarizing content) and learning (such as understanding and promoting solutions to community problems or creating collaborations with community stakeholders).

Threaded through this news labor, an ethic of identity-aware care meant the prioritizing of listening and learning. In this chapter, I offer up a series of recommendations—summing up the learning resulting from all of these projects aimed at trust building to help the profession and all the change agents improve and be more effective. Finally, I make an argument for a major perspective shift away from the typical distancing of journalists, especially those who worked at for-profit newsrooms spurred by competitiveness and territoriality, and toward a holistic, networked approach that privileges collaboration, information sharing, and innovation born from expansive thinking and consideration of marginalized folx. Indeed, when I was doing a pre-book talk in April 2022, I was asked what incentive commercial news outlets had to adopt such a theory, and my answer was this: The status quo no longer works, and they have to do something or they will die out. Ah, but will it work? We have no idea as of this writing.

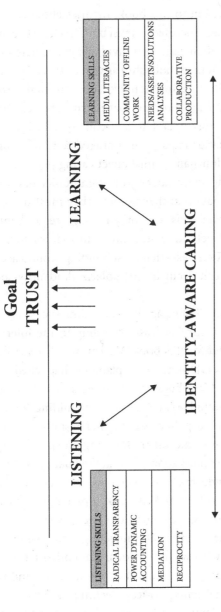

Goal
TRUST

LISTENING

LEARNING

IDENTITY-AWARE CARING

THROUGH ENGAGEMENT PRACTICES

LISTENING SKILLS
RADICAL TRANSPARENCY
POWER DYNAMIC ACCOUNTING
MEDIATION
RECIPROCITY

LEARNING SKILLS
MEDIA LITERACIES
COMMUNITY OFFLINE WORK
NEEDS/ASSETS/SOLUTIONS ANALYSES
COLLABORATIVE PRODUCTION

FOUR NEW ROLES FOR JOURNALISTS	
RELATIONSHIP BUILDER	COMMUNITY CONVERSATION FACILITATOR
COMMUNITY COLLABORATOR	PROFESSIONAL NETWORK BUILDER

Figure 6.1 Trust building with identity-aware care.

A Theory of Identity-Aware and Care-Based Trust Building in Engagement Journalism

As we learned in the introduction to this book, theories about trust have spanned decades and disciplines. Theories on trust building tend to consider power dynamics broadly but often assume individuals participate in trust building in similar ways.[6] From the scholarship as well as this evidence, we know trust to be relational at its core. In this book, I challenged the existing thinking around the kinds of trust building that journalists were trained to do and interrogated how trust operated as a construct in journalists' thinking about audience relationships. I encouraged a reimagining of trust building in news work. Journalists must enact caring practices based on identities and on listening to compete with communicators seeking to be trusted in public information exchange—and they must do so over and over in a process that never ends. It is only through regular, intense, and intentional listening—to each other, to content, to sources, to brands, within communities, and to ourselves—that trust building around accurate and meaningful information can occur in this polarized, identity-specific environment.

The journalism industry and all of its agents—including subsidiaries and affiliates—have accepted this theory, at least according to the interviews, surveys, and focus groups I did for this book. We can see that a collective evolution of norms and protocols around this explanation happened at what I believed to be a critical mass. Many books over the years have documented parts of this transformation around this theory of trust building, with some concentrating on how networked publics were either responsible or supportive or demanding of change[7] and others focusing on specific engagement practice evolutions.[8] Still others zoomed in on the nuance of changing roles and purposes of the industry.[9] But when we viewed all of these transformations in aggregate, as I did in this book, a paradigmatic pattern emerged that demonstrated how a significant value system overhaul has been in the works. I have argued that the central connecting components of this trust building extend beyond what we have known from other trust theory scholarship. For journalism in Western countries, these expanding values underscored an ethic of care via listening-to-learn techniques and demanded a keen awareness of identity (identity work, identity biases, identity politics and ideologies, etc.) as any individual or organization or profession or institution achieved authority over public information.

Relationships built on an ethic of care (e.g., via engaged listening). Journalists care, of course, and always have. Sometimes as a young reporter, I lamented the professional choice I had made as I watched my former classmates bring home checks with six figures and have weekends off. But I always came back to the higher calling bit; for me, this "higher calling" was the result of two kinds of caring that I felt keenly: I cared to make a difference in people's lives, and I cared about having an informed democracy. And journalism was a way I could do both. So I stayed, year after year, caring for 13 years in one newsroom and then another and another.

Journalists listen, of course, and always have. Listening was my favorite part of the job. I had always loved listening to stories. As a reporter, I got to record them, channel them as accurately as possible, and tell them to others. I felt that through this caring and listening, I gave my sources and their stories legitimacy.

By offering up the disagreements that populated our public discourse, I engaged in civic care.[10] We know from scholarship that listening with care can "enhance legitimacy claims, increase levels of trust, help deal with disagreements, improve representation, and refine deliberation."[11] But for me, the caring through listening stopped at the production of content because, ultimately, I was not trained to care further. I tracked what happened to the story, documenting any letters to the editor or comments or—much more seldom—any policy change that occurred because of what I wrote. But in terms of the people I had talked to, the caring became more abstract for me. To be honest, this type of listening generated more transactional and perhaps even extractive qualities than I would have admitted at that time. The particular caring and listening I have laid out in this book, however, and the kind that is being practiced and advocated by many in this built environment toward trust building has been a caring involving a more committed engagement on behalf of individual reporters as well as their newsrooms and the entire press.

For those studying care in a journalism context, how to care in this way could play out in many different ways. For journalism care theorists Hossain and Aucoin, these were

(a) social constructing context; (b) promoting dialogue through human values; (c) designing vision that incorporates all people in a community, including the most vulnerable or voiceless among us and seeing how caring about one another can change our journalist narratives; (d) reframing those narratives that can change for the better the version of reality that is accepted by societies; (e) embedding iterativity that gives voice to and shows compassion toward the Other and calling the journalists to self-reflexivity or constant questioning throughout ethical decision making; and (f) making processes and outcomes transparent, for only through transparency can journalists gain and maintain the trust of their readers and viewers.[12]

This was a more proactive version of listening than the kind I practiced in the living rooms and coffee shops of my reporting days. Listening for this caring must not only be "prophetic" (i.e., listening by suspending reaction) but also listening to co-create meaning between all the listening and speaking parties through empathetic dialogue.[13] This requires quite a bit more than taking notes and re-creating story. In the literature around the ethic of care, listening plays an essential role in being attuned, attentive, engrossed, empathetic, understanding, patient, caring, discriminating, astute, open-minded, curious, persistent, and courageous.[14] Importantly, in failing to listen in these ways, we fail to learn.[15] And when we fail to learn as journalists, we fail as journalists completely.

In these kinds of caring and listening, journalists can become "a solvent of power," as we learned from the rhetorician Andrew Dobson in his book called *Listening for Democracy: Recognition, Representation, Reconciliation*, which I discussed in Chapter 4. Here we come back to power, which must always be at the forefront of any discussion involving journalists and trust building. To be a "solvent of power," journalists cede power—the power to tell stories, to control stories—by remaining silent and allowing others to amplify their voices, to tell their own stories. For reporters, this might look like allowing sources to look over their quotes, collaborating with folx to co-produce stories, or avoiding the typical hierarchical source structure in favor of something more neighborhood-based and less official. In this process, journalists themselves can become vulnerable, sharing with constituents their own challenges, talking through difference, and learning about their own inhibitions to trusting relationship building. "Communication opens up the possibility of creating a relationship in which risk itself becomes relational," wrote Dobson about how being a solvent of power might work.[16]

Furthermore, all of this must be intentional on the part of the journalist and explicit on the part of the source or community member. When Dobson wrote that listening needs to be more than checking a box certifying that we allowed people to speak,[17] it resonated with me, personally and professionally, in terms of moving away from a transactional kind of information exchange in favor of something more deliberate and co-creative. Over and over, these change agents in the emergent trust-focused built environment—from the individual actors to the organizational training and the developing culture—prefaced this reflexive, engaging work as imperative to trust building.

Relationships Built through Identity Work and Engaged Listening

Journalists have identities, of course; they are just taught to hide them. No posting of political signs. No attending protests as a participant. No letting anyone know your political leanings. Some even went so far as to disenfranchise themselves, so committed they were to maintain objective appearances. Nonetheless, as the scholarship around care and listening as part of democracy has attested to, all identities and ideologies get in the way of active listening because they cause us to hear according to these categories within us or that have been socially constructed to be applied to us.[18] Journalists had always put people into boxes: politician, activist, witness, regular person, victim, hero, crackpot, etc. Indeed, they have internalized the word "agenda" so much that everyone is suspect and they question everyone's ulterior motives. When I asked all the journalists I have surveyed over the past few years if they agreed that everyone has an agenda, 54% checked either "strongly agree" or "somewhat agree," and more than 40% strongly agreed or somewhat agreed that they do not trust most people. When we asked journalists about how their own identities influenced their reporting, some did not acknowledge that they themselves operated with agendas innate to their identities and ideologies. Most important, these identity constructs can interfere with reporters' capacity to listen and therefore to care in anything more than an abstract manner. For example, we know from Chapter 4 how people have underestimated, undercounted, and ignored Black women in particular. And many white journalists specifically do not realize how their whiteness permeates every decision and interaction they conduct.

However, as we saw in Chapter 3, more and more journalists in small to midsize newsrooms considered their various identities as they went about their jobs, listening to themselves and understanding how their own histories could influence their work—with the increasing number of journalists of color leading the way. More and more, these journalists were putting their identities at the forefront of their job, not only trying to be transparent about who they were but also working to consider their own identities in relation to the identities of their sources and constituents. For example, at the *Texas Tribune*, management recognized their newsroom comprised mostly white, left-leaning reporters—identities that meant they failed to understand the true appeal of Trump to conservatives in rural communities.[19] These journalists recognized that to build trust, they needed to work within communities, and to work within communities, they had to approach their job with their whole being. In this built environment, identity work—that is, efforts to appreciate their biases and privileges, thinking about how people identify in reporting, etc.—must become a fundamental value for journalists and not merely an extracurricular practice, as had typically been the case in mainstream reporting. This was why Hearken's Bridget Thoreson started off all of their Citizens Agenda trainings with a session on personal identities and why journalism engagement consultant Malii Witten threaded her Bahá'í Faith throughout her trainings, which prioritized unity and equity and asked that people engage—care—with their whole being, with all of their identities, and in concert with others' identities.

It was also part of the reason why engagement consultant Fiona Morgan quit newsrooms to get her MA in public policy, train in bias and privilege, and work on journalism projects that helped communities improve themselves by amplifying all voices and changing problematic any status quo. As mentioned in an earlier chapter, in 2015 Morgan became the Journalism Program director at the national advocacy organization Free Press in New Jersey and worked to reinvent local journalism through a project called News Voices. Morgan advocated the building of trust within communities through listening, inclusivity, collaboration, and consensus shaping. For me, Morgan and her various collaborators were part of a sea change operating at both the individual and organizational levels of this industry as well as the more metadiscursive plane within which they and other change agents intentionally work to transform mainstream journalism from its flailing norms and protocols of a dying commercial industry to one prioritizing engagement, collaboration, and connection in the stewarding of a different kind of democratic public forum of deliberation and civic dialogue.

In our interview, Morgan talked about her time at News Voices as trying to get the profession to move away from this obsession with objectivity to focus on identities. For her, trust was caught up in whether reporters could appreciate how people moved in the world and how the world moved for or against them:

> You start talking to people who are affected by racial injustice about de-mocracy, that does not land very well. [Democracy] is not really an in-trinsic goal for people who need basic human rights and dignity. So if things that I associate with democracy as being intrinsic to human rights and dignity, I think there's a sense of, like, what democracy for whom? Because when did we ever have that? Don't talk to me about democracy. Let's talk about meeting these basic needs. . . . We realized that we couldn't create a constituency for journalism, if people didn't feel like journalism was showing up for them. So we had to back way up and start working on the reckoning: the reckoning of how journalism has hurt people, how journalism is part of systems of oppression, that it's part of a struc-tural, a whole big set of structures. And that that has helped people in communities of color, and honestly, communities all over the place, in-cluding conservatives, see journalism as part of the power structure. And that's when you have to go, "Okay, so maybe if . . . I build a constituency for journalism, that's actually kind of self-serving for journalism. What am I really here for?"

Here we have another spin on the age-old question "What are journalists for?" asked over and over, perhaps most famously by Jay Rosen (of Citizens Agenda most recently) in his book about public journalism back in 2001. But in public journalism, reporters were still in control, and we were not talking so much about "identities" in the newsrooms of the 1990s as we were talking about "transparency" and "civic journalism" and the idea of integrating jour-nalism *into the democratic process*, not about whether or not that democratic process itself was problematic fundamentally. What Morgan surfaced here was that this fundamental fact needed to be understood: journalism not only propped up systems of oppression but was *itself a system of oppression*.[20] Continuing to focus on objectivity would fail to highlight the much more salient and devastating reality that objectivity, even as an ideal, was keeping reporters from practicing an ethic of care that was identity aware, with a power lens.

But what might this new value system look like? I have spent the previous chapters revealing how the profession and its adjacent actors have worked to establish a new system of norms and routines around engagement. And I have also reported how several of my own projects fared. With help from my various research teams over the years, I offer a series of recommendations for trust-building work either in the newsroom or in a journalism school. In Chapter 2, I offered a list of engagement strategies for journalists and journalism students to employ—techniques proven to build trust through experimentation of the dozens of entities and projects informing this book. The following recommendations are more about how to implement those strategies, given the structural, fiscal, political, cultural, and other constraints in both newsrooms and universities.

To begin, it is suggested that those working in journalistic arenas, including professors, undergo an accounting of what is working and what is not within the practices already established. In this reckoning, it is important to evaluate frankly how prepared the players involved are to be part of the change, identify holdouts, and work to establish the new paradigm as part of the core missions, asking a series of questions: Has everyone undergone identity/bias/privilege training in an ongoing manner? What did an audit of sources/databases/authors/speakers reveal about representation to date? What process for restorative justice has been taken, such as apologies for stereotypes and/or microaggressions or a response protocol going forward? This evaluation needs to be public to demonstrate transparency, authenticity, and good intentions.

Once a commitment has been made to embrace change, it is important to outline some goals around trust building (What does success look like? Who are the target communities?), followed by how that success will be logged and measured. And finally, an absolutely key step in this work is ensuring the work will not be extractive and exploitative (e.g., the journalists/students are the only ones benefiting) but will be done in cooperation with and from within communities. How can this trust-building work be reciprocal and mutually beneficial? How can this work be in service to community, at a fundamental level? As one American Press Institute 2018 report stated, "[L]istening alone is not enough. Newsrooms must demonstrate how what they hear changes their behavior, guides their coverage in responsive ways and opens up new routines that can make journalism more inclusive, participatory and, ideally, sustainable."[21]

The following more specific suggestions come from myriad sources within this research, including the trust-focused case studies, the focus groups, interviews, and surveys, the leaders and participants in the Citizens

Agenda project, and the participant journalism professors and students in the Journalism Educator Collaborative.[22] These also reflect some of the dozens of recommendations already out there in industry reports about trust building from places like Tow Center,[23] the Agora Journalism Center,[24] and the American Press Institute,[25] as well as scholarship such as Andrea Wenzel's book *Community-Centered Journalism* and a growing number of books like Mónica Guzmán's 2022 *I Never Thought of It That Way.*

Recommendations

- Build on existing relationships and use them to expand into new groups and communities.
- Build for the long term via the institution. Instructors, students, and reporters come and go, so trust building needed to be something institutionally encouraged and enacted. When a trusted reporter leaves or a community-based-learning class ends, make sure a plan is in place to keep that community relationship active within the newsroom/department. Making sure this trust work is done across the organization—and not shoved onto one person—will help.
- Get uncomfortable and then be creative. Said one of our Citizens Agenda trainees, "When you're . . . out of your comfort zone, you start to think more out of the box. You think creatively, your mind is open, your heart is open and you're down to kind of go along and try different things."
- Nuance your trust-building skill set according to the kinds of communities you want to enter. Different demographics will need different kinds of strategies.
- Follow through. One of the biggest failures of the Citizens Agenda work was how little time and effort went into actually publishing the results of the Citizens Agenda or into reconnecting with people who had participated, as this newsroom reported: "We also never published a main Citizens Agenda explanation to readers, part of the model process and something we planned to do, due to time and resource constraints." J-school professors also mentioned their limited time in a semester to keep up the trust building, especially for students who leave the community when they leave the course and the university. In these cases, it is important that someone be charged with following through with the communities to let them know what happened to their words and their efforts with the engagement.

- Find people within your organization who are on board with the change in protocols and try to bypass those who will throw up obstacles. Eventually critical masses of adopters will force change at structural levels, even with people resistant to such change—or at least one hopes.
- Provide specific examples and anecdotes to students/co-workers about how to implement strategies and techniques to trust build.
- Build in more time than you think you will need to both reconceptualize traditional priorities like deadlines and to understand how much time engagement work takes. From our journalists implementing Citizens Agenda: "I would start using it earlier. I was worried about the timing with the primary and the election, but I wish we had just started collecting reader questions and issues in January. We could have noted every story we did that came from those questions/issues raised. I also wanted to tie the information we gathered to a newsletter campaign, but with the short time window, it just didn't come together."
- Appreciate the importance of partnerships and networks, both at the story production level and at the source level when trust building.
- Work cross-culturally as much as possible, having reporters and students report in Spanish, for example (using a translator if necessary).
- Reconsider what success looks like. Document all kinds of metrics, not just story clicks or number of sources. Qualitative responses are important as well. Ask students and reporters to keep a log of what they did for the story—including what did not go in the story—to publish alongside content (and to use for grading purposes). Expect some failure, emphasizing the learning from that failure. Use what you end up with, creatively: "Once we agreed to do a more modified approach—allowing me to use initial responses from the People's Agenda (PA) to quiz candidates and shape my coverage in the pre-primary period over the summer, rather than waiting until we had collected all of the responses we wanted to begin incorporating the PA into my reporting—it made things a lot easier."
- Make everyone responsible for engagement work. This will also help ensure there is sustainability going forward.
- Offer choices within the work by allowing journalists, students, the project partners, and community members multiple pathways to participate and that identify concrete ways to be involved. Make sure that, for example, times for hosted discussions consider work schedules and also provide babysitting, translation, transportation, and food.

- Keep on keeping on, even if you fall off the work for a while during hectic times. "The main thing that helped us overcome challenges was to remember that even if you miss a deadline or fall off the roadmap, do the next right thing to get back at it. Now that we have a draft agenda, it should be easier to keep going." This is not an "all or nothing" endeavor.
- Think outside the box in terms of connecting within communities. Linking up with community leaders to gain access to neighborhoods is only one option. Other options are placing suggestion boxes and QR codes around neighborhoods and libraries with specific feedback instructions; setting up tables at food pantries, farmers' markets, libraries; hosting small dinner parties in people's homes; doing Slack or Discord channels or other kinds of messaging platforms.
- Partner with entities whose skill sets would be useful and important to trust-building work, such as a marketing department or a nonprofit that works with multimedia or youth organizations. But remember that each individual also has a skill set to share.
- Communicate, communicate, communicate. Not only with your team members and editors/professors but also with your sources and communities: what you are doing, when, how, and why, and also what you are *not* doing and why.
- Constantly check yourself and the work that you are doing. Does it offer up a sense of belonging for all? Are there embedded microaggressions? Why did you ask that question that way? Why did you choose that source? Are there broad representations in the content, thinking not just about race but also about disabilities, sexuality/gender, and other typically marginalized identities? Is it produced with a power lens that helps reveal problematic structures? Does it push the conversation forward in a way that helps lay down a path toward solutions? Trust building within community demands continuous self-training in identities, privileges, biases, and power.

Conclusions

As stated in the introduction of this book, the theory of trust building reflects the first major paradigm shift in mainstream journalism in more than a century. Trust building in journalism used to envelop a series of actions around transparency in reporting, intense neutrality aiming for unsullied objectivity, and longevity around credibility with a broad acceptance of authority. Engagement meant numbers of clicks or shares, letters to the editor, and other one-way communication patterns with audiences. Today trust building embodies engagement practices toward relationship building, as in this comprehensive definition from the nonprofit Impact Architects, a social change agency providing research and advising to various entities, including many media companies: "Engaged journalism is an inclusive practice that prioritizes the information needs and wants of the community members it serves, creates collaborative space for the audience in all aspects of the journalistic process, and is dedicated to building and preserving trusting relationships between journalists and the public."[26]

Collaboration, community, relationships—the buzzwords of the built environment framed the many reports coming out of this built environment.[27] The key activity in this work has been listening; for example, in "How a Culture of Listening Strengthens Reporting and Relationships," the American Press Institute defined listening as "The process of seeking out the information needs, feedback and perspectives of the people in our areas of coverage. In particular, this emphasis on listening is meant to expand our attention to people and communities who feel alienated or have traditionally been marginalized by news coverage."[28] Over the past decade, a stark rise in hatred toward immigrants, people of color, and "others" globally as well as the discovery that mainstream journalists were startlingly disconnected from conservatives and other groups of people have laid bare the need to examine community polarization and difference within news brands. More and more we see explicit missions around expanding audiences and amplifying voices not typically heard in mainstream news.[29] And with those missions has come a commitment to understand how different identities—their politics, their ideologies, their biases and privileges—influence newsmaking and news content. As newsrooms have watched their subscriptions dwindle, publishers and editors noted the relevancy declines and understood the intense need to change.[30]

Through all of it is the ubiquitous presence of identity emphasis—a trend being captured by recent scholarship. In their 2022 book about the concept of autonomy in journalism, Henrik Örnebring and Michael Karlsson explore the historical underpinnings of how the mainstream Western press ended up perpetuating systems of oppression through objectivity. They argue that the value of autonomy was "paradoxical" in that "autonomy, intended to enable journalists to work in a professional fashion and empower them in relation to other social actors, has often done the ideological work of constraint and exclusion." The authors call for new thinking around what autonomy should actually mean for the transforming Western press, suggesting it is a concept that is relational, bounded, and actively constructed. The conception of an autonomous press was born when white, propertied, educated men reigned supreme and artificially declared themselves to be the very definition of independent, rational, and credible; other beings could not be autonomous for they did not reach full personhood.

> For most of U.S. history, the state only extended citizen's rights to male, white, landed gentry. Black people did not get full citizen rights until the 1960s. So who comprises the public and how far does—and should— journalism's loyalty to this public stretch? Sometimes journalists and observers of journalism frame this loyalty issue as a conflict between giving people what they want versus giving them what they need: if citizens demand naked celebrities all the time, should journalism loyally provide that? This framing underplays the importance of questioning the way actors define "the public" in the first place. The choice may not be so much about whether to give audiences naked celebrities or not, but whether to give audiences white supremacy or not.[31]

The calls for a reckoning within the mainstream Western press parallel those in many other industries and professions during the early 2000s, marked by the #MeToo movement in 2017 and the Black Lives Matter protests in 2020. As information producers throughout the globe struggle to retain authority, building trust among constituencies becomes about relationship building (moving from content transactions) where journalists show vulnerability, express respect, and engage themselves as much as they ask for engagement from audience members.

To recap, then, I restate my theory on trust building as it was being operationalized in the built environment during 2010–23 (and on) in the United States: **Trust building** happens through the nurturing of personal, organizational, and institutional relationships that people have with information, sources, news brands, journalists, and each other during what is commonly referred to as *engagement*. For trust building to occur, engagement needs to be practiced with *identity-aware care* and enacted through *listening* and *learning*. This trust building will be in constant flux in how it is practiced, what defines success, and who is responsible for the

ENGAGE   Inclusive conversations foster relationships between community members and journalists, sparking new insights.

REFLECT   Local media learn from engagement, better serves community needs. People see their lives reflected in the news.

VALUE   Public feels invested in local news coverage, devotes greater attention and support to the media. News outlets value public input.

SUSTAIN   Communities thrive when news outlets engage audiences regularly. An informed public engages in civic affairs.

Figure 6.2 Theory of change.
Sources: Free Press, Fiona Morgan, and News Voices Project.

trusting work. At the time of this writing in 2023, a critical mass of journalistic practitioners—reporters and editors as well as funders, nonprofits,
consultants, media watchers, and others—were working to shore up this
burgeoning built environment they have developed over the previous five
years. It is too soon to know if it will save the industry; this book is not about
that.[32] What we do know is that many millions of dollars from hundreds of
funders, investors, members, and newsrooms are being dedicated to shifting
away from objectivity as the foremost guiding principle in mainstream journalism in the United States and other Western countries. Instead, new values
are rising in prominence, becoming part of the fundamental norms and
routines in newsrooms—community grounded, engagement focused, identity configured, and care led.

As I consider the touchstones of this built environment, I keep going
back to Fiona Morgan of Branchhead Consulting, a pioneer in the built

HOW NEWS VOICES WORKS

We organize and build power with communities so people have a stronger voice in how local journalism can be revived, strengthened and transformed.

LISTEN   **AMPLIFY**   **BUILD**   **CHANGE**

LISTEN   Centering racial justice, we do intensive outreach, host inclusive conversations and lead forums to learn what news local communities need.

AMPLIFY   Through skill-building workshops, leadership development and newsroom engagement, we lift up vital community efforts and support quality journalism.

BUILD   We help civic groups, newsrooms and individuals pursue creative, collaborative projects that inform their communities and build lasting trust.

CHANGE   We shift the culture of local news by centering community. News consumers become constituents of journalism and find roles to play alongside journalists to strengthen local media and hold power accountable.

FP **Free Press**   News Voices   Learn more at newsvoices.org and by contacting newsvoices@freepress.net

Figure 6.3 Theory of change at work in News Voices.
Sources: Free Press, Fiona Morgan, and News Voices Project.

environment, intentionally and purposefully bringing the profession closer and closer to major revolution. In every project she did, connecting local media to their communities, to funders, and to each other, she kept in mind this paradigm shift she advocated for. She explained her theoretical framework to me as a "theory of change,"[33] having developed it in 2015 as part of her work with News Voices: New Jersey that laid out the project's underlying mission to transform journalism. As demonstrated in an illustration of the theory as it worked for News Voices (Figures 6.2 and 6.3), the participants began with the foremost activities of engaging and mobilizing people, nonprofits, community leaders, and government agents along with journalists, seeking to establish collaborations around pressing issues and identify possible policy solutions. These activities led to changes in awareness of the issues and possible resolutions, changes in capacity of actors through, for example, more diverse source relationships, changes in networks with a greater sense of shared agendas, and changes in local news content through and because of this immersive engagement between journalists and publics. This created, Morgan wrote, "a virtuous cycle" that is "developed between community engagement and reporters, resulting in better quality in local news."[34]

Outcomes included richer stories that were "more tailored" to the specific community being covered, in addition to more substantial initiatives, collaborations, and appreciation for all involved (especially journalism, as the link between local news and community was reified and fortified). News outlets should thus experience changes in resources through these collaborations as well as tested practices of community work that can be replicated for other issues. As a result, "an active network of people invested in the role of journalism can plan in building New Jersey's future."[35] In this project, I see encapsulated a how-to for the theory of trust building this built environment propels.

The Agora Journalism Center wrote a report about projects involved in trust building, figuring out new ways to be more community-centric and public-oriented. They had this to say about News Voices, which was one of the projects evaluated in the 2018 report: "For Free Press and News Voices, perhaps the clearest example of a trust-building practice is diversity. . . . Their community events are intentionally inclusive from the planning stages to the event itself, and the group of attendees is diverse. This is likely to result in communities' increasing trust in media as long as the journalists listen and, crucially, follow the stories they hear."[36]

The argument I am making in this book is that the most effective way for journalists to accomplish this listening work is to approach journalism with an identity-aware care, centering power dynamics and identity constructions, and letting those values guide any information exchange.

Of course, journalists struggle—and will always struggle—to meet these trust-building expectations, especially as the industry continually contracts and transforms. Although the vast majority of our journalists in small to midsize newsrooms accepted the new paradigm in principle, they also expressed extensive challenges to implementing this kind of trust-building work, from isolation in newsrooms in terms of mindset change to fiscal and time constraints. For example, we are seeing a major overhaul in how journalists are trained in this built environment, and it will take a while for that training to be complete—if it ever will be, for it will need to continue to evolve as communities' needs change. In addition, trust building demands consistency, and many of our change agents said the constant turnover in newsrooms inhibits true trust from building among communities; just as communities get to know one reporter, a new one takes their place. This is a huge limitation and a reason it is important to make this work part of the brand—indeed, a core part of the profession's norms—so that all reporters and editors are practicing as such, foundationally.

Another significant consideration about trust building has to do with intentionality in the public information-exchange spaces around the world. There may come a day when engagement via digital technologies is subsumed into the culture so as to become invisible—a cycle that starts with innovation but quickly progresses to capitalized commodity, whose initial promise becomes co-opted and perverted by controlling agents like corporations and governments.[37] People who engage in trust building will always have ulterior motives. I have helped categorize the very open and benevolent front stage of trust-building work.[38] Lots of work around information exchange is necessary and genuine, seeking to bolster an informed democracy. However, at the back end (stage) we have for-profit corporations hoping to monetize that trust in other, often hidden ways. At another extreme, we have malevolent political and other operatives seeking to build trust so that the misinformation they provide will be accepted as fact.[39] And still others build trust by appealing to fear and anger, playing into people's baser instincts and the groupthink we are all susceptible to.[40] If these people (and bots, political sites, pundits, conspiracy theorists, and entire countries) succeed in their endeavors (and there is much evidence to demonstrate they are succeeding, at least among certain segments of the population), the art of trust building must continue to morph and stay relevant and journalists will have to adapt.

We do know this, though: the previous ways of trust building through sustained and reliable transmission of accurate information over time no longer will foster journalistic authority.[41] The industry and its affiliates, including journalism schools, have a theory about what to do, and that work is well underway, as documented in this book. It is changing at all levels of the practice of newsmaking: the systems level of media culture and professional communities, the meso level of newsrooms and funders and J-schools, the micro individual level of the trade bloggers, consultants, reporters, publishers, journalism students, and professors. The built environment will constantly change as new technologies and audience expectations take hold. What matters, reminded our change agents, is how journalists are positioning themselves for those changes, as Fiona Morgan said to me in our interview: "So even if it feels like it's not yielding results really quickly, for good or bad, all the work that you do builds up over time. And it's that work that we should be evaluating. Unlike a lot of reporting, where it's fast-paced, and it keeps turning over, community work is cumulative." At the core of this paradigmatic shift has arisen an ethic of care, manifested through listening and in consideration of identities. Perhaps this more human-based value system for journalism will find relevancy with the changing media culture at hand.

One morning in June 2022, Sarah Gagnon[42] met me at a downtown coffeeshop in Madison to discuss our Journalism Game project, the one I described in Chapter 4 as part of a media literacy effort to get middle school kids to understand how journalistic knowledge is made. The game[43] is a text-based adventure schematic, similar to a traditional "choose-your-own-adventure" books. Explained Sarah, "Unlike some knowledge, journalistic knowledge is knowledge that is constructed objectively but also subjectively. How the community responds to the journalist during the creating of the story and the reading of the story is part of that knowledge creation. This was the concept of the game, from my point of view, and how the trust mechanic became so significant." The player would be the journalist navigating a flood in a small town, trying to meet deadlines while gathering quality content and building trust on the fly. We had already done several rounds of testing with kids, and one of the consistent pieces of feedback was "It's not fair" when they ran out of time and their story was deemed "shoddy" by the editor character. Wrote one middle schooler on their evaluation, "The least fun moment of the game for me was when you were able to pick who to talk to as a source of information but when you talk with them, they don't give you any information."

Sarah looked at me and said, "I love that, that they are getting to this 'it's not fair' understanding in the game. What they miss is that the system journalists are working under is unfair." She added that she was working on how to make sure the kids moved from the *game* not being fair to the concept that newsmaking is hard work, especially dealing with unpredictable sources and settings. Built into the game were all kinds of minefields for the reporter character that involved intense interactions with community members, with the need to build trust at every stage. Threaded throughout were constant opportunities for the reporter to work their journalism through caring acts, such as the option to help a neighbor herd their escaping chickens or to join in sandbagging the riverbank. Each time the reporter chose to give care, they were rewarded with a quality quote or access to information. Interestingly, this was not an explicit suggestion from me or the other journalist consultants but came about naturally as the game storytellers thought about how trust today might be built. Caring through every level helped the reporter overcome the assumptions people in the town made about the reporter's identities: that they were too young to be able to help or too new to the town to want to help. Caring through every level meant you built enough trust to earn information. Caring meant you won the game.

Appendix

30 Trust-Focused Initiatives Sampling: Case Studies

AGA Khan Foundation	First Draft	News Integrity Initiative
Agora Journalism Center	Google News Labs	News Voices
ANSPSCH	The Ground Truth Project/ Report For America	PRI's *The World*
Ask a . . .	Hearken	Solutions Journalism Network
Building Trust in Media in South East Europe and Turkey	Journalism That Matters	Spaceship Media
Center for Media Engagement (Engaging News Project)	Knight Commission on Media, Trust & Democracy	Trusting News
Coral Project	The Media Trust Project	Voting Block
WBEZ Chicago's *Curious City*	Melting Mountains: The Seattle-Sherman Country Road Trip	What's Next, West Virginia
Democracy Fund	Membership Puzzle Project	Year of Listening
Ethical Journalism Network	The Ground Trust Project/ Report for America	Your Voice Ohio

In this Appendix I explain the story of the multiphased methodology for this book, as it unfolded since 2018. I began with my umbrella questions: How are journalists trying to build trust with people, and how does the traditional reporting job have to change to accommodate that trust building? Then I wanted to understand how journalists as individuals in real-world newsrooms could implement that work. And finally, I hypothesized that individual journalists would go about this trust-building work differently according to their own identities, as I posed the simple but as yet unasked question: How do journalists trust people? I investigated these questions via three phases of inquiry, mixing qualitative and quantitative methods under a massive protocol from the University of Wisconsin–Madison's Institutional Review Board.[1] Sixteen undergraduate and graduate students worked on various parts, and I could not have completed this project without them. I name them all in the acknowledgments.

In the first phase, during 2018, my research team and I collected 25 complete case studies of initiatives (culled from an original 55 entities), programs, and projects aimed at rebuilding trust between journalists and their audiences to understand the common ingredients of engagement. This number later expanded to 30 as I stumbled over other projects. Using the qualitative software NVIVO, we textually analyzed all the material about these projects in the trade press, on their websites, and in social media. We also interviewed the projects' founders and directors or managers, about 28 people in all. From these projects, a long list of strategies emerged—most of them found to be successful at building trust among news audiences and most of them involving the development of individual relationships between reporters and their communities. From this list, I topologized the eight new skill sets—radical transparency, power dynamic accounting, mediation, reciprocity, media literacies, community offline work, needs/assets/solution analyses, and collaborative production—and the four new roles that journalists needed to learn: relationship builder, community collaborator, conversation facilitator, and professional network builder. For this first phase of the project, money from my endowed research chair, the Helen Firstbrook Franklin, paid for $20 Amazon gift card incentives for those we interviewed (most declined the incentive) as well as the students' time to document and analyze all of this.

We took these strategies into the second phase of the project in 2019, presenting them to reporters and editors across the nation in in-depth interviews, focus groups, and surveys, with participants mostly at small and midsize news outlets. We asked questions—Have you ever done this? Would you ever do it? Would your newsroom allow you to do this?— as well as asking them to describe their own strategies for building trust, their thoughts about engagement, and how they considered their audiences. In all we connected with 174 journalists at small to midsize news outlets (including freelancers) via a survey (106 respondents), interviews (47), and focus groups (20). We found these through (1) a Cision database of journalists that I paid to get access to; (2) requests through Twitter, several listservs, and Facebook group pages; and (3) snowball sampling from the journalists who participated. Those who interviewed with us received $25 Amazon gift cards and those who did the survey got $20. The focus groups were conducted at the Online News Association conference and the National Newspaper Association in fall 2019. I used funding from my endowed research chair for the travel, room rentals, incentives, and student workers.

In all, 65% of our sample was white, 20% Hispanic or Latino/a/x, 8% African American or Black, 10% Asian, and the rest mixed race. About 50% were 20–35, 20% 30–50, 20% 51–65, and 10% 66–75. They were evenly distributed across the United States, the majority in newsrooms with circulations between 50,000 and 150,000, but a wide variety of newsroom sizes. Sixty percent were female, 39% male, and 1% nonbinary. More than 80% had a college or postgraduate degree, most in journalism. The people we talked to said they were either Christian (44%), Jewish (5%), agnostic (13%), atheist (10%), or didn't have a religion (30%), and about 9% were "other." And though the vast majority said they leaned left politically, almost all said they tried to maintain "neutrality" by bracketing political beliefs in their jobs. About 20% of our sample identified as LGBTQ; the majority of respondents came from middle- or lower-middle-class families growing up. We also had a broad range of platforms participating with the majority in print and online, but radio and television were also well represented.

The same set of questions was used in all the interviews, surveys, and focus groups, asking participants their thoughts about what engagement meant to them, how they engaged, how they thought about building trust, obstacles to trust building, obstacles to engagement, etc. For each engagement strategy, we asked whether they already did them, were willing to do them, or would be able to do them. Open-ended questions asked about their role conceptions as a journalist. All of this data—from the Phase 1 case studies and Phase 2 of journalist interviewing—went into NVIVO, where we created a codebook breaking down the dimensions of trust, engagement, identity, care, listening, and learning. I used critical discourse analysis[2] (CDA) to appreciate how the material created an overarching professional metadiscourse of the relationship between these concepts and practice. From this material, I could understand what was feasible and not feasible in the newsrooms. I also discovered from this work that journalists' individual identities— not only racial but also their income and their journalism education—influenced how they went about engagement and other trust-building practices. And I could explore the interconnections between trust building with engaging, identity-aware, and caring practices of listening and learning as well.

Next, I wanted to apply the learning in real-world settings. The third phase happened in two parts during 2020 and 2021. In the first part, I took on the research lead with the Citizens Agenda/Election SOS project, the brainchild of New York University professor Jay Rosen of the Membership Puzzle Project with the Hearken engagement firm. Rosen was resurrecting the public journalism movement from the 1990s—an attempt to reimagine the relationship between journalists and their publics and one Rosen himself had played a key role in conceptualizing and promoting. Rosen and Hearken formed a consortium dream team with the Trusting News newsroom training program run by Joy Mayer. The Citizens Agenda Guide offered journalists a blueprint for changing election coverage, centering coverage on people's needs rather than horserace coverage. They asked me to help lead the research of the project. With grants from Democracy Fund, Solutions Journalism Network, and other funders, we trained more than a 100 journalists in engagement practices, which were formalized in the Guide as well as in my list of engagement strategies. During each of five cohorts of training from May through September 2020, I was able to give my own list of engagement strategies, separated into low-effort and high-effort categories, to the groups of journalists, derived from Phase 1 and honed during Phase 2.

At the end of 2020 and into 2021, my research team and I, along with Hearken, analyzed how it all went, doing in-depth interviews and surveys of participants to find out the challenges and successes of such a guide and my list going forward. Members of Hearken's Election SOS team conducted 21 interviews with cohort participants in February 2021. The interviews took about 45 minutes and were run from a standard script of questions about election coverage and experience in the training program. The interviewees came from 18 newsrooms. I received secondary data set approval from my Institutional Review Board to access this data in an agreement with Hearken since my team did not engage in collecting this data. In addition, my team surveyed 30 additional Citizens Agenda participants who implemented some version of Citizens Agenda in fall 2020 from 30 newsrooms:

- 11% less than 5,000 circulation, 11% 5,000–25,000, 7% 25,000–50,000, 22% 50,000–150,000, 7% 150,000–500,000, 18% more than 500,000, 25% (either don't know or not applicable)
- 32% 1–5 editorial employees, 32% 6–15, 11% 16–30, 7% 31–50, 7% 51–100, 11% more than 100
- 60% female, 32% male, 4% transgender male, 4% nonbinary
- 4% under 20, 47% 20–35, 32% 36–50, 11% 51–65, 7% 66–75

- 61% white, 14% Black, 11% Hispanic, 7% Asian, 7% mixed race
- 14% LGBTQ, 75% not LGBTQ, 11% prefer not to say or other
- 11% less than $20,000 household income, 7% $20,000–34,000, 22% $35,000–49,000, 18% $50,000–74,999, 11% $75,000–99,999, 32% over $100,000
- 67% J-school grad, 33% not
- 25% living in Northeast, 7% Northwest, 18% Southeast, 22% Southwest, 22% Midwest, 7% outside of United States

I provided $25 gift cards to interviewees from my various research funds.

In the second part of Phase 3, I developed four teaching modules for reporting instructors—Basic Engagement Strategies, Power and Privilege, Content Collaboration and Community Conversation Facilitation—based on this prior research. Included in the modules were PowerPoint presentations, in-class exercises, assignments, readings, and discussion prompts.[3] I sent out word that I had these ready for implementation in fall 2020 classrooms, hoping to get five professors interested. By the time I was done, I had a network of more than 120 journalism instructors and professors interested, and 14 instructors willing to implement some of the modules in their fall reporting courses—such was the interest in engagement work. I also taught some of the module material in my own advanced reporting class during fall 2020. After the semester, my research team and I interviewed all the professors who participated and surveyed their students, 160 in all, to document the outcomes. I provided $20 Amazon gift cards to both the professors and the students who completed the surveys, funded from my endowed research chair.

As such, I became a participant observer of these initiatives, attending engagement events, helping to train newsrooms in engagement strategies, and participating in the creation of a network of people interested in making engagement fundamental for journalism. I took all the texts of the data—transcripts, survey responses, training recordings, etc.—and again uploaded them to NVIVO, using the same coding scheme to process the material for understanding the deep concepts underneath the engagement work and also to revise the strategies for new iterations. This learning will inform, for example, work I am doing with Trusting News in 2022–23, asking newsrooms to implement small parts of these engagement, transparency, and other trust-building strategies as well as training journalists in different aspects of them. It also informed a new collaborative project between Hearken and Solutions Journalism Network ahead of the midterm November 2022 elections to train 22 newsrooms in new engagement practices for the coverage. As such, this would be considered "action-based research," which means the work is pragmatic, embedded in working newsrooms as laboratories. Furthermore, this applied research manifests what we call the Wisconsin Idea at the University of Wisconsin–Madison—that is, the notion that all the research, teaching, and service we do extends beyond the borders of campus in order to improve the world around us, outside of the academy.

I should also mention that I embarked on this book during the Trump presidency—a time of aggressive physical and political attacks on mainstream journalists as well as increased incidents of misogyny and racism throughout the United States, emboldened by the environment of hate. That tense period from 2016 to 2020 gave way to the start in March 2020 of what would be a multiyear pandemic that shut down the entire world for periods of time (a pandemic still in play at the time I am writing this). And then came the Russian attack on Ukraine and the intense worry that a World War III with nuclear weapons waited on the horizon. All of this impacted trust building and how it was being enacted in newsrooms, not to mention the capacity of journalists, journalism students, and journalism instructors everywhere. For example, the incredible pressure of all of this and what it meant for the unprecedented news cycle during fall 2020 prevented a more robust implementation of the Citizens Agenda Guide and other engagement strategies in newsrooms. We all just made the best of it. This book represents the learning from all of it, in the hopes we can work toward a more inclusive journalism that can produce a shared set of facts about public affairs in these important times.

Notes

Prologue

1. I was still working in a newsroom during my PhD program. I do not recommend that, by the way.
2. Swift, "Americans' Trust in Mass Media Sinks to New Low"; Gallup Inc. and Knight Foundation, "State of Public Trust in Local Media."
3. Quandt, "Dark Participation."
4. Bennett and Pfetsch, "Rethinking Political Communication in a Time of Disrupted Public Spheres."
5. Bennett and Livingston, "The Disinformation Order."
6. Carlson, *Journalistic Authority*; Carlson, Robinson, and Lewis, *News after Trump*.
7. See, for example, the viral article by Wesley Lowery, "A Reckoning over Objectivity, Led by Black Journalists."
8. Snider, "You're More Likely to Trust News from a Trusted Facebook Friend."
9. Editorial Board, "The Facts on Trump's Fraud Letter."
10. I will go into all of this more when I explain how scholars, particularly Joan Tronto in *Caring Democracy*, have theorized the ethic of care as the practice of the following qualities: attentiveness (knowing the needs of others by attending to others), responsibility (feeling responsible for others' care), competence (adopting an ethic of care, which requires action with appropriate resources and effort), responsiveness (adjusting our caregiving specifically for the person or entity at hand and not by simply imagining what needs we ourselves might have), and solidarity (collectively understanding and accepting that care is essential to a working democracy and a thriving humanity).

Chapter 1

1. National Newspaper Association, "Media Guide 2020." I should note that the NNA does not keep track of its members' race, gender, and age (personal communication, 2021). The photos of the board and staff are all of people who present as white, with the exception with one female-presenting person who may be a woman of color.
2. It is available at https://theevergrey.com/.
3. Its website is https://resolvephilly.org/.
4. You may note the absence of "politics" in this list of identities. The problem is very few journalists identified as conservative in the samples we drew. As such, it was difficult

to determine whether conservative journalists approached fieldwork differently than their liberal counterparts. Given that these other identities mattered—especially race and education—we can assume it would make a difference. Certainly, as I mention in Chapter 3, their *assumed* liberal status affected how sources and audiences responded to them. I plan to go deeper into this question in a future book.

5. You can read details of my methods in the appendix.

6. I asked a few working in this field to look at the list and add to it. For inclusion in the list, the initiative's primary goal had to be trust building in journalism or news. We ended up with about 55 trust-specific entities operating in 2017–21, the list is outdated, changing every day as some programs end or die, organizations align, and new opportunities emerge. Not included are dozens of organizations that have other ongoing initiatives and one-off projects that contribute to the theory of trust building today.

7. I am so excited for a book by Andrea Wenzel, tentatively titled *Making News Antiracist*, forthcoming as of this writing, that documents this part of the built environment.

8. The phrase "built environment" was settled on after much reading, thinking, and consulting with people familiar with all of this, including Drs. Regina Lawrence, Chris Anderson, Andrea Wenzel, and Anthony Nadler. I will delve into this metaphor and its limitations—as well as other terms I considered and rejected—in Chapter 2.

9. Though, as you will see in Chapter 3, the journalists we talked to thought about identity very broadly, in some cases talking about their identities as being pet owners or parents or book lovers.

10. Thank you, anonymous reviewers and readers! See my acknowledgments for those I can name.

11. I will use generic labels like "white," "Black," "Brown," "Asian," etc. to describe people's or group identities when I either do not know the specific heritage or when I want to be inclusive for groups. Whenever possible, I will use more specific identities, such as "African American" or "Mexican" or "Chinese." I capitalize all labels except "white" to signal that we are talking about constructed identities. I do not capitalize "white" in order to symbolize my rejection of the commonly capitalized "White Supremacy." This article in *The Atlantic* influenced me on this decision: Appiah, "The Case for Capitalizing the 'B' in Black."

12. To help make sure this book is not singularly "whitewashed," that is, ignorant of perspectives about this reckoning, I combined my own identity, bias, and privilege trainings with reading and teaching widely on these topics. One of my anonymous reviewers at Oxford University Press called me out in an early draft for being too dismissive of scholarship and journalism writings about journalists of color and ethnic media—something I tried to resolve in my revisions. In addition, I hired an African American scholar knowledgeable in both journalism and journalism studies, especially race and ethnicity studies, to give each chapter a "sensitivity read," looking for unintentional microaggressions, places where I missed or inaccurately assumed the perspectives of "others," or where my own positionality obscured or stunted my insights. I am sure there are still problematic statements and assumptions being made, and I apologize for those. If you see any, I would so love to hear about it so that I may learn and do better next time.

13. This is a strong statement that might put off some people. I detailed what I mean by this in my 2018 book, *Networked News, Racial Divides: How Power and Privilege Shape Public Discourse in Progressive Communities.*

14. Many scholars have begun this reckoning in other publications as well: Callison and Young (2020), *Reckoning;* Robinson, *Networked News* (2018); Ramasubramanian, "#CommunicationSoWhite"; Chakravartty et al., "#CommunicationSoWhite"; Ng, White, and Saha, "#CommunicationSoWhite"; Usher, *News for the Rich, White, and Blue.*

15. You can download the Citizens Agenda guide from the Hearken website, at least as of 2022: https://www.thecitizensagenda.org/download. You can read a bit about what we did in this medium post and this Hearken report: Thoreson, "Citizens Agenda in Action"; Thoreson et al., "Election SOS."

16. The four modules are currently titled "Power & Privilege," "Content Collaboration," "Community Conversation Facilitation," and "Basic Engagement Strategies." They include PowerPoint presentations, readings, assignments, classroom exercises, handouts, discussion prompts, and other material for reporting instructors, and they can be found at https://suerobinson.org/teaching/. Feel free to take whatever you need for them, simply crediting The Journalism Educator Collaborative.

17. Maras, *Objectivity in Journalism;* Mindich, *Just the Facts;* Ward, "Inventing Objectivity."

18. Brenan, "Americans' Trust in Media Dips to Second Lowest on Record."

19. Edelman, "2021 Edelman Trust Barometer."

20. Gottfried, "Republicans Less Likely to Trust Their Main News Source If They See It as 'Mainstream.'"

21. Fioroni, "Skeptics or Cynics?"

22. Gallup Inc. and Knight Foundation, "State of Public Trust in Local Media."

23. Brenan, "Americans' Trust in Media Dips to Second Lowest on Record."

24. Carlson, Robinson, and Lewis, *News after Trump;* Carlson, *Journalistic Authority.*

25. Pew Research Center, "Black, White and Hispanic Americans Give Very Different Reasons for Why They Feel the News Media Don't Understand Them."

26. Husband, "Minority Ethnic Media as Communities of Practice"; Yu, "Ethnic Media as Communities of Practice"; Matsaganis and Katz, "How Ethnic Media Producers Constitute Their Communities of Practice"; Matsaganis, Katz, and Ball-Rokeach, *Understanding Ethnic Media.*

27. Ornebring, "Anything You Can Do, I Can Do Better?"; Kohring and Matthes, "Trust in News Media"; Furlan, "Who Can You Trust?"

28. See the Aspen Institute report by Rousseau et al., "Not So Different after All"; Hauser and Benoit-Barne, "Reflections on Rhetoric, Deliberative Democracy, Civil Society, and Trust"; and Lenard, *Trust, Democracy, and Multicultural Challenges.* All of these highlight the proposition that this level of trust depends on taking a risk, despite feeling vulnerable.

29. Gopal, "Understanding Trust to Strengthen Democracy."

30. Pew Research Center, "Trends and Facts on Newspapers"; Hare, "The Coronavirus Has Closed More Than 70 Local Newsrooms across America."

31. Some follow-up studies have shown that most people think of cable news when asked about "news media"; in fact, when specifically asked about their local paper, they report significantly higher levels of trust.

32. Quandt, "Dark Participation"; Carlson, Robinson, and Lewis, *News after Trump*.

33. Gopal, "Understanding Trust to Strengthen Democracy."

34. Kilgore, "Trump's Long Campaign to Steal the Presidency"; Woodward, "AP Fact Check."

35. U.S. Department of Homeland Security, "National Terrorism Advisory System Bulletin."

36. Enten, "Polls Show Majority of Republicans Mistakenly Think the 2020 Election Wasn't Legitimate."

37. National Intelligence Council, "Foreign Threats to the 2020 US Federal Elections."

38. See Belair-Gagnon, Nelson, and Lewis, "Audience Engagement, Reciprocity, and the Pursuit of Community Connectedness in Public Media Journalism" (2018).

39. Batsell, *Engaged Journalism*, 145.

40. Mersey, Malthouse, and Calder, "Focusing on the Reader."

41. Belair-Gagnon, Nelson, and Lewis, "Audience Engagement, Reciprocity, and the Pursuit of Community Connectedness in Public Media Journalism" (2018), 558.

42. Nelson and Schmidt, "Taking the Audience Seriously?"; Nelson, *Imagined Audiences*; Schmidt, Nelson, and Lawrence, "Conceptualizing the Active Audience."

43. Again, see Nelson and Schmidt, "Taking the Audience Seriously?," for a fuller accounting of the differences between these kinds of engagement.

44. Guzmán, "What Exactly Is Engagement and What Difference Does It Make?"

45. Lawrence et al., "Building Engagement."

46. Xia, Robinson, Zahay, and Freelon, "The Evolving Journalistic Roles on Social Media." Thank you to *Journalism Practice* for allowing me to use parts of that article in this book.

47. Lewis, Holton, and Coddington, "Reciprocal Journalism," 229.

48. Ferrucci, "Networked," 11.

49. Uslaner and Brown, "Inequality, Trust, and Civic Engagement."

50. McManus and Mosca, "Strategies to Build Trust and Improve Employee Engagement."

51. Xia et al., "The Evolving Journalistic Roles on Social Media"; Molyneux and Mourão, "Political Journalists' Normalization of Twitter"; Van der Wurff and Schoenbach, "Civic and Citizen Demands of News Media and Journalists"; Neilson, "'I Don't Engage.'"

52. Nelson, *Imagined Audiences*; Quandt, "Dark Participation"; Schmidt, Nelson, and Lawrence, "Conceptualizing the Active Audience"; Schmidt and Lawrence, "Engaged Journalism and News Work"; Wenzel, "Public Media and Marginalized Publics"; Schmidt and Lawrence, "Putting Engagement to Work."

53. Schmidt, Nelson, and Lawrence, "Conceptualizing the Active Audience"; Nelson, *Imagined Audiences*.

54. Nelson, "The Next Media Regime."

55. Hearken, "Our Founding Story."

56. Brandel, "Newsrooms Are Focused on Innovating the Distribution of News"; Hearken, "Our Founding Story."

57. Ore, "Whiteness as a Racialized Space."

58. Newkirk, *Within the Veil*; Dolan, "Whiteness and News"; Blaagaard, "Journalism of Relation."

59. Smith, "Inside the Revolts Erupting in America's Big Newsrooms."

60. Smith, "Inside the Revolts Erupting in America's Big Newsrooms."

61. National Advisory Commission on Civil Disorders, *The Kerner Report*; Tully, Vraga, and Smithson, "News Media Literacy, Perceptions of Bias, and Interpretation of News"; Woods, Prince, and Chideya, "If Journalists Value Diversity Why Are Newsrooms So White?"

62. Friedlich, "Lessons from The Philadelphia Inquirer's Content Audit."

63. *New York Times*, "Making a More Diverse, Equitable and Inclusive New York Times."

64. Jensen, "Kessler Interview Puts Spotlight on How to Cover Racist Viewpoints."

65. And, of course, the opposite is also true: how we *receive* attempts at engagement is also shaped by our identities—this we have known.

66. Black, Brown, and other journalists of color working at ethnic publications have long centered identity in coverage decisions. I will talk about this more in the next chapter as well. For a discussion of this, see Andrea Wenzel's *Community-Centered Journalism*, especially 31–33.

67. Brown, "Philadelphia Inquirer Journalists Walk Out over 'Buildings Matter, Too' Headline."

68. Giddens, *Modernity and Self-Identity*, 53.

69. Castells, *The Power of Identity*.

70. Atske et al., "7 Facts about Black Americans and the News Media."

71. Wilner et al., "News Distrust among Black Americans Is a Fixable Problem."

72. Gallup Inc. and Knight Foundation, "American Views 2020."

73. Mitchell et al., "How Americans Get Their News."

74. Shah and Thornton, *Newspaper Coverage of Interethnic Conflict*; Squires, "Rethinking the Black Public Sphere"; Squires, *African Americans and the Media*; Atton, *Alternative Media*; Srinivasan, "Indigenous, Ethnic and Cultural Articulations of New Media."

75. Robinson, *Networked News* (2018); Callison and Young, *Reckoning* (2020).

76. Clardy, "Civic Tenderness as a Response to Child Poverty in America," 319.

77. As the same time as I was reading about an ethic of care, I was writing another book with two friends (see Carlson, Robinson, and Lewis, *News after Trump*) and was grappling with what a moral voice in journalism might sound like. I took my first stabs at how that might play out in that publication and am advancing it for this project, using an identity-aware ethic of care as the moral vessel to journalistic practice.

78. Gilligan, *In a Different Voice*.

79. Tronto, *Moral Boundaries*.

80. Cannon, *Black Womanist Ethics*.

81. Collins, *Black Feminist Thought*.

82. Jackson, "Black Psychology," 247–49.

83. Nobles, "Extended Self," 19.

84. Bloom, *Jewish Relational Care A–Z*.

85. Susan and Michael, *Care, Community and Citizenship*. See also Howard, Lopez-Franco, and Wheeler, "Participatory Monitoring and Accountability and the Sustainable Development Goals."

86. Shaw, Howard, and Franco, "Building Inclusive Community Activism and Accountable Relations through an Intersecting Inequalities Approach," 10.
87. For more about the supposed dichotomy between behaving according to a sense of justice and with an ethic of care, check out especially McBride, "The Ethics of Justice and Care in the American Media"; Young and Allen, *Justice and the Politics of Difference*; Tronto, *Caring Democracy*; Held and Oberbrunner, *Justice and Care*.
88. We see this play out in the US criminal justice system: a criminal must serve time as a form of justice, where many people who break the law have done so because they have lacked the necessary caring to be productive (e.g., lacking food, money, housing, sobriety, education, guidance).
89. Mindich, *Just the Facts*; Powell, *Racing to Justice*.
90. Tronto, *Moral Boundaries*; Tronto, *Caring Democracy*.
91. This chapter is based off a journal article I published with some of the research team in *Journalism Studies*, in 2021 with Kelly Jensen and Carlos Dávalos. Thank you to *Journalism Studies* for allowing us to reprint some of it.
92. Hearken, "The Citizens Agenda."
93. See https://suerobinson.org/teaching/.
94. Here I give a shoutout to UW-Madison undergraduate research scholar, Rachel Reingold, for her help with these interviews, coding, and analyses.
95. These numbers are arbitrary and do not indicate either ranking or chronology.
96. Graves, "Deciding What's True," 8.
97. Vos and Craft, "The Discursive Construction of Journalistic Transparency"; Haapanen, "Problematising the Restoration of Trust through Transparency"; Karlsson, "Rituals of Transparency."
98. Wenzel, *Community-Centered Journalism*; Wenzel, "Making News Antiracist"; Belair-Gagnon, Nelson, and Lewis, "Audience Engagement, Reciprocity, and the Pursuit of Community Connectedness in Public Media Journalism" (2018); Konieczna, *Journalism without Profit*.
99. Wenzel, "Making News Antiracist"; Callison and Young, *Reckoning*.
100. Beverly et al., "Video and Recap."
101. Ferrucci, "Exploring Public Service Journalism"; Lamuedra, Martín, and Broullón-Lozano, "Normative and Audience Discourses on Public Service Journalism at a 'Critical Juncture'"; Riaz, "Journalism Crisis."
102. Hooley, "What's Working."
103. Vasquez, "Is Movement Journalism What's Needed During This Reckoning over Race and Inequality?"; Simonton, "Out of Struggle."
104. Vasquez, "Is Movement Journalism What's Needed During This Reckoning over Race and Inequality?"
105. Varma, "Evoking Empathy or Enacting Solidarity with Marginalized Communities?"; Varma, "Solidarity in U.S. Journalism."
106. I am leaving out public journalism from the late 1990s because I am only exploring the contemporary movements still in play, ones that are organized and intentionally built out at the time of this writing in 2023. However, it goes without saying that many of these movements had their genesis in the public journalism movement that

died in the early 2000s. Ferrucci, "Public Journalism No More"; Ferrucci, Nelson, and Davis, "From 'Public Journalism' to 'Engaged Journalism.'"

107. Belair-Gagnon, Nelson, and Lewis, "Audience Engagement, Reciprocity, and the Pursuit of Community Connectedness in Public Media Journalism" (2019); Batsell, *Engaged Journalism*; Schmidt and Lawrence, "Putting Engagement to Work"; Guzmán, "What Exactly Is Engagement and What Difference Does It Make?"

108. Bass, "The Evolution of Solutions Journalism"; Solutions Journalism Network website; Powers and Curry, "No Quick Fix."

109. I say "most" because I hesitate to lump the fact-checking industry in with all of these, as it is focused on content. However, part of my argument is that consumers and journalists alike are being asked to be hyperfocused on engaging with all parts of journalism, including the content. The fact-checking profession has not only used technology and other affordances to debunk misinformation but has also created vast networks and collaborations within the news media and also with audiences to focus attention on these endeavors—all in the name of building trust in mainstream information through media literacy.

110. See the website https://www.solutionsjournalism.org/ for more information.

111. Varma, "Evoking Empathy or Enacting Solidarity with Marginalized Communities?"; Varma, "Solidarity in Action."

112. So much has been written showing how the press not only enabled but made room for these problematic politicians, but start with White's *The Branding of Right-Wing Activism* and Carlson, Robinson, and Lewis' *News after Trump*.

Chapter 2

1. Indeed, journalism studies scholarship has already begun documenting this incredible and ubiquitous shift, as Nelson and Schmidt point out in their 2022 ICA paper, "Taking the Audience Seriously."

2. Cassidy, "Media Culpa?"

3. Ingber, "The U.S. Now Ranks as a 'Problematic' Place for Journalists."

4. Hendrickson, "Local Journalism in Crisis."

5. The challenges with public journalism were well catalogued and analyzed: Voakes, "Civic Duties"; Haas and Steiner, "Public Journalism"; Ferrucci, "Public Journalism No More." Although certainly this current movement may have been seeded in that time period, I see what is happening now as much more integrated at all levels of the industry with much more money and participation. Furthermore, public journalism centered a very particular public—an ideal and informationally engaged public. Although focus groups of engaged community members helped develop, source, and critique stories, public journalism did not really involve a paradigm shift in terms of a value system or evolution in practices fundamentally. Ferrucci would disagree: Ferrucci, Nelson, and Davis, "From 'Public Journalism' to 'Engaged Journalism.'" They suggest that the "spirit" of public journalism has endured in

engagement journalism, and I do agree. But this trust-focused built environment far expands this original notion, entailing a much more expansive view of what we mean by "the public."

6. Many worried the term "Citizens" in the title would turn off some of the very people they hoped to reach: undocumented immigrants. As such, Rosen and the team encouraged newsrooms to pick whatever name they wanted, and many did; for example, as one Midwestern news outlet chose "Peoples Agenda."

7. One of the biggest disappointments and challenges related to the research part of this project was that it was not well funded. My university and department funded small parts of it (some interviews, the survey) through my endowed chair as well as a big internal award called the H. I. Romnes Faculty Fellowship. But it was not enough to really evaluate how much the trainings changed actual content. Democracy Fund helped Hearken with the trainings and newsroom incentives but declined to include money to formally evaluate the outcomes. Regina Lawrence, while keeping abreast of the project, faded to the background as she became editor of *Political Communication* and her work took her in other directions. I stayed on the project for this book as Hearken agreed that I could sit in on all the trainings and have access to the data from training surveys and other materials for this book, as long as I also shared my data with them and provided my expertise where warranted. I wrote more about this participant observation and community-based research in the appendix as well as in Chapters 5 and 6.

8. But none from the Global South, Russia, or Asia. These were all Western projects, largely, though some of their work extended into other geographic realms. A significant limitation, this data was very Western-centric.

9. Special thanks to Dr. Regina Lawrence at the Agora Journalism Center and the University of Oregon for helping me frame this chapter in a journal article we did together. I am not sure she is convinced that this is the right term for what we are seeing, but she certainly pushed me to be more precise and sophisticated in my justification.

10. Tronto, *Caring Democracy.*

11. First Draft News, "About."

12. Crunchbase, "First Draft News."

13. First Draft News, "About."

14. Called Verificado.uy: First Draft News, "Verificado.UY."

15. First Draft News, "Vaccines and Misinformation."

16. Morgan, "Residents and Reporters Discuss Inequity in Charlotte."

17. See https://mediareparations.org/about/.

18. Kaklauskas and Gudauskas, "Intelligent Decision-Support Systems and the Internet of Things for the Smart Built Environment."

19. Jackson, Dannenberg, and Frumkin, "Health and the Built Environment"; Lopez, *The Built Environment and Public Health.*

20. Kaklauskas and Gudauskas, "Intelligent Decision-Support Systems and the Internet of Things for the Smart Built Environment"; Shrouf and Miragliotta, "Energy Management Based on Internet of Things."

21. Thank you to Dr. Regina Lawrence from the University of Oregon for spending a lot of time talking this out with me throughout 2021. She worked really hard to convince me "ecosystem" was not the word we needed to describe the engagement work happening in the field. One gorgeous morning in September 2021, I happened to be in Portland, and she met me at an eclectic coffee shop where we Zoomed with Dr. Chris Anderson from the University of Leeds to discuss the term and its possible replacements. What fun it all was.

22. In journalism studies alone, check out Goddard, "Towards an Archaeology of Media Ecologies"; Ramos et al., "Mapping Emerging News Networks"; Wiard, "News Ecology and News Ecosystems"; Anderson, Coleman, and Thumin, "How News Travels; Domingo, Masip, and Wahl-Jorgensen, "Mapping the Digital News Ecosystem"; Graeff, Stempeck, and Zuckerman, "The Battle for 'Trayvon Martin'"; Kelly, "Parsing the Online Ecosystem"; Picard, "Twilight or New Dawn of Journalism?"; Ruotsalainen and Heinonen, "Media Ecology and the Future Ecosystemic Society."

23. Nadler, "Nature's Economy and News Ecology," 833.

24. Personal communication, 2022.

25. Quick shoutout here to Andrea and Tony, who both had toddlers at home and were navigating the pandemic, child care, *and* this conceptualization session. I was in awe.

26. Basta and Moroni, *Ethics, Design and Planning of the Built Environment*; Yaneva and Zaera-Polo, *What Is Cosmopolitical Design?*; Fleming and Roberts, *Sustainable Design for the Built Environment*; Villanueva et al., "Bringing Local Voices into Community Revitalization"; Villanueva, "Designing a Chinatown Anti-Displacement Map and Walking Tour with Communication Asset Mapping."

27. Powell, *Racing to Justice*; Capers, "The Racial Architecture of Criminal Justice."

28. An, Orlando, and Rodnyansky, "The Physical Legacy of Racism"; Fu, "Can Buildings Be Racist?"

29. Mindich, *Just the Facts*; Reese, "The News Paradigm and the Ideology of Objectivity"; Schudson, *Discovering the News*.

30. Tuchman, "Objectivity as Strategic Ritual."

31. See every movement, from the muckrakers in the early 1900s to the New Journalists in the 1960s and 1970s.

32. I could not find anything that applied the term "built environment" specifically to the far-right media machine of disinformation, but that is basically what it was, beginning with the 1990s talk radio shows. For a few of the many commentaries describing this thriving machine, see Carlson, Robinson, and Lewis, *News after Trump*; Brock, *The Republican Noise Machine*; Froehlich, *A Disinformation-Misinformation Ecology*.

33. Wenzel, "Making News Antiracist."

34. Attia, *Net Zero Energy Buildings (NZEB) Concepts, Frameworks and Roadmap for Project Analysis and Implementation*.

35. Knight Commission on Trust, Media, and Democracy, 2019.

36. Frederick, "Podcast: Craigslist Founder's Giving to Democracy and Journalism."

37. After his gift to CUNY, the school renamed itself the Craig Newmark Graduate School of Journalism at the City University of New York. In the wake of that announcement, Newmark came under a lot of flak since many blamed him for contributing to

journalism's demise; indeed, one study showed that Craigslist alone cost newspapers about $5 billion in classifieds revenue between 2000 and 2007, according to a *New York Times* article about the endowment. Nonetheless, as a major philanthropist Newmark was a huge influencer and networker in this built environment since the beginning of its blossoming. I note also that CUNY has been an innovator in journalism engagement, especially the MA Engagement (formerly Social Journalism) program run by Dr. Carrie Brown and started in 2014. Peiser, "Craigslist Founder Gives $20 Million to CUNY Journalism School."

38. Karlsson, *Transparency and Journalism.*
39. Robinson, *Networked News, Racial Divides.*
40. Guzmán, *I Never Thought of It That Way.*
41. Holton, Lewis, and Coddington, "Interacting with Audiences"; Bélair-Gagnon, Nelson, and Lewis, "Audience Engagement, Reciprocity, and the Pursuit of Community Connectedness in Public Media Journalism," May 28, 2019.
42. Bulger and Davison, "The Promises, Challenges, and Futures of Media Literacy"; Mason, Krutka, and Stoddard, "Media Literacy, Democracy, and the Challenge of Fake News."
43. Wenzel, "Public Media and Marginalized Publics"; Wenzel, *Community-Centered Journalism.*
44. Bass, "The Evolution of Solutions Journalism"; Gutsche and Brennen, *Journalism Research in Practice*; Wenzel, *Community-Centered Journalism.*
45. Hatcher and Thayer, "Assessing Collaboration in One Media Ecosystem"; Konieczna, "Reimagining Newsroom Collaboration"; Nettlefold and Pecl, "Engaged Journalism and Climate Change"; Konieczna, *Journalism without Profit.*
46. Robinson and Lawrence, "The Trust-Building News Ecosystem."
47. Lawrence, Radcliffe, and Schmidt, "Practicing Engagement," 1238. See also Lawrence et al., "Building Engagement."
48. Wenzel, *Community-Centered Journalism.*
49. Moon and Lawrence, "Disseminator, Watchdog and Neighbor?"
50. Heyamoto and Milbourn, "The 32 Percent Project."
51. Even when it was something I really, really wanted to do, like hanging with this really cool city council woman at her mountainside ski condo in Maine. Sigh. That one still smarts. I mean, it reportedly had a jacuzzi and everything. I am not suggesting that reporters should now accept those kinds of invitations from city councilors, but I do want to underscore that the rules are changing and participating in the lived experiences of typically marginalized community members would now be a valuable and essential thing to do.
52. Lewis, Holton, and Coddington, "Reciprocal Journalism," 229.
53. Poepsel, "Thematic Analysis of Journalism Engagement in Practice."
54. Schmidt and Lawrence, "Engaged Journalism and News Work."
55. Poepsel, "Thematic Analysis of Journalism Engagement in Practice."
56. Gans, *Deciding What's News*; Tuchman, "Objectivity as Strategic Ritual"; Zelizer, "Journalists as Interpretive Communities."
57. Robinson, Xia, and Zahay, "Public Political Talk on Twitter and Facebook."

58. Chaskin, "Building Community Capacity."
59. Saegert, "Building Civic Capacity in Urban Neighborhoods."
60. Chaskin, "Building Community Capacity."
61. Elliott and Kaufman, "Building Civic Capacity to Resolve Environmental Conflicts."
62. Naparstek and Haskell, "Neighborhood Approaches to Urban Capacity Building"; Holley, "Emerging Ethnic Agencies."
63. Hankins and Martin, "Contextualizing Neighbourhood Activism"; Coates, "Solidarity"; Mocca and Osborne, "'Solidarity Is Our Weapon'"; Scholz, "Solidarity."
64. Varma, "Evoking Empathy or Enacting Solidarity with Marginalized Communities?"
65. Varma, "Solidarity Journalism."
66. Varma, "Evoking Empathy or Enacting Solidarity with Marginalized Communities?"; Varma, "Solidarity in U.S. Journalism"; Varma, "Solidarity Journalism."
67. Pech and Leibel, "Writing in Solidarity," 152.
68. Tronto, *Caring Democracy*, 19.
69. Gladstone, "When Black Journalists Are Barred from Covering Black Lives Matter Protests."
70. Tronto, *Caring Democracy*.
71. Schifrin, "Local Newsrooms across the Country Are Closing."
72. Here I am playing off the now famous line of Jay Rosen's back in 2006 describing "citizen journalists" as "the people formerly known as the audience." Rosen, "The People Formerly Known as the Audience."

Chapter 3

1. Gannett was the largest newspaper chain in the United States at the time. I worked at two Gannett properties during my 13-year stint as a reporter, the *Burlington Free Press* in Vermont and the *Courier Post* in New Jersey.
2. Mensing, "College and University Journalism Education."
3. Weaver, *The American Journalist*; Weaver et al., *The American Journalist*; Weaver and Wilnat, "Introduction."
4. Check out Society of Professional Journalists, "Society of Professional Journalists"; Reuters Institute for the Study of Journalism; Kovach and Rosenstiel, *The Elements of Journalism*.
5. Rodríguez, "Incorporating a Critique of Coloniality"; Mignolo, "Epistemic Disobedience, Independent Thought and Decolonial Freedom," 1.
6. This actually comes from Santiago Castro-Gomez's book *Hybris del Punto Cero*, but I got it from Rodríguez, "Incorporating a Critique of Coloniality," 23. She was applying this critique of colonialism to the Eurocentric philosophies upon which the practice of mainstream journalism and mass communication in the United States was based.
7. Lewis, "Perspective," 73.

8. So much research exists on this, but start with Catherine Squires's *African Americans and the Media*, Libby Lewis's *The Myth of Post-Racialism in Television News*, Marian Meyers's *African American Women in the News*, Robert Entman's *Projections of Power*, Sarah Jackson's *Black Celebrity, Racial Politics, and the Press*, and Angela Wagner's "Watching the Watchdogs." See also Forde and Bedingfield, *Journalism and Jim Crow*.

9. National Advisory Commission on Civil Disorders, *The Kerner Report*, 389.

10. American Society of News Editors, "The ASNE Newsroom Diversity Survey." Similarly, a 2018 Pew Research Center report showed that 77% of U.S. journalists were white and 61% were male—lower than the national job force average: Grieco, "Newsroom Employees Are Less Diverse Than U.S. Workers Overall."

11. Gottfried et al., "Journalists Give Industry Mixed Reviews on Newsroom Diversity, Lowest Marks in Racial and Ethnic Diversity."

12. Jones, "The Great Remove"; Henningham, "Political Journalists' Political and Professional Values"; Correa, "Does Class Matter?"

13. Hassell, Holbein, and Miles, "Journalists May Be Liberal, but This Doesn't Affect Which Candidates They Choose to Cover."

14. Henningham, "Political Journalists' Political and Professional Values," 321.

15. Corcoran, "The Political Preferences and Value Orientations of Irish Journalists."

16. Tang and Lee, "Hong Kong Journalists' Attitude towards Social Protests."

17. Patterson and Donsbagh, "News Decisions."

18. Gottfried, "Republicans Less Likely to Trust Their Main News Source If They See It as 'Mainstream' "; Jurkowitz et al., "Democrats Report Much Higher Levels of Trust in a Number of News Sources Than Republicans."

19. Kennedy, Middleton, and Ratcliffe, "Introduction."

20. Doane, "Rethinking Whiteness Studies"; Omi and Winant, *Racial Formation in the United States*; Powell, *Racing to Justice*.

21. Dolan, "Whiteness and News," 201.

22. Dolan, "Whiteness and News," 204–5.

23. In her 2021 book *News for the Rich, White and Blue,* Nikki Usher detailed more than 10 years of research on how legacy media remain white and elite and increasingly out of reach for most in the United State.

24. Newkirk, *Within the Veil*, 7.

25. Newkirk, *Within the Veil*, 39.

26. Jackson, *Black Celebrity, Racial Politics, and the Press*.

27. Farhi and Izade, "NPR Is Losing Some of Its Black and Latino Hosts."

28. Newkirk, *Within the Veil*, 22. See also Squires, *Dispatches from the Color Line*; Freelon et al., "How Black Twitter and Other Social Media Communities Interact with Mainstream News"; Wagner, "Watching the Watchdogs."

29. Converse, "The Nature of Belief Systems in Mass Publics (1964)," 3.

30. Converse, "The Nature of Belief Systems in Mass Publics (1964)"; Tang and Lee, "Hong Kong Journalists' Attitude towards Social Protests"; Peffley and Hurwitz, "A Hierarchical Model of Attitude Constraint."

31. Tang and Lee, "Hong Kong Journalists' Attitude towards Social Protests," 58.

32. Newkirk, *Within the Veil*, 33–37. See also Polyak and Donnelly, "Advancing Diversity, Equity, and Inclusion in Journalism."

33. Squires, *Dispatches from the Color Line*, 186.

34. Mastin, Campo, and Frazer, "In Black and White"; Holt, "Afterword"; Shah and Thornton, *Newspaper Coverage of Interethnic Conflict*; Shah, "Toward More Inclusive News"; van Dijk, *Racism and the Press*; Wilson, *Black Journalists in Paradox*.

35. In *The Elements of Journalism,* Kovach and Rosenstiel write that journalists' "first obligation is to the truth" and include a discussion about these terms.

36. Cook and Hegtvedt, "Distributive Justice, Equity, and Equality"; Duclos, "Equity and Equality."

37. Brogan, "A 'Perfect Storm.'"

38. Manafy, "The Media Industry's #MeToo Moment."

39. This all came just after the 2016 U.S. presidential election of Donald Trump, whose rise in popularity among working-class, rural, and suburban people had been completely missed by American journalists. So another kind of reckoning about political identity had also been happening for mainstream newsrooms, which had begun hiring reporters to find, talk to, and understand their communities' Trumpers. Holmes, "George Floyd Killing Sparks Protests across US."

40. As recounted in Allissa Richardson's *Bearing Witness While Black*, x.

41. Holmes, "George Floyd Killing Sparks Protests across US."

42. Nieman Lab; Smith, "Inside the Revolts Erupting in America's Big Newsrooms."

43. As Richardson pointed out in her excellent book, *Bearing Witness While Black*, Jewish people have a similar tradition of witnessing as a way to cope with trauma and push for reparation. Core to this witnessing, we must remember, is that this kind of journalism often brings havoc and danger to the person attending to the trauma. Note, too, that Pamela Newkirk also provided evidence of this in *Within the Veil*.

44. Richardson, *Bearing Witness While Black*, 24.

45. Welch, "Journalists Abandoning 'Objectivity' for 'Moral Clarity' Really Just Want to Call People Immoral."

46. Tom Rosenstiel identified as a white man who worked at the American Press Institute, writing a lot of reports and books about journalism, including cowriting the well-known *Elements of Journalism*, in which he expressly stated that objectivity was not a viable ideal and played up balance and fairness, proportionality, and truthfulness instead: Kovach and Rosenstiel, *The Elements of Journalism*.

47. *New York Times*, "Making a More Diverse, Equitable and Inclusive New York Times"; Robertson, "New York Times Calls for Workplace Changes in Diversity Report."

48. Even *Saturday Night Live* lampooned Vermont as one of the whitest states in the nation: Corwin, "'Laugh Because It's Funny.'"

49. Len-Ríos and Perry, *Cross-Cultural Journalism and Strategic Communication*. A "fault line," according to Len-Ríos and Perry, marks the identities and other arenas of difference that can create polarization. It is a paradigm developed by the Missouri School of Journalism to force reporters to be more introspective about how identities inform stories while helping people toward understanding of divisive topics.

50. Again, all of them considered themselves liberal or independent and, further, reported that they tried to keep their personal politics out of their job.
51. Smith, Allen, and Danley, "'Assume the Position'"; Smith, "Black Faculty Coping with Racial Battle Fatigue"; Fasching-Varner et al., *Racial Battle Fatigue in Higher Education*.
52. Thoreson had left Hearken and was at the Institute for Nonprofit News in 2022.
53. The election guide can be downloaded here: https://www.thecitizensagenda.org/download. The 2020 effort was detailed in Thoreson, "Citizens Agenda in Action."
54. Robinson, *Networked News, Racial Divides: How Power and Privilege Shape Public Discourse in Progressive Communities*.
55. See not only my 2018 book *Networked News, Racial Divides*, but also David Mindich's *Just the Facts* or *Reckoning* by Candis Callison and Mary Lynn Young.
56. Hamington, "Caring, Journalism, and the Power of Particularism"; Hekman, *Moral Voices, Moral Selves*.
57. Hamington, *Embodied Care*.
58. Gilligan and Ward, "Forward," in *Race-ing Moral Formation*, x.
59. As in "Comfort the afflicted and afflict the comfortable," a popular phrase of mainstream journalists who saw their job as enforcing equity. Also see Siddle Walker and Snarey, *Race-ing Moral Formation*; Kohlberg, *The Philosophy of Moral Development*.
60. All the essays in Siddle Walker and Snarey, *Race-ing Moral Formation* work well to explain these intersecting values.
61. Hamington, *Embodied Care*, 96.
62. Steiner and Okrusch, "Care as a Virtue for Journalists"; Hossain and Aucoin, "The Ethics of Care as a Universal Framework for Global Journalism," October 2, 2018.
63. Steiner and Okrusch, "Care as a Virtue for Journalists," 114–15.
64. Hossain and Aucoin, "The Ethics of Care as a Universal Framework for Global Journalism," November 1, 2018, 204.
65. McBride, "The Ethics of Justice and Care in the American Media."
66. Hamington gets at this idea a bit in *Embodied Care*: "If morality is relational as care ethics proposes, then we cannot simply be passive and wait to form relations, we need seek out a relational understanding with unfamiliar others. In other words, global citizenry in a cosmopolitan world requires sympathetic, connected knowledge of others where we endeavor to form deep and disruptive knowledge of others. Such knowledge can be described as 'disruptive' in the sense that it jars us from the routines and patterns of our day to draw attention and emotive reactions" (97, 100).
67. Hamington, "Caring, Journalism, and the Power of Particularism," 96–97.
68. Hamington, "Caring, Journalism, and the Power of Particularism"; Examining Ethics Podcast, "A Spirit of Care with Maurice Hamington."
69. Kang, "Identity-Centered Multicultural Care Theory."
70. Thayer-Bacon, *Relational "(e)Pistemologies"*; Thayer-Bacon, "The Power of Caring."
71. Hecht, "A Research Odyssey"; Hecht et al., "A Communication Theory of Identity."
72. Carey, *Communication as Culture*.
73. This, of course, is not meant to say that journalists who follow more traditional mandates around engagement with audiences don't also care about people or even

perform nurturing roles in their private lives. It is only to make the distinction around these divergent professional values guiding reporting work these days.

74. You can read more about these follow-ups in the appendix on the overall methods for this book.

75. Not everyone, though. For many, thinking about marginalized communities during the fall 2020 election cycle was something not in the bandwidth at a time of the ongoing pandemic and the intense campaign between Donald Trump and Joe Biden. I will talk more about that in the next few chapters.

Chapter 4

1. Parts of this chapter first appeared in a journal article; thanks to *Journalism Studies* for allowing me to reprint some of it. Robinson, Jensen, and Dávalos, " 'Listening Literacies' as Keys to Rebuilding Trust in Journalism."

2. Carlson, Robinson, and Lewis, *News after Trump*; Pew Research Center, "In a Politically Polarized Era, Sharp Divides in Both Partisan Coalitions."

3. Field Day is a lab and studio at University of Wisconsin—Madison that researches and makes learning games, led by David Gagnon. The games' projects are built in partnerships with world-class subject experts and cohorts of teacher fellows. The games are publicly distributed for free to classrooms all over the country.

4. See the project "The Journalism Game: Scaling Journalistic Practices to Middle School Youth to Support Democracy," described in University of Wisconsin–Madison, "Baldwin Grants Awarded to Eight Projects." As of early 2023, the Journalism Game was deep in production and almost ready for testing in classrooms, planned for late spring 2023.

5. So that the intervention would be useful in several capacities within a seventh-grade curriculum.

6. Glenn, "A Content Analysis of Fifty Definitions of Listening."

7. Lundsteen, *Listening*.

8. Purdy and Borisoff, *Listening in Everyday Life*; Wolvin and Coakley, *Listening*.

9. Purdy and Borisoff, *Listening in Everyday Life*, 7.

10. Lewis and Reinsch, "Listening in Organizational Environments."

11. Most deliberation scholars suggest that without people listening to what each other is saying, true deliberation and productive public discourse cannot happen: Dobson, *Listening for Democracy*; Habermas, *Justification and Application*; Habermas, *The Theory of Communicative Action*; Goodin, *Innovating Democracy*; Levin, *The Listening Self*.

12. Dobson, *Listening for Democracy*, 106.

13. Dobson, *Listening for Democracy*; Rice, "Toward an Aristotelian Conception of Good Listening"; Rice, "Moral Perception, Situatedness, and Learning to Listen."

14. Dobson, *Listening for Democracy*, 171.

15. Levin, *The Listening Self*, 111.

16. Calder, "Democracy and Listening," 133; see also Calder, "Listening, Democracy and the Environment."
17. Fraser, *Justice Interruptus*; Fraser, *Scales of Justice*.
18. Tannen, *You Just Don't Understand*.
19. Giovanni, *Racism 101*.
20. Royster, "When the First Voice You Hear Is Not Your Own," 36.
21. Harry, "Listening to Black Women."
22. Ahmed, "Feminist Killjoys."
23. Ratcliffe, "Rhetorical Listening"; Ratcliffe, *Rhetorical Listening*.
24. Ratcliffe, *Rhetorical Listening*, 25.
25. Ratcliffe, *Rhetorical Listening*, 26, italics in original.
26. Ratcliffe, "Rhetorical Listening," 33.
27. Royston actually delved into this a bit on p. 38 of her essay "When the First Voice You Hear Is Not Your Own," writing, "The goal is not, 'You talk, I talk.' The goal is better practices so that we can exchange perspectives, negotiate meaning, and create understanding with the intent of being in a good position to cooperate, when, like now, cooperation is absolutely necessary."
28. Hobbs and Jensen, "The Past, Present, and Future of Media Literacy Education."
29. Rindfleisch, Burroughs, and Wong, "The Safety of Objects"; Maksl, Ashley, and Craft, "Measuring News Media Literacy."
30. Aufderheide, *Media Literacy*.
31. UNESCO, "Global Media and Information Literacy (MIL)."
32. Hobbs and Harris, "Restoration Ecology"; Livingston, "Media Literacy and the Challenge of New Information and Communication Technologies"; Steinbrink and Cook, "Media Literacy Skills and the 'War on Terrorism.'"
33. Brown, "Media Literacy Perspectives," 44. Scharrer, "Making a Case for Media Literacy in the Curriculum: Outcomes and Assessment."
34. Potter, *Media Literacy*, 22.
35. Hobbs and Jensen, "The Past, Present, and Future of Media Literacy Education," 9.
36. boyd, "Did Media Literacy Backfire?"; Mason, Krutka, and Stoddard, "Media Literacy, Democracy, and the Challenge of Fake News"; Williams, "Fighting 'Fake News' in an Age of Digital Disorientation"; Middaugh, "Civic Media Literacy in a Transmedia World"; Craft, Ashley, and Maksl, "News Media Literacy and Conspiracy Theory Endorsement"; Kahne and Bowyer, "Educating for Democracy in a Partisan Age"; Vraga, Tully, and Bode, "Assessing the Relative Merits of News Literacy and Corrections in Responding to Misinformation on Twitter."
37. Cohen, "Exploring Echo-Systems"; Eslami et al., "'I Always Assumed That I Wasn't Really That Close to [Her].'"
38. van Dijck, Poell, and Waal, *The Platform Society*, 63, 71, 65–66, 67.
39. Eslami et al., "'I Always Assumed That I Wasn't Really That Close to [Her]'"; Noble, *Algorithms of Oppression*.
40. Cohen, "Exploring Echo-Systems," 148.
41. Fleming, "'Truthiness' and Trust"; Maksl, Ashley, and Craft, "Measuring News Media Literacy"; Paisana, Pinto-Martinho, and Cardoso, "Trust and Fake News."

42. Maksl, Ashley, and Craft, "Measuring News Media Literacy."

43. boyd, "Did Media Literacy Backfire?"

44. Peters, "Even Better Than Being Informed," 175.

45. Peters, "Even Better than Being Informed."

46. Peters, "Even Better than Being Informed"; Edgerly and Vraga, "Deciding What's News."

47. We conceptualized this typology in a journal article: Robinson, Jensen, and Dávalos, "'Listening Literacies' as Keys to Rebuilding Trust in Journalism."

48. See Checkology, "The News Literacy Project."

49. Peet, "Knight Foundation, Aspen Institute Launch Trust, Media and Democracy Initiative."

50. Green-Barber, "Impact Report."

51. Basically this category evokes Manuel Castells's "mass self-communicator," the person now equipped with plenty of digital platforms to share information with the world, in *The Power of Identity*.

52. Center for Media, Data and Society, "CMDS Media Specialists Train Representatives of Press Councils of Southeast Europe and Turkey on Online Media Ethics."

53. Newton, "Understanding News?"

54. Ethical Journalism Network, "Facebook Reveals Plan to Tackle Spread of Fake News Online."

55. Libin, "Relative Truths."

56. Bunton, "Your Voice Ohio to Host 'The Opioid Epidemic' in WCH Feb. 19."

57. Ciobanu, "Seattle's KUOW Is Hosting 'Ask a . . .' Conversations to Foster Empathy and Understanding between Communities."

58. Newton, "Understanding News?"

59. Seale, "4 Ways Google News Lab Is Driving Innovation in Newsrooms."

60. Ethical Journalism Network, "Facebook Reveals Plan to Tackle Spread of Fake News Online."

61. Robinson, Jensen, and Dávalos, "'Listening Literacies' as Keys to Rebuilding Trust in Journalism."

62. UNESCO, "Press Clubs Are a Perfect Platform to Debate Media's Role in Governance and Sustainable Development."

63. To give you an idea of how much money is being funneled into these trust-building projects right now, Craig Newmark alone was responsible for infusing more than $40 million between 2015 and 2020 journalism initiatives like these.

64. Ingram, "Facebook Partners with Craig Newmark to Fund Journalism Trust Project."

65. Wenzel, "Public Media and Marginalized Publics."

66. One of my fantastic graduate students working in the different iterations of the data collection for the book, Kelly Jensen, was a UW-Madison Communication Arts student at the time studying literacy.

67. And also the European Journalism Centre to regrant to newsrooms across Europe to support their Engaged Journalism Accelerator program. See https://engagedjournalism.com/.

68. de Aguiar, "Beyond Mountains, There Are Mountains."

69. Rinaldi, *In Dialogue with Reggio Emilia*, 65.
70. Sevenhuijsen, *Citizenship and the Ethics of Care*.
71. Tronto, *Caring Democracy*, 18.
72. Sevenhuijsen, *Citizenship and the Ethics of Care*, 182.
73. Tronto, *Moral Boundaries*; Tronto, *Caring Democracy*.
74. Sevenhuijsen, *Citizenship and the Ethics of Care*, 185.
75. Sevenhuijsen, *Citizenship and the Ethics of Care*, 185.
76. Young, "Communication and the Other."
77. Vraga, Tully, and Bode, "Assessing the Relative Merits of News Literacy and Corrections in Responding to Misinformation on Twitter," 160.
78. Paisana, Pinto-Martinho, and Cardoso, "Trust and Fake News"; Silverstone, "Complicity and Collusion in the Mediation of Everyday Life."
79. Tronto, *Moral Boundaries*.
80. de Aguiar, "Beyond Mountains, There Are Mountains."
81. Independence Media: https://independencemedia.org/.
82. de Aguiar, "Refilling Our Well."

Chapter 5

1. Hearken, "The Citizens Agenda Guide."
2. The brilliant Dr. Wang helped me with several parts of these studies. At the time he was at the University of Wisconsin-Madison and then began a postdoctoral position at the University of Kansas as of 2023.
3. Hearken, "Election SOS."
4. All but one (in the United Kingdom) were in the United States, as the modules were geared to journalism as practiced and taught in the United States. I hoped to change that as the database of modules and the Journalism Educators Collaborative grow.
5. It is important to remember that fall 2020 remained a virtual, COVID-19 pandemic semester, and many students and professors were in crisis at some point, usually having to do with the pandemic or its challenges in some way. But we still received some good learning out of it. I scaled up the project thanks to a UW-Madison grant about inequities in the 2021–22 academic year with seven journalism school/newsroom collaborations in the United States. For my class as well as with the grant, I worked with a nonprofit affiliate of MIT called Cortico and its conversation program, Local Voices Network. However, the collection and analysis of that data came too late to be included in this book.
6. More about the methods can be found in the appendix. We worked with Max Resnik, Colleen Butler, Mathias Lemos Costillo, Kelly Paola, and their colleagues at Cortico and the Local Voices Network.
7. Dewey, *The Public and Its Problems*.
8. The events and dialogue from this meeting were written by Bridget Thoreson and verified by Rosen and Brandel.

9. Fallows, "The Media Learned Nothing from 2016"; Patterson, "News Coverage of the 2016 General Election."

10. All of this made possible by support from Democracy Fund, Trusted Elections Find Project, and the American Press Institute.

11. Or policymakers—many newsrooms used the guide in non-election ways such as COVID coverage.

12. Hearken conducted 21 interviews with Election SOS participants, and I was given Institutional Review Board approval to access their data. In addition, we interviewed another five journalists while surveying 32. We reviewed the content of three Citizens Agenda projects after the primaries in 2020. Alas, we did not have enough funding and resources to do a pre- or postcontent analysis of the actual coverage of these newsrooms during fall 2020, which would have given us a better idea of how much the trainings changed coverage. That said, the evaluation with the participants provided further evidence of the robust networking and new commitment from the industry toward trust building through engagement work. The public Hearken Election SOS report can be found here: Thoreson et al., "Election SOS."

13. Remember that Citizens Agenda as a guide was out by fall 2019 and so many newsrooms were already using it before COVID hit the United States and the world shut down in March 2020.

14. BINJ Online, "The BINJ Citizens Agenda for New Hampshire Primary Coverage."

15. Thoreson et al., "Election SOS," 20–21.

16. "Local Voices Network."

17. Boston Institute for Non-Profit Journalism, "Manchester Divided," 2020.

18. Kiesel, "A Disabled Reporter Walks into a Democratic Primary Event . . ."

19. As I mentioned in the introductory chapter, I could not do audience studies or even a comprehensive textual analysis of content because of resource constraints.

20. This is the focus of my next set of studies, in partnership with a quantitative political scientist named Joshua Darr of Louisiana State University. We are doing a seris of mixed-methods (focus groups, listening sessions, experiments, and targeted suveys) with audiences to test whether the industry retraining is having any impact on news consumers.

21. Craig Newmark Graduate School of Journalism. Website. https://www.journalism.cuny.edu/about-us/

22. Germantown Info Hub, "The Germantown Info Hub Is a Community Journalism Project That Shares Information and Stories of and for Germantown."

23. She is also author of Community-Centered Journalism, which I cite throughout this book.

24. Special thanks to DeNeen Brown, a professor at University of Maryland and a Washington Post reporter, for a huge chunk of the Power & Privilege materials.

25. I had hoped to get money for them via a grant, and I had several proposals out, but then COVID happened and many of the foundations switched their priorities. I did manage some Amazon gift cards, though, thanks to my endowed research professorship money and the UW-Madison's School of Journalism & Mass Communication.

26. We ended up with twelve interviews and 165 student surveys. You can read more about what we did in the appendix. Thanks especially to UW-Madison undergraduate student Rachel Reingold for being my research partner on these.

27. Fun fact: Lisa Miller was actually one of my journalism teachers when I was an undergraduate student at University of New Hampshire back in the late 1990s. We never forget our teachers.

28. Spillman, Kuban, and Smith, "Words du Jour."

29. Eschenfelder, "But Can They Write?"

30. Foust and Bradshaw, "Pushing Boundaries."

31. Thier, "Opportunities and Challenges for Initial Implementation of Solutions Journalism Coursework"; Wenger, Owens, and Cain, "Help Wanted"; Nelson and Lewis, "Training Social Justice Journalists"; Huntsberger and Stavitsky, "The New 'Podagogy.'"

32. We surveyed 165 students, as mentioned earlier. More detail of sampling and methods is in the appendix.

33. Some respondents also offered more traditional concepts for journalism and engagement, for instance, "I believe that the goal of journalism should be reporting the truth, and nothing but the truth. Journalists are called to provide unbiased, information to inform and connect with audiences" and "Engagement is about whether or not the journalistic piece has been absorbed and taken into consideration by the audience." Nonetheless we saw a significant shift in the paradigm J-school students were adopting.

34. This is a Hearken term: Thoreson, "Public-Powered Journalism in Practice."

35. We gave our participants the option of being named or not.

36. In 2022, several states had or were preparing laws forbidding the teaching of critical race theory—something that the Trump administration had expressly prohibited in its last year in office, 2020: Schwartz, "Trump Tells Agencies to End Trainings on 'White Privilege' and 'Critical Race Theory'"; Flaherty, "Legislating against Critical Race Theory, with Curricular Implications in Some States."

37. Tronto, *Caring Democracy*.

38. DACA referred to "Deferred Action for Childhood Arrivals," which was the status given to the children of immigrants without legal documentation to be in the United States. This was a status that allowed these children sanctuary here and was conferred by then President Barack Obama's administration in June 2012.

39. A common complaint that has always existed about journalists is that they care only about getting the story.

40. Thoreson et al., "Election SOS," 21.

41. Carlson, Robinson, and Lewis, *News after Trump*.

42. Thoreson et al., "Election SOS," 27.

43. Giroux, "Spectacles of Race and Pedagogies of Denial"; Giroux, *The Public in Peril*; Gutsche, *Elevating Problems of Journalistic Power in an Age of Post-Truth*.

44. Len-Ríos and Perry, *Cross-Cultural Journalism and Strategic Communication*; Daniels and Blom, *Teaching Race*; Ellis, Voakes, and Bergen, *News for US*.

45. Brown Kilgo, "Radically Transforming Programs and Syllabi," 10.

Chapter 6

1. Institute for Nonprofit News, "Bridget Thoreson Joins the INN Member Collaborations Team."
2. Brandel, "A New Chapter for Hearken, a New Chapter for Me."
3. I discussed these in Chapter 2.
4. U.S. Department of Homeland Security, "National Terrorism Advisory System Bulletin."
5. Mayer brought me on as a researcher for the Road to Pluralism project, along with Joshua Darr, a political communication scholar from Louisiana State University. At the time of this writing, we were all still collecting data and collaborating.
6. Though, of course, not all. See for, example, Iris Young's work on inclusion in deliberation, *Inclusion and Democracy*.
7. Russell, "Digital Communication Networks and the Journalistic Field"; Castells, *The Rise of the Network Society*; Robinson, *Networked News, Racial Divides: How Power & Privilege Shape Public Discourse in Progressive Communities*.
8. Wenzel, *Community-Centered Journalism*; Nelson, *Imagined Audiences*; Xia et al., "The Evolving Journalistic Roles on Social Media"; Schmidt and Lawrence, "Putting Engagement to Work"; Poepsel, "Thematic Analysis of Journalism Engagement in Practice."
9. Xia, Robinson, Zahay, and Freelon, "The Evolving Journalistic Roles on Social Media"; Hanitzsch and Vos, "Journalistic Roles and the Struggle over Institutional Identity"; Holton, Lewis, and Coddington, "Interacting with Audiences"; Finneman, Heckman, and Walck, "Reimagining Journalistic Roles"; Dilday, "Journalists Can Help People Tell Their Own Stories by Talking Less, Listening More."
10. "Civic care" comes from Miller, "Caring to Disagree."
11. Dobson, *Listening for Democracy*, 106.
12. Buzzanell, "Feminist Discursive Ethics"; Hossain and Aucoin, "The Ethics of Care as a Universal Framework for Global Journalism," November 1, 2018, 207.
13. Dobson, *Listening for Democracy*, 68.
14. Rice, "Toward an AristoTelian Conception of Good Listening," 151.
15. Forester, "Planning in the Face of Power," 109.
16. Dobson, *Listening for Democracy*, 7, 126.
17. Dobson, *Listening for Democracy*, 171.
18. Dobson, *Listening for Democracy*.
19. Ember, "News Outlets Rethink Usage of the Term 'Alt-Right.'"
20. This is not a new idea. Many scholars have declared the mainstream press itself to be a system colluding with white supremacy since its origins. See, for example, Callison and Young, *Reckoning*; Haywood, "Fight for a New America"; Forde and Bedingfield, *Journalism and Jim Crow*; Robinson, *Networked News, Racial Divides: How Power & Privilege Shape Public Discourse in Progressive Communities*; Mindich, *Just the Facts*.
21. Goins, "How a Culture of Listening Strengthens Reporting and Relationships."
22. Some of these also came directly from the report by Hearken in the wake of Citizens Agenda: Thoreson et al., "Election SOS."
23. Wenzel et al., "Journalism across Divides?"

24. See, for example, Garcia McKinley and Green-Barber, "Engaged Journalism."
25. See, for example, Goins, "How a Culture of Listening Strengthens Reporting and Relationships."
26. Green-Barber, "Towards a Useful Typology of Engaged Journalism."
27. In a June 2018 report from the Agora Journalism Center, "The 32 Percent Project," Lisa Heyamoto and Todd Milbourn argued that trust in journalism happens in the same way trust occurs in other industries, and that all kinds of trust must have these six characteristics: authenticity, transparency, positivity, diversity, consistency, and shared mission. However, scholarship on trust has not generally mentioned factors such as diversity or a shared mission, and I see these as being key parts of this new trust-focused built environment.
28. Goins, "How a Culture of Listening Strengthens Reporting and Relationships."
29. To be clear, many news organizations over the past decades have sought to amplify marginalized voices. What is different is that this has become a ubiquitous, explicitly stated mission as part of the profession.
30. Carlson, Robinson, and Lewis, *News after Trump*.
31. Örnebring and Karlsson, "Journalistic Autonomy," 20, 53–54.
32. Jacob Nelson, *Imagined Audiences,* would tell us we may never know as audiences ultimately are unknowable.
33. The theory of change emerged in the 1990s as a way to help evaluate when things, people, or places transform, to understand not the origin of the problem or even its solution, but to provide an explanation for the methods involved in changing. As Fiona Morgan did in the News Voices graphic, the theory of change often manifests in a flow chart that tracks the possible pathways to resolution given a set of potential variables (e.g., "If this, then that"). It has had application in a variety of industries, from finance to organizations. See, for example, Theory of Change Community, "What Is Theory of Change?"
34. Morgan, "Listen to People Who Care," Paragraph 14.
35. Morgan, "Listen to People Who Care."
36. Goins, "How a Culture of Listening Strengthens Reporting and Relationships," 50.
37. Marvin, *When Old Technologies Were New*.
38. Goffman, *The Presentation of Self in Everyday Life*; Stalder, "Between Democracy and Spectacle."
39. Quandt, "Dark Participation."
40. Wahl-Jorgensen, *Emotions, Media and Politics*; Holton, Bélair-Gagnon, and Royal, "The Human Side of (News) Engagement Emotion, Platform and Individual Agency."
41. For one major statement on journalistic authority and its decline, check out Carlson, *Journalistic Authority*.
42. Just as a reminder, Sarah Gagnon was Field Day Lab creative director for the Journalism Game project we won a grant for in 2020. Field Day is a lab and studio at UW-Madison that researches and makes learning games. Lead by David Gagnon, their games' projects are built in partnerships with world-class subject experts and cohorts of teacher fellows. Their games are publicly distributed for free to classrooms all over the country.
43. The game will be available in 2023, from this website: https://fielddaylab.wisc.edu/.

Appendix

1. An Institutional Review Board is an organization within a research university that oversees all research being done on or involving "human subjects," such as interviews.
2. I draw from both Fairclough and van Dijk's version of CDA, because I am interested in how a concept like trust is operationalized within the language of the journalistic profession, especially in how structural inequities innate in the institution of the press manifest in production, social, and other practices. This involved multiple readings, first identifying the broad themes, then crunching those themes for symbols, metaphors, and other meanings in a series of ever-deepening interpretations. In the application of CDA, we could see how conceptions of power and identity influence the ways of journalism and news content, and especially in the building of audience relationships. See Fairclough, Mulderrig, and Wodak, "Critical Discourse Analysis"; Fairclough, *Critical Discourse Analysis*; van Dijk, "Ideology and Discourse Analysis"; van Dijk, *Discourse and Context.*
3. You can find these here (feel free to use whatever you want from them, citing the Journalism Educator Collaborative): https://suerobinson.org/teaching/.

References

Ahmed, Sara. "Feminist Killjoys (and Other Willful Subjects)." *The Scholar and Feminist Online* 8, no. 3 (Summer 2010). https://sfonline.barnard.edu/polyphonic/print_ah med.htm.

American Society of News Editors. "The ASNE Newsroom Diversity Survey." November 15, 2018. https://members.newsleaders.org/diversity-survey-2018.

An, Brian, Anthony W. Orlando, and Seva Rodnyansky. "The Physical Legacy of Racism: How Redlining Cemented the Modern Built Environment." SSRN, Rochester, NY, September 1, 2019. https://doi.org/10.2139/ssrn.3500612.

Anderson, C. W., Stephen Coleman, and Nancy Thumim. "How News Travels: A Comparative Study of Local Media Ecosystems in Leeds (UK) and Philadelphia (US)." In *Local Journalism: The Decline of Newspapers and the Rise of Digital Media*, edited by Rasmus Kleis Nielson, 73–98. London: I.B. Tauris & Co., 2015.

Appiah, Kwame Anthony. "The Case for Capitalizing the 'B' in Black." *The Atlantic*, June 18, 2020. https://www.theatlantic.com/ideas/archive/2020/06/time-to-capitalize-black and-white/613159/.

Atske, Sara, Michael Barthel, Galen Stocking, and Christine Tamir. "7 Facts about Black Americans and the News Media." Pew Research Center, August 7, 2019. https://www. pewresearch.org/fact-tank/2019/08/07/facts-about-black-americans-and-the-news-media/.

Attia, Shady. *Net Zero Energy Buildings (NZEB) Concepts, Frameworks and Roadmap for Project Analysis and Implementation*. Oxford: Butterworth-Heinemann, 2018. https://doi.org/10.1016/B978-0-12-812461-1.00002-2.

Atton, Chris. *Alternative Media*. Sage, 2001.

Aufderheide, Patricia. *Media Literacy: A Report of the National Leadership Conference on Media Literacy*. Aspen Institute, Communications and Society Program, 1993. https://eric.ed.gov/?id=ED365294.

Balloch, Susan, and Michael Hill. *Care, Community and Citizenship: Research and Practice in a Changing Policy Context*. Policy Press, 2007.

Bass, Tasia. "The Evolution of Solutions Journalism." *Solutions Journalism: A Review and Analysis of Patterns* (blog), December 12, 2019. https://medium.com/solutionsjournal ism/the-evolution-of-solutions-journalism-f7a917eba5df.

Basta, Claudia, and Stefano Moroni, eds. *Ethics, Design and Planning of the Built Environment*. New York: Springer, 2013.

Batsell, Jake. *Engaged Journalism: Connecting with Digitally Empowered News Audiences*. New York: Columbia University Press, 2015.

Belair-Gagnon, Valerie, Jacob L. Nelson, and Seth C. Lewis. "Audience Engagement, Reciprocity, and the Pursuit of Community Connectedness in Public Media Journalism." *Journalism Practice* 13, no. 5 (May 28, 2019): 558–75. https://doi.org/10.1080/17512786.2018.1542975.

Bennett, W. Lance, and Livingston, Steven. "The Disinformation Order: Disruptive Communication and the Decline of Democratic Institutions." *European Journal of Communication* 33, no. 2 (2018): 122–39.

Beverly, Juliet, Leah Donnella, Cassie Haynes, and Robert Samuels. "Video and Recap: What Would Antiracist Journalism Look Like?" *Journalism Institute* (blog), July 14, 2020. https://www.pressclubinstitute.org/event/what-would-antiracist-journal ism-look-like/.

BINJ Online. "The BINJ Citizens Agenda for New Hampshire Primary Coverage." January 2020. https://binjonline.com/2020/01/23/the-binj-citizens-agenda-for-new-hampsh ire-primary-coverage/.

Blaagaard, Bolette. "Journalism of Relation: Social Constructions of 'Whiteness' and Their Implications in Contemporary Danish Journalistic Practice and Production." VBN, 2009. https://vbn.aau.dk/en/publications/journalism-of-relation-social-constr uctions-of-whiteness-and-thei.

Bloom, Jack H., ed. *Jewish Relational Care A–Z: We Are Our Other's Keeper.* New York: Routledge, 2006.

Boston Institute for Non-Profit Journalism. "Manchester Divided." Website, 2020. //binjonline.com/manchesterdivided/.

boyd, d. "Did Media Literacy Backfire?" Data & Society: Points, January 5, 2017. https://points.datasociety.net/did-media-literacy-backfire-7418c084d88d.

Brandel, Jennifer. "A New Chapter for Hearken, a New Chapter for Me." *Medium* (blog), June 28, 2020. https://medium.com/we-are-hearken/a-new-chapter-for-hearken-a-new-chapter-for-me-af123d2ee4b7.

Brandel, Jennifer. "Newsrooms Are Focused on Innovating the Distribution of News. The Process, Not So Much." *Medium* (blog), April 23, 2019. https://medium.com/we-are-hearken/newsrooms-are-focused-on-innovating-the-distribution-of-news-the-proc ess-not-so-much-802d7b5d8e77.

Brenan, Megan. "Americans' Trust in Media Dips to Second Lowest on Record." Gallup, October 7, 2021. https://news.gallup.com/poll/355526/americans-trust-media-dips-second-lowest-record.aspx.

Brock, David. *The Republican Noise Machine: Right-Wing Media and How It Corrupts Democracy.* Three Rivers Press, 2005.

Brogan, Dylan. "A 'Perfect Storm.'" *Isthmus*, February 3, 2022. https://isthmus.com/news/cover-story/a-perfect-storm/?fbclid=IwAR3IPwMOLZBVMzUVRvZQ6VqkJgeTY EAqkx7Uq5lFUslk73cNZFtDLfM6oC8.

Brown, Lee. "Philadelphia Inquirer Journalists Walk Out over 'Buildings Matter, Too' Headline." *New York Post*, June 4, 2020. https://nypost.com/2020/06/04/philadelphia-inquirer-journalists-walk-out-over-deeply-offensive-headline/.

Brown, James A. "Media Literacy Perspectives." *Journal of Communication* 48 (1998): 44–57. https://doi-org.ezproxy.library.wisc.edu/10.1111/j.1460-2466.1998.tb02736.x.

Brown Kilgo, Danielle. "Radically Transforming Programs and Syllabi." In *Teaching Race: Struggles, Strategies, and Scholarship for the Mass Communication Classroom*, by George L. Daniels and Robin Blom, 3–14. Lanham, MD: Rowman & Littlefield, 2021. https://rowman.com/ISBN/9781538154557/Teaching-Race-Struggles-Strategies-and-Scholarship-for-the-Mass-Communication-Classroom.

Bulger, Monica, and Patrick Davison. "The Promises, Challenges, and Futures of Media Literacy." *Journal of Media Literacy Education* 10, no. 1 (May 9, 2018): 1–21.

Bunton, A. "Your Voice Ohio to Host 'The Opioid Epidemic' in WCH Feb. 19." *The Record Herald*, January 22, 2018. https://www.recordherald.com/news/22413/your-voice-ohio-to-host-the-opioid-epidemic-in-wch-feb-19.

Buzzanell, P. "Feminist Discursive Ethics." In *The Handbook of Communication Ethics*, edited by G. Cheney, S. May, and D. Munshi, 64–83. New York: Routledge, 2011.

Calder, Gideon. "Democracy and Listening." In *Problems of Democracy: Language and Speaking*, edited by Mary-Ann Crumplin, 125–35. New York: Inter-Disciplinary Press, 2011.

Calder, Gideon. "Listening, Democracy and the Environment." *In-Spire Journal of Law, Politics and Societies* 4, no. 2 (2009): 26–41.

Callison, Candis, and Mary Lynn Young. *Reckoning: Journalism's Limits and Possibilities*. New York: Oxford University Press, 2020.

Cannon, Katie. *Black Womanist Ethics*. Atlanta, GA: Scholar's Press, 1988.

Capers, Bennett. "The Racial Architecture of Criminal Justice." *SMU Law Review* 74 (2021): 405.

CapRadio. "Bloomberg Stumped in Sacramento, So We Asked Him Your Questions on Climate Change, Homelessness." February 3, 2020. https://www.capradio.org/145429.

Carey, James W. *Communication as Culture*. Routledge, 1989. https://books.google.com/books/about/Communication_as_Culture.html?id=AcSufbsE7TwC.

Carlson, Matt. *Journalistic Authority: A Relational Approach*. New York: Columbia University Press, 2017.

Carlson, Matt, Sue Robinson, and Seth C. Lewis. *News after Trump: Confronting Journalism's Crisis of Relevance in a Changed Media Culture*. Oxford: Oxford University Press, 2021.

Cassidy, John. "Media Culpa? The Press and the Election Result." *The New Yorker*, November 11, 2016. https://www.newyorker.com/news/john-cassidy/media-culpa-the-press-and-the-election-result.

Castells, Manuel. *The Power of Identity*. Vol. 2. Blackwell, 2009. https://doi.org/10.1002/9781444318234.

Castells, Manuel. *The Rise of the Network Society: The Information Age: Economy, Society, and Culture*. Vol. 1. 2nd edition. Chichester: Wiley-Blackwell, 2009.

Castro-Gomez, Santiago. *Hybris del Ponto Cero*. Bogotá: Pontificia Universidad Javeriana, 2014.

Center for Media, Data and Society. "CMDS Media Specialists Train Representatives of Press Councils of Southeast Europe and Turkey on Online Media Ethics," June 21, 2016. https://cmds.ceu.edu/article/2016-06-21/cmds-media-specialists-train-repr esentatives-press-councils-southeast-europe-and.

Chakravartty, Paula, Rachel Kuo, Victoria Grubbs, and Charlton McIlwain. "#CommunicationSoWhite." *Journal of Communication* 68, no. 2 (April 1, 2018): 254–66. https://doi.org/10.1093/joc/jqy003.

Chaskin, Robert J. "Building Community Capacity: A Definitional Framework and Case Studies from a Comprehensive Community Initiative." *Urban Affairs Review* 36, no. 3 (January 1, 2001): 291–323. https://doi.org/10.1177/10780870122184876.

Checkology. "The News Literacy Project." Accessed May 30, 2021. http://get.checkol ogy.org/.

Ciobanu, M. "Seattle's KUOW Is Hosting 'Ask a . . .' Conversations to Foster Empathy and Understanding between Communities." Journalism, February 16, 2018. https://www.journalism.co.uk/news/seattle-s-kuow-is-hosting-ask-a-conversations-to-fos ter-empathy-and-understanding-between-communities-/s2/a717754/.

Clardy, Justin Leonard. "Civic Tenderness as a Response to Child Poverty in America." In *Philosophy and Child Poverty: Reflections on the Ethics and Politics of Poor Children and Their Families*, edited by Nicolás Brando and Gottfried Schweiger, 303–21. Springer Nature, 2019. https://www.academia.edu/44593372/Civic_Tenderness_as_a_Response_to_Child_Poverty_in_America.

Coates, Rodney. "Solidarity." In *The Blackwell Encyclopedia of Sociology*, edited by George Ritzer, 4620–23. New York: John Wiley & Sons, 2007. https://doi.org/10.1002/978140 5165518.wbeoss209.

Cohen, James. "Exploring Echo-Systems: How Algorithms Shape Immersive Media Environments." *Journal of Media Literacy Education* 10, no. 2 (November 27, 2018): 139–51. https://doi.org/10.23860/JMLE-2018-10-2-8.

Collins, Patricia Hill. *Black Feminist Thought: Knowledge, Consciousness, and the Politics of Empowerment*. New York: Routledge, 2008.

Converse, Philip E. "The Nature of Belief Systems in Mass Publics (1964)." *Critical Review* 18, nos. 1–3 (January 2006): 1–74. https://doi.org/10.1080/08913810608443650.

Cook, Karen S., and Karen A. Hegtvedt. "Distributive Justice, Equity, and Equality." *Annual Review of Sociology* 9 (1983): 217–41.

Corcoran, Mary P. "The Political Preferences and Value Orientations of Irish Journalists." *Irish Journal of Sociology* 13, no. 2 (November 1, 2004): 23–42. https://doi.org/10.1177/079160350401300203.

Correa, Teresa. "Does Class Matter? The Effect of Social Class on Journalists' Ethical Decision Making." *Journalism & Mass Communication Quarterly* 86, no. 3 (September 1, 2009): 654–72. https://doi.org/10.1177/107769900908600312.

Corwin, Emily. "'Laugh Because It's Funny . . . Cry Because It's True': SNL Sketch Skewers Lack of Diversity in Vt." Vermont Public Radio, October 2, 2018. https://www.vpr.org/vpr-news/2018-10-02/laugh-because-its-funny-cry-because-its-true-snl-sketch-skewers-lack-of-diversity-in-vt.

Craft, Stephanie, Seth Ashley, and Adam Maksl. "News Media Literacy and Conspiracy Theory Endorsement." *Communication and the Public* 2, no. 4 (December 1, 2017): 388–401. https://doi.org/10.1177/2057047317725539.

Crunchbase. "First Draft News." Accessed May 29, 2021. https://www.crunchbase.com/organization/first-draft-news.

Daniels, George L., and Robin Blom, eds. *Teaching Race: Struggles, Strategies, and Scholarship for the Mass Communication Classroom*. Lanham, MD: Rowman & Littlefield, 2021.

de Aguiar, Molly. "Beyond Mountains, There Are Mountains." *News Integrity Initiative* (blog), January 12, 2020. https://medium.com/news-integrity-initiative/beyond-mountains-there-are-mountains-93ba75964aa.

de Aguiar, Molly. "Refilling Our Well." *Independence Media* (blog), January 2022. https://independencemedia.org/.

Dewey, John. *The Public and Its Problems*. Athens, OH: Swallow Press, 1954.

Dilday, Erika. "Journalists Can Help People Tell Their Own Stories by Talking Less, Listening More: 'Our Role Is Facilitator Instead of Interpreter, Catalyst Instead of Judge.'" *Nieman Reports* 74, no. 4 (Fall 2020): 1–7.

Doane, Ashley. "Rethinking Whiteness Studies." In *White Out*, edited by Ashley "Woody" Doane and Eduardo Bonilla-Silva, 3–20. United Kingdom: Routledge, 2003.

Dobson, Andrew. *Listening for Democracy: Recognition, Representation, Reconciliation*. Oxford: Oxford University Press, 2014.

Dolan, Kevin M. "Whiteness and News: The Interlocking Social Construction of 'Realities.'" University of Illinois at Urbana-Champaign, 2011. https://www.ideals.illin ois.edu/handle/2142/24404.

Domingo, David, Pere Masip, and Karin Wahl-Jorgensen. "Mapping the Digital News Ecosystem: Professional Journalism, New Producers and Active Audiences in the Digital Public Sphere." European Science Foundation, Annual Meeting in Barcelona, Spain, May 2013.

Duclos, Jean-Yves. "Equity and Equality." SSRN, Rochester, NY, September 1, 2006. https://doi.org/10.2139/ssrn.923598.

Edelman. "2021 Edelman Trust Barometer." 2021. https://www.edelman.com/trust/2021-trust-barometer.

Edgerly, S., and Emily K. Vraga. "Deciding What's News: News-ness as an Audience Concept for the Hybrid Media Environment." *Journalism & Mass Communication Quarterly*, no. 97 (2020): 416–34.

Editorial Board, The. "The Facts on Trump's Fraud Letter." *Wall Street Journal*, October 28, 2021. https://www.wsj.com/articles/the-facts-on-donald-trumps-fraud-letter-2020-election-11635449578.

Elliott, Michael, and Sanda Kaufman. "Building Civic Capacity to Resolve Environmental Conflicts." *Environmental Practice* 5, no. 3 (September 1, 2003): 265–72. https://doi. org/10.1017/S146604660303566X.

Ellis, Paula Lynn, Paul S. Voakes, and Lori Bergen. *News for US.* CA: Cognella, 2022. https://titles.cognella.com/news-for-us-9781516548514.

Ember, Sydney. "News Outlets Rethink Usage of the Term 'Alt-Right.'" *New York Times*, November 29, 2016. https://www.nytimes.com/2016/11/28/business/media/news-outl ets-rethink-usage-of-the-term-alt-right.html.

Enten, Harry. "Polls Show Majority of Republicans Mistakenly Think the 2020 Election Wasn't Legitimate." CNN, April 11, 2021. https://www.cnn.com/2021/04/11/politics/ voting-restrictions-analysis/index.html.

Entman, Robert. *Projections of Power: Framing News, Public Opinion, and U.S. Foreign Policy.* Chicago: University of Chicago Press, 2003.

Eschenfelder, Christine C. "But Can They Write? Television News Industry Assessment of the Skills of Broadcast Journalism Students and Recent Graduates." *Journalism & Mass Communication Educator* 75, no. 2 (Summer 2020): 226–32. https://doi.org/10.1177/ 1077695819884172.

Eslami, Motahhare, Aimee Rickman, Kristen Vaccaro, Amirhossein Aleyasen, Andy Vuong, Karrie Karahalios, Kevin Hamilton, and Christian Sandvig. "'I Always Assumed That I Wasn't Really That Close to [Her]': Reasoning about Invisible Algorithms in News Feeds." In Proceedings of the 33rd Annual ACM Conference on Human Factors in Computing Systems (CHI '15). Association for Computing Machinery, New York, 2015. https://doi.org/10.1145/2702123.2702556.

Ethical Journalism Network. "Facebook Reveals Plan to Tackle Spread of Fake News Online." *Arab News*, April 10, 2017. https://www.arabnews.com/node/1082136/media.

Examining Ethics Podcast. "A Spirit of Care with Maurice Hamington." The Prindle Institute for Ethics. Podcast. April 28, 2021. https://examiningethics.org/2021/04/ maurice-hamington/.

Fairclough, Norman. *Critical Discourse Analysis: The Critical Study of Language.* 2nd edition. Harlow: Routledge, 2010.

Fairclough, Norman, Jane Mulderrig, and Ruth Wodak. "Critical Discourse Analysis." In *Discourse Studies: A Multidisciplinary Introduction*, edited by T. A. van Dijk, 357–78. London: Sage, 2011.

Fallows, James. "The Media Learned Nothing from 2016." *The Atlantic*, September 15, 2020. https://www.theatlantic.com/ideas/archive/2020/09/media-mistakes/616222/.

Farhi, Paul, and Elahe Izade. "NPR Is Losing Some of Its Black and Latino Hosts. Colleagues See a Larger Crisis." *Washington Post*, January 5, 2022. https://www.washingtonpost.com/lifestyle/media/audie-cornish-npr-all-things-considered/2022/01/05/48e2d306-6d86-11ec-aaa8-35d1865a6977_story.html.

Fasching-Varner, Kenneth J., Katrice A. Albert, Roland W. Mitchell, and Chaunda Allen. *Racial Battle Fatigue in Higher Education: Exposing the Myth of Post-Racial America*. Lanham, MD: Rowman & Littlefield, 2014.

Ferrucci, Patrick. "Exploring Public Service Journalism." *Journalism & Mass Communication Quarterly* 94, no. 1 (Spring 2017): 355–70. https://doi.org/10.1177/1077699016681968.

Ferrucci, Patrick. "Networked: Social Media's Impact on News Production in Digital Newsrooms." *Newspaper Research Journal* 39, no. 1 (March 26, 2018): 6–17.

Ferrucci, Patrick. "Public Journalism No More: The Digitally Native News Nonprofit and Public Service Journalism." *Journalism* 16, no. 7 (October 1, 2015): 904–19. https://doi.org/10.1177/1464884914549123.

Ferrucci, Patrick, Jacob L Nelson, and Miles P. Davis. "From 'Public Journalism' to 'Engaged Journalism': Imagined Audiences and Denigrating Discourse." *International Journal of Communication* 14, no. 9 (2020): 1586–604.

Finneman, Teri, Meg Heckman, and Pamela E. Walck. "Reimagining Journalistic Roles: How Student Journalists Are Taking On the U.S. News Desert Crisis." *Journalism Studies* 23, no. 3 (March 2022): 338–55. https://doi.org/10.1080/1461670X.2021.2023323.

Fioroni, Sarah. "Skeptics or Cynics? Age Determines How Americans View the News Media." Knight Foundation (blog), September 21, 2021. https://knightfoundation.org/articles/skeptics-or-cynics-age-differences-in-how-americans-view-the-news-media/.

First Draft News. "About." Accessed May 29, 2021. https://firstdraftnews.org:443/about/.

First Draft News. "Vaccines and Misinformation: Get the Support You Need." Accessed May 29, 2021. https://firstdraftnews.org:443/project/vaccines-and-misinformation-get-the-support-you-need/.

First Draft News. "Verificado.UY." Accessed May 29, 2021. https://firstdraftnews.org:443/project/verificado-uy/.

Flaherty, Colleen. "Legislating against Critical Race Theory, with Curricular Implications in Some States." *Inside Higher Ed*, June 9, 2021. https://www.insidehighered.com/news/2021/06/09/legislating-against-critical-race-theory-curricular-implications-some-states.

Fleming, Jennifer. "'Truthiness' and Trust: News Media Literacy Strategies in the Digital Age." In *Media Literacy: New Agendas in Communication*, by K Tyner, 124–46. New York: Routledge, 2009. https://knightfoundation.org/reports/indicators-of-news-media-trust/.

Fleming, Rob, and Saglinda H. Roberts. *Sustainable Design for the Built Environment*. London: Routledge, 2019.

Forde, Kathy Roberts, and Sid Bedingfield, eds. *Journalism and Jim Crow: White Supremacy and the Black Struggle for a New America.* Champaign: University of Illinois Press, 2021. https://www.press.uillinois.edu/books/?id=65stx8ft9780252044106.

Forester, John. "Planning in the Face of Power." *Journal of the American Planning Association* 48, no. 1 (March 31, 1982): 67–80. https://doi.org/10.1080/0194436820 8976167.

Foust, James C., and Katherine A. Bradshaw. "Pushing Boundaries: How Coding Is (and Isn't) Taught in Accredited Journalism Programs." *Journalism & Mass Communication Educator* 75, no. 3 (September 2020): 335–47. https://doi.org/10.1177/107769582 0912953.

Fraser, Nancy. *Justice Interruptus: Critical Reflections on the "Postsocialist" Condition.* New York: Routledge, 1997.

Fraser, Nancy. *Scales of Justice: Reimagining Political Space in a Globalizing World.* New York: Columbia University Press, 2009.

Frederick. "Podcast: Craigslist Founder's Giving to Democracy and Journalism." *The Chronicle of Philanthropy*, August 23, 2018. https://www.philanthropy.com/article/ podcast-craigslist-founders-giving-to-democracy-and-journalism/.

Freelon, Deen, Lori Lopez, Meredith D. Clark, and Sarah J. Jackson. "How Black Twitter and Other Social Media Communities Interact with Mainstream News." SocArXiv, August 5, 2018. https://doi.org/10.31235/osf.io/nhsd9.

Friedlich, Jim. "Lessons from The Philadelphia Inquirer's Content Audit—Lenfest Institute." Lenfest Institute for Journalism (blog), February 12, 2021. https://www.lenfe stinstitute.org/diverse-growing-audiences/what-we-learned-from-an-independent-diversity-audit-of-more-than-3000-philadelphia-inquirer-stories/.

Froehlich, Thomas J. *A Disinformation-Misinformation Ecology: The Case of Trump. Fake News Is Bad News—Hoaxes, Half-Truths and the Nature of Today's Journalism.* IntechOpen, 2020. https://doi.org/10.5772/intechopen.95000.

Fu, Albert S. "Can Buildings Be Racist? A Critical Sociology of Architecture and the Built Environment." *Sociological Inquiry*, no. 92 (2021): 442–65. https://doi.org/10.1111/ soin.12478.

Furlan, Patrizia. "Who Can You Trust? Medical News, the Public and What Reporters Think about Public Relations Sources." *Pacific Journalism Review* 18, no. 2 (October 2012): 102–17.

Gallup Inc. and Knight Foundation. "American Views 2020: Trust, Media and Democracy." November 9, 2020. https://knightfoundation.org/wp-content/uploads/2020/08/Ameri can-Views-2020-Trust-Media-and-Democracy.pdf.

Gallup Inc. and Knight Foundation. "State of Public Trust in Local Media." October 29, 2019. https://knightfoundation.org/reports/state-of-public-trust-in-local-news/.

Gans, Herbert. *Deciding What's News: A Study of CBS Evening News, NBC Nightly News, Newsweek, and Time.* Chicago: Northwestern Press, 1979.

Garcia McKinley, Eric, and Lindsay Green-Barber. "Engaged Journalism: Practices for Building Trust, Generating Revenue, and Fostering Civic Engagement." Media Impact Funders, January 31, 2019. https://mediaimpact.issuelab.org/resource/engaged-jou rnalism-practices-for-building-trust-generating-revenue-and-fostering-civic-eng agement.html.

Germantown Info Hub. "The Germantown Info Hub Is a Community Journalism Project That Shares Information and Stories of and for Germantown." Accessed June 10, 2021. https://germantowninfohub.org/.

Giddens, Anthony. *Modernity and Self-Identity: Self and Society in the Late Modern Age*, 35. Stanford, CA: Stanford University Press, 1991.

Gilligan, Carol. *In a Different Voice: Psychological Theory and Women's Development*. Cambridge, MA: Harvard University Press, 2016.

Gilligan, Carol, and Janie Ward. "Foreward." In *Race-ing Moral Formation: African American Perspectives on Care and Justice*, edited by Vanessa Siddle Walker and John R. Snarey, ix–xiii. New York: Teachers College Press, 2004.

Giovanni, Nikki. *Racism 101*. New York: William Morrow, 1994.

Giroux, Henry A. "Spectacles of Race and Pedagogies of Denial: Anti-Black Racist Pedagogy under the Reign of Neoliberalism." *Communication Education* 52 (2003): 191–211.

Giroux, Henry A. *The Public in Peril: Trump and the Menace of American Authoritarianism*. London: Routledge, 2017.

Gladstone, Brook. "When Black Journalists Are Barred from Covering Black Lives Matter Protests." *On the Media*, WNYC, July 23, 2021. https://www.wnycstudios.org/podcasts/otm/segments/black-journalist-was-barred-covering-blm-protests-on-the-media.

Glenn, Ethel C. "A Content Analysis of Fifty Definitions of Listening." *International Listening Association. Journal* 3, no. 1 (January 1, 1989): 21–31. https://doi.org/10.1207/s1932586xijl0301_3.

Goddard, Michael. "Towards an Archaeology of Media Ecologies: 'Media Ecology,' Political Subjectivation and Free Radios." *Fibreculture Journal* 17 (2011). https://seventeen.fibreculturejournal.org/fcj-114-towards-an-archaeology-of-media-ecologies-%e2%80%98media-ecology%e2%80%99-political-subjectivation-and-free-radios/.

Goffman, Erving. *The Presentation of Self in Everyday Life*. New York: Anchor, 1959.

Goins, Cole. "How a Culture of Listening Strengthens Reporting and Relationships." American Press Institute, September 4, 2018. https://www.americanpressinstitute.org/publications/how-a-culture-of-listening-strengthens-reporting-and-relationships/.

Goodin, Robert E. *Innovating Democracy: Democratic Theory and Practice after the Deliberative Turn*. Oxford: Oxford University Press, 2008. https://doi.org/10.1093/acprof:oso/9780199547944.001.0001.

Gopal, Srik. "Understanding Trust to Strengthen Democracy." *Democraey Fund* (blog), August 21, 2017. https://democracyfund.org/idea/understanding-trust-to-strengthen-democracy/.

Gottfried, Jeffrey. "Republicans Less Likely to Trust Their Main News Source If They See It as 'Mainstream'; Democrats More Likely." Pew Research Center (blog), July 1, 2021. https://www.pewresearch.org/fact-tank/2021/07/01/republicans-less-likely-to-trust-their-main-news-source-if-they-see-it-as-mainstream-democrats-more-likely/.

Gottfried, Jeffrey, Amy Mitchell, Mark Jurkowitz, and Jacob Liedke. "Journalists Give Industry Mixed Reviews on Newsroom Diversity, Lowest Marks in Racial and Ethnic Diversity." Pew Research Center's Journalism Project (blog), June 14, 2022. https://www.pewresearch.org/journalism/2022/06/14/journalists-give-industry-mixed-reviews-on-newsroom-diversity-lowest-marks-in-racial-and-ethnic-diversity/.

Graeff, Erhardt, Matt Stempeck, and Ethan Zuckerman. "The Battle for 'Trayvon Martin': Mapping a Media Controversy Online and Off-Line." *First Monday* 19, no. 2 (January 28, 2014). https://doi.org/10.5210/fm.v19i2.4947.

Graves, Lucas. "Deciding What's True: Fact-Checking Journalism and the New Ecology of News." PhD dissertation, Columbia University, 2013.

Green-Barber, Lindsay. "Impact Report: N.J. Voting Block." Center for Cooperative Media and The Center for Investigative Reporting, 2017.

Green-Barber, Lindsay. "Towards a Useful Typology of Engaged Journalism." *The Impact Architects* (blog), October 18, 2018. https://medium.com/the-impact-architects/towards-a-useful-typology-of-engaged-journalism-790c96c4577e.

Grieco, Elizabeth. "Newsroom Employees Are Less Diverse Than U.S. Workers Overall." November 2, 2018. https://www.pewresearch.org/fact-tank/2018/11/02/newsroom-employees-are-less-diverse-than-u-s-workers-overall/.

Gutsche, Robert E., and Bonnie Brennen, eds. *Journalism Research in Practice: Perspectives on Change, Challenges, and Solutions*. New York: Routledge, 2020.

Gutsche, Robert E. "Elevating Problems of Journalistic Power in an Age of Post-Truth." *Journalism & Mass Communication Educator* 74 (2019): 1–9.

Guzmán, Mónica. *I Never Thought of It That Way*. Penguin Random House, 2022. https://www.penguinrandomhouse.com/books/691561/i-never-thought-of-it-that-way-by-monica-guzman/.

Guzmán, Mónica. "What Exactly Is Engagement and What Difference Does It Make?" American Press Institute (blog), May 2, 2016. https://www.americanpressinstitute.org/publications/reports/strategy-studies/what-is-engagement/.

Haapanen, Lauri. "Problematising the Restoration of Trust through Transparency: Focusing on Quoting." *Journalism* 23, no. 4 (April 2022): 875–91. https://doi.org/10.1177/1464884920934236.

Haas, Tanni, and Linda Steiner. "Public Journalism: A Reply to Critics." *Journalism* 7, no. 2 (May 1, 2006): 238–54. https://doi.org/10.1177/1464884906062607.

Habermas, Jürgen. *Justification and Application: Remarks on Discourse Ethics*. Polity Press, 1993. https://www.wiley.com/en-us/Justification+and+Application%3A+Remarks+on+Discourse+Ethics-p-9780745616391.

Habermas, Jürgen. *The Theory of Communicative Action*. Vol. 1: *Reason and the Rationalization of Society*. Translated by Thomas McCarthy. Boston: Beacon Press, 1985.

Hamington, Maurice. "Caring, Journalism, and the Power of Particularism." *Metropolitan State College of Denver*, Expositions: Interdisciplinary Studies in the Humanities, no. 5 (2011): 94–102.

Hamington, Maurice. *Embodied Care: Jane Addams, Maurice Merleau-Ponty, and Feminist Ethics*. New York: Routledge, 2004.

Hanitzsch, Thomas, and Tim P. Vos. "Journalistic Roles and the Struggle over Institutional Identity: The Discursive Constitution of Journalism." *Communication Theory* 27, no. 2 (May 1, 2017): 115–35. https://doi.org/10.1111/comt.12112.

Hankins, Katherine B., and Deborah G. Martin. "Contextualizing Neighbourhood Activism: Spatial Solidarity in the City." In *Handbook of Urban Geography*, edited by Tim Schwanen and Ronald van Kempen, 411–27. United Kingdom: Edward Elgar Publishing, 2019.

Hassell, Hans, John Holbein, and Matthew Miles. "Journalists May Be Liberal, but This Doesn't Affect Which Candidates They Choose to Cover." *Washington Post*, April 10, 2020. https://www.washingtonpost.com/politics/2020/04/10/journalists-may-be-liberal-this-doesnt-affect-which-candidates-they-choose-cover/.

Hare, Kristen. "The Coronavirus Has Closed More Than 70 Local Newsrooms across America. And Counting." *Poynter* (blog), April 26, 2021. https://www.poynter.org/locally/2021/the-coronavirus-has-closed-more-than-60-local-newsrooms-across-america-and-counting/.

Harry, Sydette. "Listening to Black Women: The Innovation Tech Can't Crack." *Wired*, January 11, 2021. https://www.wired.com/story/listening-to-black-women-the-innovation-tech-cant-figure-out/.

Hatcher, John A., and Dana Thayer. "Assessing Collaboration in One Media Ecosystem." *Journalism Practice* 11, no. 10 (December 2017): 1283–301. https://doi.org/10.1080/17512786.2016.1254059.

Hauser, Gerard A., and Chantal Benoit-Barne. "Reflections on Rhetoric, Deliberative Democracy, Civil Society, and Trust." *Rhetoric and Public Affairs* 5 (2002): 261–75.

Haywood, D'Westwood. "Fight for a New America." In *Journalism and Jim Crow: White Supremacy and the Black Struggle for a New America*, edited by Kathy Roberts Forde and Sid Bedingfield, 57–82. Champaign: University of Illinois Press, 2021.

Hearken. "The Citizens Agenda Guide." Hearken and Membership Puzzle Project, 2020. https://pages.wearehearken.com/the-citizens-agenda.

Hearken. "Election SOS: Supporting Journalists to Provide Better Election Coverage." Accessed May 25, 2021. https://electionsos.com/.

Hearken. "Our Founding Story." Accessed May 21, 2021. https://wearehearken.com/founding-story/.

Hecht, Michael L. "A Research Odyssey: Toward the Development of a Communication Theory of Identity." *Communications Monographs*, June 2, 2009, 76–82. https://doi.org/10.1080/03637759309376297.

Hecht, Michael L., Jennifer R. Warren, Eura Jung, and Janice L. Krieger. "A Communication Theory of Identity: Development, Theoretical Perspective, and Future Directions." In *Theorizing and Intercultural Communication*, edited by William B. Gudykunst, 257–78. London: Sage Publications Ltd., 2005.

Hekman, Susan J. *Moral Voices, Moral Selves: Carol Gilligan and Feminist Moral Theory*. University Park, PA: Penn State University Press, 1996. https://www.amazon.com/Moral-Voices-Selves-Gilligan-Feminist/dp/0271014849.

Held, Virginia, and Carol W. Oberbrunner. *Justice and Care: Essential Readings in Feminist Ethics*. Boulder, CO: Routledge, 1995.

Hendrickson, Clara. "Local Journalism in Crisis: Why America Must Revive Its Local Newsrooms." Report. Brookings, November 12, 2019. https://www.brookings.edu/research/local-journalism-in-crisis-why-america-must-revive-its-local-newsrooms/.

Henningham, John. "Political Journalists' Political and Professional Values." *Australian Journal of Political Science* 30, no. 2 (July 1, 1995): 321–34. https://doi.org/10.1080/00323269508402339.

Heyamoto, Lisa, and Todd Milbourn. "The 32 Percent Project: How Citizens Define Trust and How Journalists Can Earn It." Agora Journalism Center, June 2018. https://journalism.uoregon.edu/files/imported/2018-Agora-Report-Update.pdf.

Hobbs, R. J., and J. A. Harris. "Restoration Ecology: Repairing the Earth's Ecosystems in the New Millennium." *Restoration Ecology* 9, no. 2 (2001): 239–46. https://doi.org/10.1046/j.1526-100x.2001.009002239.x.

Hobbs, Renee, and Amy Jensen. "The Past, Present, and Future of Media Literacy Education." *Journal of Media Literacy Education* 1, no. 1 (2009): 1–11.

Holley, Lynn C. "Emerging Ethnic Agencies." *Journal of Community Practice* 11, no. 4 (October 1, 2003): 39–57. https://doi.org/10.1300/J125v11n04_03.

Holmes, Oliver. "George Floyd Killing Sparks Protests across US: At a Glance Guide." *The Guardian*, May 30, 2020. http://www.theguardian.com/us-news/2020/may/30/george-floyd-protests-latest-at-a-glance-white-house.

Holt, Thomas C. "Afterword: Mapping the Black Public Sphere." In *The Black Public Sphere*, edited by The Black Public Sphere Collective, 325–28. Chicago: University of Chicago Press, 1995.

Holton, Avery E., Valérie Bélair-Gagnon, and Cindy Royal. "The Human Side of (News) Engagement Emotion, Platform and Individual Agency." *Digital Journalism* 9, no. 8 (2021): 1184–89. https://doi.org/10.1080/21670811.2021.1930086.

Holton, Avery E., Seth C. Lewis, and Mark Coddington. "Interacting with Audiences: Journalistic Role Conceptions, Reciprocity, and Perceptions about Participation." *Journalism Studies* 17, no. 7 (October 2, 2016): 849–59. https://doi.org/10.1080/1461670X.2016.1165139.

Hooley, Erin. "What's Working: Service Journalism Is Having a Moment—RJI." Reynolds Journalism Institute, February 10, 2020. https://rjionline.org/news/whats-working-service-journalism-is-having-a-moment/.

Hossain, Mohammad Delwar, and James Aucoin. "The Ethics of Care as a Universal Framework for Global Journalism." *Journal of Media Ethics* 33, no. 4 (October 2, 2018): 198–211. https://doi.org/10.1080/23736992.2018.1509713.

Hossain, Mohammad Delwar, and James Aucoin. "The Ethics of Care as a Universal Framework for Global Journalism." *Journal of Media Ethics*, November 1, 2018. https://www.tandfonline.com/doi/abs/10.1080/23736992.2018.1509713.

Howard, Jo, Erika Lopez-Franco, and Joanna Wheeler. "Participatory Monitoring and Accountability and the Sustainable Development Goals: A Learning Report of the Participate Network." April 2017. https://opendocs.ids.ac.uk/opendocs/handle/20.500.12413/13326.

Huntsberger, Michael, and Alan Stavitsky. "The New 'Podagogy': Incorporating Podcasting into Journalism Education." *Journalism & Mass Communication Educator* 61, no. 4 (Winter 2007): 397–410.

Husband, Charles. "Minority Ethnic Media as Communities of Practice: Professionalism and Identity Politics in Interaction." *Journal of Ethnic and Migration Studies* 31, no. 3 (May 1, 2005): 461–79. https://doi.org/10.1080/13691830500058802.

Ingber, Sasha. "The U.S. Now Ranks as a 'Problematic' Place for Journalists." NPR (blog), April 18, 2019. https://www.npr.org/2019/04/18/714625907/the-u-s-now-ranks-as-a-problematic-place-for-journalists.

Ingram, Matthew. "Facebook Partners with Craig Newmark to Fund Journalism Trust Project." *Fortune*, April 3, 2017. https://fortune.com/2017/04/03/facebook-newmark-trust/.

Institute for Nonprofit News. "Bridget Thoreson Joins the INN Member Collaborations Team." April 23, 2021. https://inn.org/news/bridget-thoreson-to-lead-inn-member-collaborations/.

International Federation of Journalists. "USA: Black Journalists Barred from Covering BLM Protests." June 9, 2020. https://www.ifj.org/media-centre/news/detail/category/press-releases/article/usa-black-journalists-barred-from-covering-blm-protests.html.

Jackson, Gerald Gregory. "Black Psychology: An Avenue to the Study of Afro-Americans." *Journal of Black Studies* 12, no. 3 (1982): 241–60.

Jackson, Richard J., Andrew L. Dannenberg, and Howard Frumkin. "Health and the Built Environment: 10 Years After." *American Journal of Public Health* 103, no. 9 (2013): 1542–44.

Jackson, Sarah. *Black Celebrity, Racial Politics, and the Press: Framing Dissent.* Routledge, 2014.

Jensen, Elizabeth. "Kessler Interview Puts Spotlight on How to Cover Racist Viewpoints." NPR (blog), August 13, 2018. https://www.npr.org/sections/publiceditor/2018/08/13/638153970/kessler-interview-puts-spotlight-on-how-to-cover-racist-viewpoints.

Jones, Sarah. "The Great Remove." *Columbia Journalism Review* (Spring/Summer, 2018). https://www.cjr.org/special_report/journalism-class.php/.

Jurkowitz, Mark, Amy Mitchell, Elisa Shearer, and Mason Walker. "Democrats Report Much Higher Levels of Trust in a Number of News Sources Than Republicans." Pew Research Center, January 24, 2020. https://www.journalism.org/2020/01/24/democrats-report-much-higher-levels-of-trust-in-a-number-of-news-sources-than-republicans/.

Kahne, Joseph, and Benjamin Bowyer. "Educating for Democracy in a Partisan Age: Confronting the Challenges of Motivated Reasoning and Misinformation." *American Educational Research Journal* 54, no. 1 (February 1, 2017): 3–34. https://doi.org/10.3102/0002831216679817.

Kaklauskas, A., and R. Gudauskas. "Intelligent Decision-Support Systems and the Internet of Things for the Smart Built Environment." In *Start-up Creation*, edited by Fernando Pacheco-Torgal, Erik Rasmussen, Claes-Göran Granqvist, Volodymyr Ivanov, Arturas Kaklauskas, and Stephen Makonin, 413–49. Woodhead, 2016. https://doi.org/10.1016/B978-0-08-100546-0.00017-0.

Kang, SoYoung. "Identity-Centered Multicultural Care Theory: White, Black, and Korean Caring." *Educational Foundations* 20, no. 3–4 (2006): 35–49.

Karlsson, Michael. "Rituals of Transparency." *Journalism Studies* 11, no. 4 (August 1, 2010): 535–45. https://doi.org/10.1080/14616701003638400.

Karlsson, Michael. *Transparency and Journalism: A Critical Appraisal of a Disruptive Norm.* London: Routledge, 2021.

Kelly, John. "Parsing the Online Ecosystem: Journalism, Media, and the Blogosphere." In *Transitioned Media*, edited by Gali Einav, 93–108. The Economics of Information, Communication and Entertainment. New York: Springer, 2010. http://link.springer.com/chapter/10.1007/978-1-4419-6099-3_7.

Kennedy, Tammie M., Joyce Irene Middleton, and Krista Ratcliffe. "Introduction: Oxymoronic Whiteness—From the White House to Ferguson." In *Rhetorics of Whiteness*, edited by Tammie M. Kennedy, Joyce Irene Middleton, and Krista Ratcliffe, 1–16. Carbondale: Southern Illinois University Press, 2017.

Kiesel, Laura. "A Disabled Reporter Walks into a Democratic Primary Event . . ." *BINJ*, February 2, 2020. https://binjonline.com/2020/02/11/a-disabled-reporter-walks-into-a-democratic-primary-event/.

Kilgore, Ed. "Trump's Long Campaign to Steal the Presidency: A Timeline." *Intelligencer*, October 25, 2021. https://nymag.com/intelligencer/article/trump-campaign-steal-presidency-timeline.html.

Knight Commission on Trust, Media and Democracy. [Report]. John S. and James L. Knight Foundation and the Aspen Institute. 2019. https://csreports.aspeninstitute.org/Knight-Commission-TMD/2019/report.

Kohlberg, Lawrence. *The Philosophy of Moral Development: Moral Stages and the Idea of Justice.* San Francisco: Harper & Row, 1981.

Kohring, Matthias, and Jörg Matthes. "Trust in News Media: Development and Validation of a Multidimensional Scale." *Communication Research* 34, no. 2 (April 1, 2007): 231–52. https://doi.org/10.1177/0093650206298071.

Konieczna, Magda. *Journalism without Profit: Making News When the Market Fails.* Oxford: Oxford University Press, 2018.

Konieczna, Magda. "Reimagining Newsroom Collaboration: How Two European News Nonprofits Are Inviting Citizens In." *Journalism Practice* 14, no. 5 (June 2020): 592–607. https://doi.org/10.1080/17512786.2020.1757490.

Kovach, Bill, and Tom Rosenstiel. *The Elements of Journalism: What Newspeople Should Know and the Public Should Expect.* New York: Three Rivers Press, 2014.

Lamuedra, María, Concha Mateos Martín, and Manuel A. Broullón-Lozano. "Normative and Audience Discourses on Public Service Journalism at a 'Critical Juncture': The Case of TVE in Spain." *Journalism Studies* 20, no. 11 (September 2019): 1528–45. https://doi.org/10.1080/1461670X.2018.1528880.

Lawrence, Regina G., Eric Gordon, Andrew DeVigal, Caroline Mellor, and Jonathan Elbaz. "Building Engagement: Supporting the Practice of Relational Journalism." Agora Journalism Center, April 2019. file:///Users/robinson4/Downloads/building_engagement_201904.pdf.

Lawrence, Regina G., Damian Radcliffe, and Thomas R. Schmidt. "Practicing Engagement: Participatory Journalism in the Web 2.0 Era." *Journalism Practice* 12, no. 10 (2018): 1220–40. https://doi.org/10.1080/17512786.2017.1391712.

Lenard, Patti Tamara. *Trust, Democracy, and Multicultural Challenges.* University Park: Pennsylvania State University Press, 2012. https://www.psupress.org/books/titles/978-0-271-05253-3.html.

Len-Ríos, Maria E., and Earnest L. Perry, eds. *Cross-Cultural Journalism and Strategic Communication: Storytelling and Diversity.* 2nd edition. New York: Routledge, 2019.

Levin, Michael. *The Listening Self: Personal Growth, Social Change and the Closure of Metaphysics.* Routledge, 1989.

Lewis, Elliott. "Perspective: When the Lecturer Is Biracial or Multiracial." In *Teaching Race: Struggles, Strategies and Scholarship for the Mass Communication Classroom*, edited by George L. Daniels and Robin Blom, 70–75. Lanham, MD: Rowman & Littlefield, 2021.

Lewis, Libby. *The Myth of Post-Racialism in Television News.* Routledge, 2017.

Lewis, Marilyn H., and N. Reinsch. "Listening in Organizational Environments." *Journal of Business Communication* 25, no. 3 (1988): 49–67.

Lewis, Seth C., Avery E. Holton, and Mark Coddington. "Reciprocal Journalism." *Journalism Practice* 8, no. 2 (March 4, 2014): 229–41. https://doi.org/10.1080/17512786.2013.859840.

Libin, S. "Relative Truths." *Journalism That Matters* (blog), 2005. https://journalismthatmatters.org/fetzer1/.

Livingston, Steven. "Media Literacy and the Challenge of New Information and Communication Technologies." *Communication Review* 7, no. 1 (2004): 3–14.

"Local Voices Network." Accessed May 26, 2021. https://lvn.org.

Lopez, Russell P. *The Built Environment and Public Health.* John Wiley & Sons, 2012.

Lowery, Wesley. "A Reckoning over Objectivity, Led by Black Journalists." *New York Times*, June 23, 2020. https://www.nytimes.com/2020/06/23/opinion/objectivity-black-journalists-coronavirus.html.

Lundsteen, Sara W. *Listening: Its Impact on Reading and the Other Language Arts.* Urbana, IL: National Council of Teachers of English, 1971. https://eric.ed.gov/?id=ED078420.

Maksl, Adam, Seth Ashley, and Stephanie Craft. "Measuring News Media Literacy." *Journal of Media Literacy Education* 6, no. 3 (March 15, 2015): 29–45.

Manafy, Michelle. "The Media Industry's #MeToo Moment." *MediaShift*, December 28, 2017. http://mediashift.org/2017/12/media-industrys-metoo-moment/.

Maras, Steven. *Objectivity in Journalism*. Cambridge, UK: Polity Press, 2013.

Marvin, Carolyn. *When Old Technologies Were New: Thinking about Electric Communication in the Late Nineteenth Century*. Reprint edition. New York: Oxford University Press, 1990.

Mason, Lance E., Dan Krutka, and Jeremy Stoddard. "Media Literacy, Democracy, and the Challenge of Fake News." *Journal of Media Literacy Education* 10, no. 1 (2018): 1–10.

Mastin, Teresa, Shelly Campo, and M. Somjen Frazer. "In Black and White: Coverage of U.S. Slave Reparations by the Mainstream and Black Press." *Howard Journal of Communications* 16, no. 3 (July 1, 2005): 201–23. https://doi.org/10.1080/1064617050 0207956.

Matsaganis, Matthew D., and Vikki S. Katz. "How Ethnic Media Producers Constitute Their Communities of Practice: An Ecological Approach." *Journalism* 15, no. 7 (2014): 926–44.

Matsaganis, Matthew D., Vikki S. Katz, and Sandra J. Ball-Rokeach. *Understanding Ethnic Media: Producers, Consumers, and Societies*. London: Sage Publications, 2011.

McBride, Kelly. "The Ethics of Justice and Care in the American Media." *Poynter* (blog), August 16, 2002. https://www.poynter.org/archive/2002/the-ethics-of-justice-and-care-in-the-american-media/.

McManus, Joseph, and Joseph Mosca. "Strategies to Build Trust and Improve Employee Engagement." *International Journal of Management & Information Systems* 19, no. 1 (January 22, 2015): 37–42. https://doi.org/10.19030/ijmis.v19i1.9056.

Mensing, Donica. "College and University Journalism Education." In *The International Encyclopedia of Journalism Studies*, edited by Tim P. Vos, Folker Hanusch, Dimitra Dimitrakopoulou, Margaretha Geertsema-Sligh, and Annika Sehl, 1–10. Wiley, 2019. https://doi.org/10.1002/9781118841570.iejs0006.

Mersey, Rachel Davis, Edward C. Malthouse, and Bobby J. Calder. "Focusing on the Reader: Engagement Trumps Satisfaction." *Journalism & Mass Communication Quarterly* 89, no. 4 (December 1, 2012): 695–709. https://doi.org/10.1177/107769901 2455391.

Meyers, Marian. *African American Women in the News: Gender, Race, and Class in Journalism*. Routledge, 2013.

Middaugh, Ellen. "Civic Media Literacy in a Transmedia World: Balancing Personal Experience, Factual Accuracy and Emotional Appeal as Media Consumers and Circulators." *Journal of Media Literacy Education* 10, no. 2 (November 27, 2018): 33–52. https://doi.org/10.23860/JMLE-2018-10-2-3.

Mignolo, Walter D. "Epistemic Disobedience, Independent Thought and Decolonial Freedom." *Theory, Culture & Society* 26, nos. 7–8 (December 1, 2009): 159–81. https://doi.org/10.1177/0263276409349275.

Miller, Joshua P. "Caring to Disagree: Democratic Disagreement as Civic Care." *Polity* 44, no. 3 (2012): 400–425.

Mindich, David. *Just the Facts: How "Objectivity" Came to Define American Journalism*. New York: NYU Press, 2000.

Mitchell, Amy, Jeffrey Gottfried, Michael Barthel, and Elisa Shearer. "How Americans Get Their News." Pew Research Center, July 7, 2016. https://www.journalism.org/2016/07/07/pathways-to-news/.

Mocca, Elisabetta, and Stephen Osborne. "'Solidarity Is Our Weapon': Social Mobilisation in Scotland in the Contest of the Post-Political Condition." *Antipode* 51, no. 2 (2019): 620–41.

Molyneux, Logan, and Rachel R. Mourão. "Political Journalists' Normalization of Twitter: Interaction and New Affordances." *Journalism Studies* 20, no. 2 (February 2019): 248–66. https://doi.org/10.1080/1461670X.2017.1370978.

Moon, Young Eun, and Regina G. Lawrence. "Disseminator, Watchdog and Neighbor? Positioning Local Journalism in the 2018 #FreePress Editorials Campaign." *Journalism Practice* (September 30, 2021): 1–19. https://doi.org/10.1080/17512786.2021.1981150.

Morgan, Fiona. "Listen to People Who Care." *Medium* (blog), March 2, 2016. https://medium.com/free-press/listen-to-people-who-care-6d6008dfaf40.

Morgan, Fiona. "Residents and Reporters Discuss Inequity in Charlotte." *Free Press*, 2017. https://www.freepress.net/our-response/advocacy-organizing/stories-field/residents-and-reporters-discuss-inequity-charlotte.

Nadler, Anthony. "Nature's Economy and News Ecology." *Journalism Studies* 20, no. 6 (April 26, 2019): 823–39. https://doi.org/10.1080/1461670X.2018.1427000.

Naparstek, Arthur J., and Chester D. Haskell. "Neighborhood Approaches to Urban Capacity Building." *Journal of Urban Affairs* 3, no. 1 (December 1, 1981): 46–55. https://doi.org/10.1111/j.1467-9906.1981.tb00123.x.

National Advisory Commission on Civil Disorders. *The Kerner Report*. Princeton, NJ: Princeton University Press, 2016. https://www-degruyter-com.ezproxy.library.wisc.edu/document/doi/10.1515/9781400880805/html.

National Intelligence Council. "Foreign Threats to the 2020 US Federal Elections," March 10, 2021. https://www.dni.gov/files/ODNI/documents/assessments/ICA-declass-16MAR21.pdf.

National Newspaper Association. "Media Guide 2020." 2020.

Neilson, Tai. "'I Don't Engage': Online Communication and Social Media Use among New Zealand Journalists." *Journalism* 19, no. 4 (September 14, 2016): 536–52. https://doi.org/10.1177/1464884916667871.

Nelson, Jacob L. *Imagined Audiences: How Journalists Perceive and Pursue the Public*. Oxford University Press, 2021.

Nelson, Jacob L. "The Next Media Regime: The Pursuit of 'Audience Engagement' in Journalism." *Journalism* 22, no. 9 (2021): 2350–67. https://doi.org/10.1177/1464884919862375.

Nelson, Jacob L., and Dan A. Lewis. "Training Social Justice Journalists." *Journalism & Mass Communication Educator* 70, no. 4 (Winter 2015): 394–406. https://doi.org/10.1177/1077695815598613.

Nelson, Jacob L., and Thomas Schmidt. "Taking the Audience Seriously? The Normative Construction of Engaged Journalism." *International Journal of Communication* 16 (2022): 21.

Nettlefold, Jocelyn, and Gretta T. Pecl. "Engaged Journalism and Climate Change: Lessons From an Audience-Led, Locally Focused Australian Collaboration." *Journalism Practice* 16, no. 1 (February 2022): 19–34. https://doi.org/10.1080/17512786.2020.1798272.

Newkirk, Pamela. *Within the Veil: Black Journalists, White Media*. New York: NYU Press, 2002.

Newton, Eric. "Understanding News? We're Not Even Close." *Trust, Media & Democracy* (blog), July 13, 2018. https://medium.com/trust-media-and-democracy/understanding-news-were-not-even-close-1770c7f89954.

New York Times. "Making a More Diverse, Equitable and Inclusive New York Times." February 24, 2021. https://www.nytco.com/company/diversity-and-inclusion/a-call-to-action/.

Ng, Eve, Khadijah Costley White, and Anamik Saha. "#CommunicationSoWhite: Race and Power in the Academy and Beyond." *Communication, Culture and Critique* 13, no. 2 (June 1, 2020): 143–51. https://doi.org/10.1093/ccc/tcaa011.

Nieman Lab. *Twitter,* June 11, 2020. https://twitter.com/NiemanLab/status/12710838 49188081665.

Noble, Safiya Umoja. *Algorithms of Oppression: How Search Engines Reinforce Racism.* New York: NYU Press, 2018.

Nobles, Wade W. "Extended Self: Rethinking the So-Called Negro Self-Concept." *Journal of Black Psychology* 2, no. 2 (February 1, 1976): 15–24. https://doi.org/10.1177/0095798 47600200205.

Omi, Michael, and Howard Winant. *Racial Formation in the United States.* 3rd edition. New York: Routledge, 2014.

Ore, Ersula. "Whiteness as a Racialized Space." In *Rhetorics of Whiteness: Postracial Hauntings in Popular Culture, Social Media, and Education,* edited by Tammie M. Kennedy, Joyce Irene Middleton, and Krista Ratcliffe, 256–70. Carbondale: Southern Illinois University Press, 2017.

Ornebring, H. "Anything You Can Do, I Can Do Better? Professional Journalists on Citizen Journalism in Six European Countries." *International Communication Gazette* 75, no. 1 (2013): 35–53.

Ornebring, Henrik, and Michael Karlsson. *Journalistic Autonomy—The Genealogy of a Concept.* Columbia: University of Missouri Press, 2022.

Paisana, Miguel, Ana Pinto-Martinho, and Gustavo Cardoso. "Trust and Fake News: Exploratory Analysis of the Impact of News Literacy on the Relationship with News Content in Portugal." *Communication & Society* 33, no. 2 (April 2020): 105–17. https://doi.org/10.15581/003.33.2.105-117.

Patterson, Thomas. "News Coverage of the 2016 General Election: How the Press Failed the Voters." Shorenstein Center (blog), December 7, 2016. https://shorensteincenter.org/news-coverage-2016-general-election/.

Patterson, Thomas E., and Wolfgang Donsbagh. "News Decisions: Journalists as Partisan Actors." *Political Communication* 13, no. 4 (October 1, 1996): 455–68. https://doi.org/10.1080/10584609.1996.9963131.

Pech, Garry, and Rhona Leibel. "Writing in Solidarity: Steps toward an Ethic of Care for Journalism." *Journal of Mass Media Ethics* 21, nos. 2–3 (August 1, 2006): 141–55. https://doi.org/10.1080/08900523.2006.9679730.

Peet, Lisa. "Knight Foundation, Aspen Institute Launch Trust, Media and Democracy Initiative." *Library Journal,* October 19, 2017. https://www.libraryjournal.com?detailStory=knight-foundation-aspen-institute-launch-trust-media-democracy-initiative.

Peffley, Mark A., and Jon Hurwitz. "A Hierarchical Model of Attitude Constraint." *American Journal of Political Science* 29, no. 4 (1985): 871–90.

Peiser, Jaclyn. "Craigslist Founder Gives $20 Million to CUNY Journalism School." *New York Times,* June 11, 2018. https://www.nytimes.com/2018/06/11/business/media/craigslist-cuny-journalism-school.html.

Peters, Chris. "'Even Better than Being Informed': Satirical News and Media Literacy." In *Rethinking Journalism,* edited by Chris Peters and M. J. Broersma, 173–88. London: Routledge, 2012.

Pew Research Center. "Black, White and Hispanic Americans Give Very Different Reasons for Why They Feel the News Media Don't Understand Them." June 24, 2020. https://www.pewresearch.org/wp-content/uploads/2020/06/ft_2020.06.25_misund erstood_02b.png.

Pew Research Center. "In a Politically Polarized Era, Sharp Divides in Both Partisan Coalitions." December 2019. https://www.pewresearch.org/politics/2019/12/17/in-a-politically-polarized-era-sharp-divides-in-both-partisan-coalitions/.

Pew Research Center. "Trends and Facts on Newspapers: State of the News Media." July 9, 2019. https://www.journalism.org/fact-sheet/newspapers/.

Picard, Robert G. "Twilight or New Dawn of Journalism?" *Journalism Studies* 15, no. 5 (September 3, 2014): 500–510. https://doi.org/10.1080/1461670X.2014.895530.

Poepsel, Mark. "Thematic Analysis of Journalism Engagement in Practice—International Symposium on Online Journalism." *#ISOJ 2021* 11, no. 1 (2021): 65–88.

Polyak, Michelle, and Katie Donnelly. "Advancing Diversity, Equity, and Inclusion in Journalism." Democracy Fund, 2019. https://democracyfund.org/wp-content/uplo ads/2020/06/2019_DF_AdvancingDEIinJournalism.pdf.

Potter, James. *Media Literacy*. 4th edition. Sage, 1875.

Powell, John A. *Racing to Justice: Transforming Our Conceptions of Self and Other to Build an Inclusive Society*. Bloomington: Indiana University Press, 2012.

Powers, Elia, and Alex Curry. "No Quick Fix: How Journalists Assess the Impact and Define the Boundaries of Solutions Journalism." *Journalism Studies* 20, no. 15 (December 2019): 2237–57. https://doi.org/10.1080/1461670X.2019.1586565.

Purdy, Michael, and Deborah Borisoff. *Listening in Everyday Life: A Personal and Professional Approach*. Lanham, MD: University Press of America, 1997.

Quandt, Thorsten. "Dark Participation." *Media and Communication* 6, no. 4 (November 8, 2018): 36–48. https://doi.org/10.17645/mac.v6i4.1519.

Ramasubramanian, Srivi. "#CommunicationSoWhite: Two-Year Anniversary Reflections—Part 1." *Dr. Srivi Website* (blog), May 4, 2020. https://www.drsrivi.com/post/communicationsowhite-two-year-anniversary-reflections-part-1.

Ramos, Daniel, Mehmet Hadi Gunes, Donica Mensing, and David M. Ryfe. "Mapping Emerging News Networks: A Case Study of the San Francisco Bay Area." In *Complex Networks*, edited by Ronaldo Menezes, Alexandre Evsukoff, and Marta C. González, 237–44. Studies in Computational Intelligence. Berlin: Springer, 2013. https://doi.org/10.1007/978-3-642-30287-9_25.

Ratcliffe, Krista. "Rhetorical Listening: A Trope for Interpretive Invention and a 'Code of Cross-Cultural Conduct.'" *College Composition and Communication* 51, no. 2 (1999): 195–224. https://doi.org/10.2307/359039.

Ratcliffe, Krista. *Rhetorical Listening: Identification, Gender, Whiteness*. Carbondale: Southern Illinois University Press, 2005.

Reese, Stephen D. "The News Paradigm and the Ideology of Objectivity: A Socialist at the Wall Street Journal." *Critical Studies in Mass Communication* 7 (1990): 390–409.

Reuters Institute for the Study of Journalism. Accessed May 23, 2021. https://reutersinstit ute.politics.ox.ac.uk/.

Riaz, Saqib. "Journalism Crisis: Proposing Public-Service Model of Press." *Global Media Journal: Pakistan Edition* 10, no. 1 (Spring 2017): 108–39.

Rice, Suzanne. "Moral Perception, Situatedness, and Learning to Listen." *Learning Inquiry* 1, no. 2 (August 1, 2007): 107–13. https://doi.org/10.1007/s11519-007-0012-2.

Rice, Suzanne. "Toward an Aristotelian Conception of Good Listening." *Educational Theory* 61, no. 2 (2011): 141–53. https://doi.org/10.1111/j.1741-5446.2011.00396.x.

Richardson, Allissa V. *Bearing Witness While Black: African Americans, Smartphones, and the New Protest #Journalism*. New York: Oxford University Press, 2020. http://ebook central.proquest.com/lib/wisc/detail.action?docID=6187368.

Rinaldi, Carlina. *In Dialogue with Reggio Emilia: Listening, Researching and Learning*. London: Routledge, 2005.

Rindfleisch, Aric, James Burroughs, and Nancy Wong. "The Safety of Objects: Materialism, Existential Insecurity, and Brand Connection." *Journal of Consumer Research* 36 (June 1, 2009): 1–16. https://doi.org/10.1086/595718.

Robertson, Katie. "New York Times Calls for Workplace Changes in Diversity Report." *New York Times*, February 24, 2021. https://www.nytimes.com/2021/02/24/business/media/new-york-times-workplace-diversity.html.

Robinson, Sue. *Networked News, Racial Divides: How Power and Privilege Shape Public Discourse in Progressive Communities*. Cambridge: Cambridge University Press, 2018. https://www.cambridge.org/core/books/networked-news-racial-divides/18A23CA56 AD93C14F8302AA73B7B34BB.

Robinson, Sue, Kelly Jensen, and Carlos Dávalos. "'Listening Literacies' as Keys to Rebuilding Trust in Journalism: A Typology for a Changing News Audience." *Journalism Studies* 22, no. 9 (July 4, 2021): 1219–37. https://doi.org/10.1080/14616 70X.2021.1937677.

Robinson, Sue, and Regina G. Lawrence. "The Trust-Building News Ecosystem: Changing Journalist Roles and Skill Sets." International Communication Assocation, Annual Meeting, Paris, May 31, 2022.

Robinson, Sue, Yiping Xia, and Megan Zahay. "Public Political Talk on Twitter and Facebook: The View from Journalists." Knight Foundation, December 2019. https://knightfoundation.org/reports/public-political-talk-on-twitter-and-facebook-the-view-from-journalists/.

Rodríguez, Ilia. "Incorporating a Critique of Coloniality." In *Teaching Race: Struggles, Strategies, and Scholarship for the Mass Communication Classroom*, edited by George L. Daniels and Robin Blom, 15–34. Lanham, MD: Rowman & Littlefield, 2021. https://rowman.com/ISBN/9781538154557/Teaching-Race-Struggles-Strategies-and-Scho larship-for-the-Mass-Communication-Classroom.

Rosen, Jay. "The People Formerly Known as the Audience." *PressThink* (blog), June 27, 2006. http://archive.pressthink.org/2006/06/27/ppl_frmr.html.

Rosen, Jay. *What Are Journalists For?* New Haven, CT: Yale University Press, 2001.

Rousseau, Denise M., Sim B. Sitkin, Ronald S. Burt, and Colin Camerer. "Not So Different after All: A Cross-Discipline View of Trust." *Academy of Management Review* 23, no. 3 (July 1, 1998): 393–404.

Royster, Jacqueline Jones. "When the First Voice You Hear Is Not Your Own." *College Composition and Communication* 47, no. 1 (1996): 29–40. https://doi.org/10.2307/ 358272.

Ruotsalainen, Juho, and Sirkka Heinonen. "Media Ecology and the Future Ecosystemic Society." *European Journal of Futures Research* 3, no. 1 (December 2015): 1–10. https://doi.org/10.1007/s40309-015-0068-7.

Russell, Adrienne. "Digital Communication Networks and the Journalistic Field: The 2005 French Riots." *Critical Studies in Media Communication* 24, no. 4 (2007): 285–302. https://doi.org/10.1080/07393180701560880.

Saegert, Susan. "Building Civic Capacity in Urban Neighborhoods: An Empirically Grounded Anatomy." *Journal of Urban Affairs* 28, no. 3 (June 1, 2006): 275–94. https://doi.org/10.1111/j.1467-9906.2006.00292.x.

Scharrer, Erica. "Making a Case for Media Literacy in the Curriculum: Outcomes and Assessment." *Journal of Adolescent and Adult Literacy* 46 (December 1, 2002): 354–58.

Schifrin, Nick. "Local Newsrooms across the Country Are Closing. Here's Why That Matters." *PBS NewsHour*, January 1, 2020. https://www.pbs.org/newshour/show/local-newsrooms-across-the-country-are-closing-heres-why-that-matters.

Schmidt, Thomas R., and Regina G. Lawrence. "Engaged Journalism and News Work: A Sociotechnical Analysis of Organizational Dynamics and Professional Challenges." *Journalism Practice* 14, no. 5 (February 27, 2020): 518–36.

Schmidt, Thomas R., and Regina G. Lawrence. "Putting Engagement to Work: How News Organizations Are Pursuing 'People-Powered Journalism.'" *Agora Journalism Center* 14, no. 5 (November 2018): 518–36.

Schmidt, Thomas R., Jacob L. Nelson, and Regina Lawrence. "Conceptualizing the Active Audience: Rhetoric and Practice in 'Engaged Journalism.'" *Journnlalism* 23, no. 1 (2022): 3–21. https://doi.org/10.1177/1464884920934246.

Scholz, Sally J. "Solidarity." In *International Encyclopedia of Ethics*, edited by Hugh LaFollette, 1–8. John Wiley & Sons, 2019. https://doi.org/10.1002/9781444367072.wbiee737.pub2.

Schudson, Michael. *Discovering the News: A Social History of American Newspapers.* New York: Basic Books, 1981.

Schwartz, Matthew. "Trump Tells Agencies to End Trainings on 'White Privilege' and 'Critical Race Theory.'" National Public Radio, September 5, 2020. https://www.npr.org/2020/09/05/910053496/trump-tells-agencies-to-end-trainings-on-white-privilege-and-critical-race-theor.

Seale, S. "4 Ways Google News Lab Is Driving Innovation in Newsrooms." International News Media Association. (blog), 2018. https://www.inma.org/blogs/conference/post.cfm/4-ways-google-news-lab-is-driving-innovation-in-newsrooms.

Sevenhuijsen, Selma. *Citizenship and the Ethics of Care: Feminist Considerations on Justice, Morality and Politics.* London: Routledge, 1998.

Shah, Hemant. "Toward More Inclusive News: Strengthening Minority Media, Transforming Journalistic Practice." In *News and Inclusion: Journalism and the Politics of Diversity Conference*, Stanford, CA, 2010.

Shah, Hemant, and Michael Thornton. *Newspaper Coverage of Interethnic Conflict: Competing Visions of America.* Thousand Oaks, CA: Sage, 2004.

Shaw, Jackie, Jo Howard, and Erika López Franco. "Building Inclusive Community Activism and Accountable Relations through an Intersecting Inequalities Approach." *Community Development Journal* 55, no. 1 (February 4, 2020): 7–25. https://doi.org/10.1093/cdj/bsz033.

Shrouf, Fadi, and Giovanni Miragliotta. "Energy Management Based on Internet of Things: Practices and Framework for Adoption in Production Management." *Journal of Cleaner Production* 100 (August 1, 2015): 235–46. https://doi.org/10.1016/j.jclepro.2015.03.055.

Siddle Walker, Vanessa, and John R. Snarey, eds. *Race-ing Moral Formation: African American Perspectives on Care and Justice. Vanessa Siddle Walker, John R. Snarey, Carol Gilligan, Janie Ward: Books.* Teachers College Press, 2004.

Silverstone, Roger. "Complicity and Collusion in the Mediation of Everyday Life." *New Literary History* 33, no. 4 (2002): 761–80. https://doi.org/10.1353/nlh.2002.0045.

Simonton, Anna. "Out of Struggle: Strengthening and Expanding Movement Journalism in the U.S. South." Project South, August 1, 2017. https://search.issuelab.org/resource/out-of-struggle-strengthening-and-expanding-movement-journalism-in-the-u-s-south.html.

Smith, Ben. "Inside the Revolts Erupting in America's Big Newsrooms." *New York Times*, June 7, 2020. https://www.nytimes.com/2020/06/07/business/media/new-york-times-washington-post-protests.html.

Smith, William A. "Black Faculty Coping with Racial Battle Fatigue: The Campus Racial Climate in a Post–Civil Rights Era." *A Long Way to Go: Conversations about Race by African American Faculty and Graduate Students* 14 (2004): 171–91.

Smith, William A., Walter R. Allen, and Lynette L. Danley. "'Assume the Position . . . You Fit the Description': Psychosocial Experiences and Racial Battle Fatigue among African American Male College Students." *American Behavioral Scientist* 51, no. 4 (2007): 551–78.

Snider, Mike. "You're More Likely to Trust News from a Trusted Facebook Friend." *USA Today*, March 21, 2007. https://www.usatoday.com/story/tech/talkingtech/2017/03/21/study-sharer-digital-news-outweighs-news-source/99447836/.

Society of Professional Journalists. "Society of Professional Journalists." Accessed May 23, 2021. https://www.spj.org/index.asp.

Solutions Journalism Network. Accessed November 12, 2021. https://www.solutionsjournalism.org/.

Spillman, Mary, Adam J. Kuban, and Suzy J. Smith. "Words du Jour: An Analysis of Traditional and Transitional Course Descriptors at Select J-Schools." *Journalism & Mass Communication Educator* 72, no. 2 (Summer 2017): 198–211. https://doi.org/10.1177/1077695816650118.

Squires, Catherine. *African Americans and the Media*. Cambridge, UK: Polity Press, 2009.

Squires, Catherine. *Dispatches from the Color Line: The Press and Multiracial America*. Albany: State University of New York Press, 2007.

Squires, Catherine. "Rethinking the Black Public Sphere: An Alternative Vocabulary for Multiple Public Spheres." *Communication Theory* 12 (2002): 446–68.

Srinivasan, R. "Indigenous, Ethnic and Cultural Articulations of New Media." *International Journal of Cultural Studies* 9, no. 4 (December 1, 2006): 497–518. https://doi.org/10.1177/1367877906069899.

Stalder, Felix. "17. Between Democracy and Spectacle: The Front-End and Back-End of the Social Web." In *The Social Media Reader*, edited by Michael Mandiberg, 242–56. New York: NYU Press, 2012. https://doi-org.ezproxy.library.wisc.edu/10.18574/nyu/9780814763025.003.0021.

Staples, Brent. *Twitter*, June 4, 2020. https://twitter.com/BrentNYT/status/1268541141416325121.

Steinbrink, John E., and Jeremy W. Cook. "Media Literacy Skills and the 'War on Terrorism.'" *Clearing House: A Journal of Educational Strategies, Issues and Ideas* 76, no. 6 (July 1, 2003): 284–88. https://doi.org/10.1080/00098650309602020.

Steiner, Linda, and Chad M. Okrusch. "Care as a Virtue for Journalists." *Journal of Mass Media Ethics* 21, nos. 2–3 (August 1, 2006): 102–22. https://doi.org/10.1080/08900523.2006.9679728.

Swift, Art. "Americans' Trust in Mass Media Sinks to New Low." Gallup, Inc., September 14, 2016. https://news.gallup.com/poll/195542/americans-trust-mass-media-sinks-new-low.aspx.

Tang, Gary, and Francis L. F. Lee. "Hong Kong Journalists' Attitude towards Social Protests: A Belief System Perspective." *Media Asia* 41, no. 1 (January 2014): 55–70. https://doi.org/10.1080/01296612.2014.11690000.

Tannen, Deborah. *You Just Don't Understand: Women and Men in Conversation.* New York: William Morrow Paperbacks, 2007.

Thayer-Bacon, Barbara J. "The Power of Caring." *Philosophical Studies in Education* 2 (1997): 1–32.

Thayer-Bacon, Barbara J. *Relational "(e)Pistemologies."* New York: Peter Lang, International Academic Publishers, 2003.

Thier, Kathryn. "Opportunities and Challenges for Initial Implementation of Solutions Journalism Coursework." *Journalism & Mass Communication Educator* 71, no. 3 (September 2016): 329–43. https://doi.org/10.1177/1077695816666078.

Thoreson, Bridget. "Citizens Agenda in Action: 20 Newsrooms Turning to the Public to Focus Their 2020 Election Coverage." *We Are Hearken* (blog), August 17, 2020. https://medium.com/we-are-hearken/citizens-agenda-in-action-20-newsrooms-turning-to-the-public-to-focus-their-2020-election-coverage-bcd86a22ec0d.

Thoreson, Bridget. "Public-Powered Journalism in Practice." *Medium* (blog), December 10, 2018. https://medium.com/we-are-hearken/public-powered-journalism-in-practice-79ea463eec0d.

Thoreson, Bridget, Yemile Bucay, Anthony Cave, Kamila Jambulatova, and Lynn Walsh. "Election SOS: Newsroom Lessons in Engagement and Trust-Building from the 2020 Elections." Hearken, April 2021. https://pages.wearehearken.com/hubfs/Election%20SOS%20Report.pdf.

Tronto, Joan C. *Caring Democracy: Markets, Equality, and Justice.* New York: NYU Press, 2013.

Tronto, Joan. *Moral Boundaries: A Political Argument for an Ethic of Care.* Routledge, 2020.

Tuchman, Gaye. "Objectivity as Strategic Ritual: An Examination of Newsmen's Notions of Objectivity." *American Journal of Sociology* 77, no. 4 (1972): 660–79.

Tully, Melissa, Emily K. Vraga, and Anne-Bennett Smithson. "News Media Literacy, Perceptions of Bias, and Interpretation of News." *Journalism* 21, no. 2 (February 1, 2020): 209–26. https://doi.org/10.1177/1464884918805262.

UNESCO. "Global Media and Information Literacy (MIL): Assessment Framework: Country Readiness and Competencies." Geneva: UNESCO, 2013.

UNESCO. "Press Clubs Are a Perfect Platform to Debate Media's Role in Governance and Sustainable Development." June 4, 2018. https://en.unesco.org/news/press-clubs-are-perfect-platform-debate-media-s-role-governance-and-sustainable-development.

University of Wisconsin–Madison. "Baldwin Grants Awarded to Eight Projects." Accessed May 29, 2021. https://news.wisc.edu/baldwin-grants-awarded-to-eight-projects/.

U.S. Department of Homeland Security. "National Terrorism Advisory System Bulletin." May 14, 2021. https://www.dhs.gov/ntas/advisory/national-terrorism-advisory-system-bulletin-may-14-2021.

Usher, Nikki. *News for the Rich, White, and Blue.* New York: Columbia University Press, 2021.

Uslaner, Eric M., and Mitchell Brown. "Inequality, Trust, and Civic Engagement." *American Politics Research* 33, no. 6 (November 1, 2005): 868–94. https://doi.org/10.1177/1532673X04271903.

Van der Wurff, Richard, and Klaus Schoenbach. "Civic and Citizen Demands of News Media and Journalists: What Does the Audience Expect from Good Journalism?" *Journalism & Mass Communication Quarterly* 91, no. 3 (September 2014): 433–51. https://doi.org/10.1177/1077699014538974.

van Dijck, Jose, Thomas Poell, and Martijn Waal. *The Platform Society: Public Values in a Connective World.* Oxford: Oxford University Press, 2018.

van Dijk, T. A. *Discourse and Context: A Socio-Cognitive Approach.* New York: Cambridge University Press, 2008.

van Dijk, Teun A. "Ideology and Discourse Analysis." *Journal of Political Ideologies* 11, no. 2 (2006): 115–40. https://doi.org/10.1080/13569310600687908.

van Dijk, Teun A. *Racism and the Press.* London: Routledge, 1991.

Varma, Anita. "Evoking Empathy or Enacting Solidarity with Marginalized Communities? A Case Study of Journalistic Humanizing Techniques in the San Francisco Homeless Project." *Journalism Studies* 21, no. 12 (September 9, 2020): 1705–23. https://doi.org/10.1080/1461670X.2020.1789495.

Varma, Anita. "Solidarity in Action: A Case Study of Journalistic Humanizing Techniques in the San Francisco Homeless Project." PhD dissertation, Stanford University, 2018. https://www.proquest.com/openview/bd67e5c6d779ac56a506bfa835274ddd/1?pq-origsite=gscholar&cbl=18750&diss=y.

Varma, Anita. "Solidarity in U.S. Journalism: Social Justice Implications of How Journalists Humanize People Experiencing Homelessness." In *The Routledge Companion to Media and Poverty,* edited by Sandra B. Borden, 64–73. Routledge, 2021.

Varma, Anita. "Solidarity Journalism." Markkula Center for Applied Ethics (blog), 2020. https://www.scu.edu/ethics/focus-areas/journalism-and-media-ethics/resources/solidarity-journalism/.

Vasquez, Tina. "Is Movement Journalism What's Needed During This Reckoning over Race and Inequality?" Nieman Reports. Accessed June 23, 2022. https://niemanreports.org/articles/158195/.

Villanueva, George. "Designing a Chinatown Anti-Displacement Map and Walking Tour with Communication Asset Mapping." *Journal of Urban Design* 26, no. 1 (January 2, 2021): 14–37. https://doi.org/10.1080/13574809.2020.1782182.

Villanueva, George, Carmen Gonzalez, Minhee Son, Evelyn Moreno, Wenlin Liu, and Sandra Ball-Rokeach. "Bringing Local Voices into Community Revitalization: Engaged Communication Research in Urban Planning." *Journal of Applied Communication Research* 45, no. 5 (December 15, 2017): 474–94. https://doi.org/10.1080/00909882.2017.1382711.

Voakes, Paul. "Civic Duties: Newspaper Journalists' Views on Public Journalism." *Journalism & Mass Communication Quarterly* 76, no. 4 (1999): 756–74.

Vos, Tim P., and Stephanie Craft. "The Discursive Construction of Journalistic Transparency." *Journalism Studies* 18, no. 12 (2017): 1505–22.

Vraga, Emily, Melissa Tully, and Leticia Bode. "Assessing the Relative Merits of News Literacy and Corrections in Responding to Misinformation on Twitter." *New Media & Society* 24, no. 10 (March 3, 2021): 2354–71. https://doi.org/10.1177/1461444821998691.

Wagner, Angelia. "Watching the Watchdogs: The News Media's Role in Canadian Politics." In *The Palgrave Handbook of Gender, Sexuality, and Canadian Politics*, edited by Manon Tremblay and Joanna Everitt, 341–58. Cham, Switzerland: Springer International, 2020. https://doi.org/10.1007/978-3-030-49240-3_17.

Wahl-Jorgensen, Karin. *Emotions, Media and Politics*. Wiley, 2019.

Ward, Stephen J. A. "Inventing Objectivity: New Philosophical Foundations." In *Journalism Ethics: A Philosophical Approach*, edited by C. Meyers, 137–64. New York: Oxford University Press, 2010.

Weaver, David H. *The American Journalist: A Portrait of U.S. News People and Their Work*. Bloomington: Indiana University Press, 1986.

Weaver, David Hugh, G. Cleveland Wilhoit, Lori A. Bergen, Dan G. Drew, and Sue A. Lafky. *The American Journalist: A Portrait of U.S. News People and Their Work*. Bloomington: Indiana University Press, 1991.

Weaver, David H., and Lars Wilnat. "Introduction." In *The Global Journalist in the 21st Century*, edited by David H. Weaver and Lars Willnat, 1–5. New York: Routledge, 2012. https://www.academia.edu/3088539/David_H_Weaver_and_Lars_Willnat_2012_Introduction_In_David_H_Weaver_and_Lars_Willnat_Eds_The_Global_Journalist_in_the_21st_Century_pp_1_5_New_York_Routledge.

Welch, Matt. "Journalists Abandoning 'Objectivity' for 'Moral Clarity' Really Just Want to Call People Immoral." Reason (blog), June 24, 2020. https://reason.com/2020/06/24/journalists-abandoning-objectivity-for-moral-clarity-really-just-want-to-call-peo ple-immoral/.

Wenger, Deb Halpern, Lynn C. Owens, and Jason Cain. "Help Wanted: Realigning Journalism Education to Meet the Needs of Top U.S. News Companies." *Journalism & Mass Communication Educator* 73, no. 1 (Spring 2018): 18–36. https://doi.org/10.1177/1077695817745464.

Wenzel, Andrea. *Community-Centered Journalism: Engaging People, Exploring Solutions, and Building Trust*. Champaign: University of Illinois Press, 2020. https://www.press.uillinois.edu/books/catalog/53bmr8ea9780252043307.html.

Wenzel, Andrea. *Making News Antiracist: Reimagining Local News Systems*. New York: Columbia University Press, Forthcoming.

Wenzel, Andrea. "Public Media and Marginalized Publics: Online and Offline Engagement Strategies and Local Storytelling Networks." *Digital Journalism* 7, no. 1 (November 14, 2017): 146–63.

Wenzel, Andrea, Anthony Nadler, Doron Taussig, and Natacha Yazbeck. "Journalism across Divides? Searching for Insights from Kigali to Kentucky." Tow Center, December 2, 2021. https://www.cjr.org/tow_center_reports/journalism-across-divides-search ing-for-insights-from-kigali-to-kentucky.php/.

Theory of Change Community. "What Is Theory of Change?" Accessed July 5, 2021. https://www.theoryofchange.org/what-is-theory-of-change/.

White, Khadijah Costley. *The Branding of Right-Wing Activism: The News Media and the Tea Party*. Oxford University Press, 2018.

Wiard, Victor. "News Ecology and News Ecosystems." ResearchGate, February 2019. https://www.researchgate.net/publication/331400264_News_Ecology_and_News_Ecosystems.

Williams, R. "Fighting 'Fake News' in an Age of Digital Disorientation: Towards 'Real News.'" In *Critical Media Literacy and Fake News in Post-Truth America*, edited by C. Z. Goering and P. L. Thomas, 53–65. Brill Sense, 2018.

Wilner, Tamar, Gina Masullo, Danielle Kilgo, and Lance Bennett. "News Distrust among Black Americans Is a Fixable Problem." University of Texas at Austin. Accessed May 20, 2021. https://mediaengagement.org/research/news-distrust-among-black-americans/.

Wilson, Clint C., II. *Black Journalists in Paradox: Historical Perspectives and Current Dilemmas*. New York: Greenwood, 1991. https://search.library.wisc.edu/catalog/9998 87565702121.

Wolvin, Andrew D., and Carolyn Gwynn Coakley. *Listening*. Wm. C. Brown, 1988.

Woods, Keith, Richard Prince, and Farai Chideya. "If Journalists Value Diversity Why Are Newsrooms So White?" WYPR, March 12, 2021. https://www.wypr.org/show/midday/2021-03-12/if-journalists-value-diversity-why-are-newsrooms-so-white.

Woodward, Calvin. "AP Fact Check: Trump's False Claims, Fuel on a Day of Chaos." *AP News*, January 6, 2021. https://apnews.com/article/ap-fact-check-donald-trump-a98d72c0ccde16fa900e6053a4599cab.

Xia, Yiping, Sue Robinson, Megan Zahay, and Deen Freelon. "The Evolving Journalistic Roles on Social Media: Exploring 'Engagement' as Relationship-Building between Journalists and Citizens." *Journalism Practice* 14, no. 5 (May 27, 2020): 556–73. https://doi.org/10.1080/17512786.2020.1722729.

Yaneva, Albena, and Alejandro Zaera-Polo. *What Is Cosmopolitical Design? Design, Nature and the Built Environment*. Burlington, VT: Routledge, 2016.

Young, Iris Marion. "Communication and the Other: Beyond Deliberative Democracy." In *Democracy and Difference: Contesting the Boundaries of the Political*, by S Benhabib, 120–36. Princeton, NJ: Princeton University Press, 1996.

Young, Iris Marion. *Inclusion and Democracy*. Oxford: Oxford University Press, 2000.

Young, Iris Marion, and Danielle S. Allen. *Justice and the Politics of Difference*. Revised edition. Princeton, NJ: Princeton University Press, 2011.

Yu, Sherry S. "Ethnic Media as Communities of Practice: The Cultural and Institutional Identities." *Journalism* 18, no. 10 (November 1, 2017): 1309–26. https://doi.org/10.1177/1464884916667133.

Zelizer, Barbie. "Journalists as Interpretive Communities." *Critical Studies in Mass Communication* 10 (1993): 219–37.

Index